THE
SMART PARENTS'
GUIDE TO
SUMMER CAMPS

THE
SMART PARENTS'
GUIDE TO
SUMMER CAMPS

SHELDON SILVER

with Jeremy Solomon

THE NOONDAY PRESS

Farrar, Straus & Giroux

NEW YORK

Printed in the United States of America
Published simultaneously in Canada by HarperCollins*CanadaLtd*
Designed by Tere LoPrete
FIRST EDITION, 1991

Library of Congress Cataloging-in-Publication Data
Silver, Sheldon.
The smart parents' guide to summer camps / Sheldon Silver with
Jeremy Solomon. — 1st ed.
p.   cm.
Includes index.
1. Camps—United States—Directories.   I. Solomon, Jeremy.
II. Title.

GV193.S55   1990   796.54'2025'73—dc20   90-48100 CIP

This book is dedicated to my wife, Roberta. Her patience, co-operation, and inspiration throughout my camping years made it all possible.

ACKNOWLEDGMENTS

I wish to thank my sons Darin and Kyle for showing me how valuable the camping experience can be. They also helped to input, organize, and interpret much of the information.

I owe a great deal of gratitude to the following camp directors: Sy Alter, Ellis Marmor, Stan Rubin, Tom Jacoby, Edie Klein, and Ted Weinstein. Throughout various stages of my camping career, these individuals gave freely of their advice, expertise, and assistance. They made my work enjoyable and rewarding.

A special thanks must be given to Mickey Black, Marvin Black, and Ted Halpern. This family epitomizes the "camping tradition." Their professionalism, commitment, and passion serve as a model and inspiration for all in camping. Their support in my camping and personal life will never be forgotten.

Also special thanks go to Elisabeth Dyssegaard and Amy Einhorn at Farrar, Straus and Giroux for their patience and good humor; to R. Mark Davis; and most of all, to Sally Brickell, who got this book off the ground and helped bring it in for a smooth landing.

CONTENTS

THE
SMART PARENTS'
GUIDE TO
SUMMER CAMPS

INTRODUCTION

Nineteen years ago, I was a parent of small children, beginning my teaching career in New York City. I was offered a position as a group leader at a sleep-away camp, and I thought it might be an interesting summer job. That thought, as it turns out, was a grand understatement. Not only was it an ideal summer job, it began what would become for me a lifelong passion. For the last nineteen years I've been involved, in one capacity or another, with camp life. For the last five I've been the director of a large sleep-away camp, with primary responsibility for everything the camp provides and represents.

Recently, I heard about two former campers who met by chance thirty years later and spent an entire evening sharing and swapping camp memories. I'm not surprised. A camp experience can be so rich, so fundamental to a child's youth and to the adult he or she becomes, that it is a deep well to draw from.

As an educator, I've always enjoyed working with children and being part of their development. And I've come to regard summer camp as an ideal place to foster a child's personal growth. Camp provides a unique environment—nurturing yet fostering independence—and I continue to be amazed by what children can accomplish when they are both cared for and challenged, free from societal and parental pressures. Without exaggeration, I can say that I've watched thousands of children overcome fears, gain confidence, and become more independent through camping.

Imagine a child who was so afraid of the water that she spent the first week of camp watching other kids swim in the pool. Then imagine her standing waist-deep in the pool, alongside the counselor who worked with her every day. If that image doesn't strike you it's because you can't see her face, which is lit with pride and exhilaration. In another case, a ten-year-old boy's parents warned me that he was shy, withdrawn, and didn't make friends easily. Imagine my amusement when I had to remind this boy at lunch that he would have to let go of his best friend's hand long enough to eat.

It's fun to see adolescent boys who've just discovered their own tough "coolness" forget it long enough to don some silly outfit and sing at the top of their lungs with the other kids at a campfire. It's inspiring to watch a child do something remarkable—ride a horse, paddle a canoe, swim—for the very first time. And it is always touching to watch, at the close of a session, crying kids exchanging autographs and addresses, delighting in the warmth of deep friendships.

What I find so gratifying about camp is that the results are tangible. At camp children make tremendous strides toward self-confidence and self-esteem, mainly by having fun. I believe summer camp, with its natural setting and group living experiences, offers children an unparalleled opportunity to mature in a safe, caring environment.

This book profiles over 150 of what I consider the best sleep-away camps that exist in the United States and Canada. It is designed to make you aware of the variety of camps available for your child, and to give you a clear sense of how to choose a camp that will best suit your child's unique needs, interests, and temperament.

Is Your Child Ready?

Parents should answer this crucial question before enrolling their son or daughter in summer camp: Is my child physically, emotionally, and socially ready to attend camp? My experience has confirmed that a child may indeed be "too young for camp": too young to benefit from it, and too young to enjoy it.

My friend Ellen called me recently, distraught about her six-year-old, Amy, whom she had just enrolled in summer camp. As this was to be the young girl's first experience away from home, Ellen arranged for Amy to spend the night at her grandmother's as a trial run. Hard to say who was more miserable at 3:00 that morning—Ellen had to go fetch a hysterical, sobbing Amy from her very tired grandmother, because the child had screamed and cried from the moment she arrived. From this less than stellar trial run, Ellen concluded that six years old was too young for summer camp.

Unfortunately, there are no hard and fast rules, no easy tests or guarantees. Each child is unique and matures differently. And while age is important, maturity is the more decisive factor. I had to agree with Ellen that Amy, at six years old, was not ready to spend a summer away from home, but other children her age might be. Your determination should be based on your child's own history of adjusting to new environments such as school, day care, and sleep-overs with friends or relatives. Previous positive experiences away from home directly prepare a child for his or her first time at camp. And your child *must* express a desire and willingness to attend camp.

Twenty years ago it was not uncommon for four- and five-year-olds to be sent to summer camp; today seven is the standard age for first-timers. I would argue that even if a child is relatively mature and independent at age four, he or she may still be too young to enjoy the experience. I recently met two former campers of mine. I had been their group leader many years ago, when they were both first-timers, and both four years old. I remembered them perfectly: adorable, cherubic boys with constantly untied shoes and minuscule attention spans. No baseball game or sing-along could hold these two for long, and I spent most of that summer following behind them as they wandered off on their own magical agendas. Now teenagers, neither boy had any memories of camp at that early age. They didn't remember me, or any of their friends or counselors, and both felt they had been too young to attend camp.

The experience of another camper, five-year-old Peter, has stayed with me. Peter was terribly homesick, and his sadness lasted well beyond the usual transition period of the session's first few days. As other kids were discovering all the camp had to offer, playing and running from one activity to another, Peter would sit alone, head lowered, with tears rolling down his cheeks. His loneliness was exacerbated by the fact that Peter's bunkmates had lost patience with him and had stopped trying to include him in their games.

Homesickness is not an incurable disease; the cure is involvement. And every summer it is my great pleasure to witness countless "miraculous recoveries": long, sad faces that brighten and come alive when kids start to have fun and make new friends. To a certain extent both the malady and the cure are normal elements of a child's first summer at camp. And while involvement—the kind camp provides in spades—never fails to draw a child out of his or her funk, it is not a remedy that can be forced. I spent an inordinate amount of time with Peter, trying to distract him and lift his spirits. But Peter could think of one thing only—home—and he wasn't interested in the other kids or in having fun. His homesickness was overwhelming and debilitating, and he was just too young to overcome it. I should add that while Peter was not yet old enough for camp that summer, he returned at age seven, and for many subsequent summers, always eager to come and sorry to leave.

Regardless of age, before going to camp your child should possess basic levels of competency in caring for himself or herself. A camper should be able to tie shoelaces, cut food, shower, dress, make the bed, fold clothes, and write a letter. Without these skills, your child will be too dependent on adult supervision to benefit from camping. His or her counselors will be baby-sitters, not friends or role models. And rather than learning how to swim or hit a baseball, your child will be struggling just to keep pace with the other children.

So for a child to benefit from camp, it's imperative that he or she be able to take care of basic needs, enjoy activities, and feel comfortable in social interaction with peers. If you have serious doubts about your child's development in any of these areas, you may want to wait a year to let your child acquire the confidence and independence that will enable him or her to enjoy camp. Summer camp is a wonderful, enriching experience—a whole world for a child to discover and delight in—and once ready for it, your child will thrive there.

Preparing Your Child

Parental attitudes play a decisive role in preparing children for their first camp experience. Sometimes parents—who, overworked, may wish *they* were setting off for camp—can paint such an idealistic picture of it that a child will be unprepared for the loneliness he or she may feel, or for the fact that he or she may dislike one activity or another. Like every rich experience, camp will include elements that your children may not like, but which they may, much to their surprise and joy, come to appreciate. Even children who can't wait to get to camp may have fears and uncertainties that should be addressed before they leave.

While your child may need extra socks or underwear for camp, he or she doesn't need extra pressure. Every summer without fail I encounter a child who revolts against the intensive instruction his or her parents have specially arranged for the child. Chances are your child won't return from camp the next Jimmy Connors or Chris Evert. But what is so exciting about camp is that chances *are* very good your child will return with new interests and skills that he or she has had the good fortune to discover and foster on his or her own.

As departure day nears, you and your child may become nervous, and feelings of doubt may surface. It will help your child—and it will ultimately help you—if you are supportive and if you speak to him or her about the fun that awaits at camp. Parents should encourage their children by reminding them of the good time they had sleeping over with grandparents or friends, and of how well those experiences went. It sometimes helps to introduce your child to other children who've attended camp. And some camps provide pre-camp get-togethers for first-time campers. I am a strong advocate of these get-togethers; they let children see that there are other nervous little kids like them, and this reduces their tension considerably.

I also urge you to be honest with your child about your own feelings.

Tell your child that you will miss him or her. Tell your child you will think of him or her often, that you will write and stay in touch. Some parents arrive at camp with a few pre-written letters for their child. I make sure that the child receives one of these each day in his or her mailbox. Thus rather than relying on the mail, this child is guaranteed the boost of parental communication during those difficult first few days. You can also tell your child that you will share his or her letters with friends and members of the extended family, who will all be excited to hear news from camp. In this way your child will feel well connected to home and to loved ones, and this emotional security should help immeasurably.

How to Choose a Camp

Now that you've determined your child is ready to attend camp, the question is: Which one? This guide profiles over 150 of the best sleep-away camps in the United States and Canada. My criteria in choosing these camps from the 300 or so I considered were drawn from my long association with summer camps, and my appreciation for what, at its best, camping can provide. All camps featured are accredited by the American Camping Association (ACA). ACA accreditation signifies high-quality camping, as ACA camps are evaluated regularly and must meet stringent criteria in health, safety, personnel, programming, and facilities.

Certain camps are not profiled in this guide. These include camps located at schools, camps specializing in one activity to the exclusion of all others, and camps designed with a very specific orientation: for the physically or emotionally disabled, or for children with weight problems. But for readers interested in these camps, I've included a listing beginning on page 343 of some of the more prominent ones catering to special needs.

There are plenty of excellent camps to choose from, and no lack of factors to consider in making your decision. The primary determinant must be your own child, and his or her unique needs, interests, and temperament. Last year, when a friend asked me to recommend camps for his son, I suggested a few I thought Jeremy would enjoy. Ultimately, my friend chose a camp with an outstanding reputation, known for its structured program and competitive athletics. It was an ideal camp . . . for another child. Jeremy is a creative child, interested in drama and the arts. My friend soon began to receive the infamous "Come get me, I hate it here" letters. After a few weeks he was forced to rescue his son, and Jeremy returned home confused and somewhat defeated. In choosing a camp, be true to your child. Sending your son or daughter to one that is wrong for him or her defeats the purpose of camp, which is to build, not shatter, a child's self-esteem and confidence.

The Primary Factors

Your main considerations in choosing a camp will be type (single sex or coed), fees, size, geographical location, length of session, and program emphasis and philosophy. I offer the following guidelines and suggestions, and while I hope you find them useful, I would caution that my comments should not overrule your better understanding of your child's own needs.

Type of camp: There are unique advantages to both single-sex and coed camps. Single-sex camps allow children to learn new skills and expand their horizons without the added social pressure imposed by proximity to the opposite sex. This pressure can be a factor even for relatively young—seven- or eight-year-old—children. As a director of a boys camp, I've come to appreciate the freedom single-sex camps can provide children, including the freedom to develop strong, close friendships with peers of the same sex, friendships that might not develop in the competition of a coed environment.

On the other hand, coed camps might be more appropriate for some children, especially older children whose interests and orientation have already expanded to include the opposite sex. In deciding between single-sex and coed camps, keep in mind that many single-sex camps have brother/sister camp arrangements whereby special activities are shared between the two camps. These arrangements vary depending on the distance between the camps and the philosophy behind their programs. Also keep in mind that siblings should almost always be kept together, unless they have very different needs in terms of a camp's program or emphasis. And finally, if you are considering sending your child to a single-sex camp for a few years and then switching to a coed camp, be advised that such a change can be traumatic for a child who has come to identify with a camp, its director, and its other campers.

Fees: Your budget will be your guide here. However, you should note that a camp's "tuition fee" may be misleading. Many camps charge extra fees for horseback riding, canteen (a camp store for candy, batteries, etc.) purchases, insurance, special trips, and other items. Extra fees are optional, but it's important to determine exactly what is, and what is not, included in the basic tuition fee. Consider how much these "extra" activities add to the overall camp program, and whether you or your child would deem them fundamental to the camp experience.

Should you wish to take advantage of these extra activities, factor in the relevant fees when considering the overall cost of each camp. Especially for older children, camps are increasingly designing programs to include special trips, and these can raise the costs considerably. Transportation to camp is generally not included in tuition, but some camps do provide free transportation to and from the nearest major metropolitan area.

Every summer I receive calls from parents complaining that if they were to buy every item on the recommended clothing and provisions list, the expense would exceed tuition. These lists are guides, and parents should use their best judgment and common sense to edit them as they see fit.

As you read through these entries, please keep in mind that the fees listed are for 1990 and are subject to change.

Geographical location: Most camps are situated in lovely, rustic settings with clean air and starry night skies, and you'll find it difficult to rate one over another on the relative merits of their settings. The real importance of a camp's location, I've found, is psychological. Many parents are reassured to know that, no matter how rarely this happens, if necessary they could drive for an hour or two to be with their child. In most cases, parents will send their children to a camp that is relatively close by for the reassurance this provides, and because the areas and natural landscapes are familiar to them.

Length of session: This question will be determined by your schedule and your child's. I would suggest, however, that a four-week session is the minimum for a complete camp experience, with time to adjust, time to develop friendships, and time to sample the extraordinary range of activities most camps offer.

Program emphasis and philosophy: These are essential components in your choice of a camp to best suit your child. Issues such as intensity of competition, freedom to choose versus assigned activities, and which activities are emphasized over others must be clarified and understood.

"Structured" and "elective" are terms frequently used to describe camp programs. Structured programs are designed with planned and precisely scheduled activities. Some camps require a camper to participate in most or all planned activities and not be back in his or her bunk reading a comic book. This type of program ensures exposure to a wide variety of activities, and campers in a structured environment have an opportunity to sample everything a camp provides.

Elective programs offer a camper the freedom to choose which activities he or she wants to participate in. This approach encourages independent decisionmaking and enables a camper to concentrate on one or two activity areas. Many camps provide a combination of structured and elective schedules.

I usually recommend that parents consider their child's age and number of years at camp in deciding how structured a program they want for him or her. I would suggest that younger children do better with more structured programs. Children away from home for the first time have enough pressure in adjusting to their environment. Forcing them to make too many decisions puts additional weight on small shoulders. My own experience supports the notion that young campers should be exposed to everything a camp has to offer. Older campers, especially children who have attended camp for a few years, are more aware and focused in their interests, and they may prefer the freedom of an elective program.

Since my background is in physical education and sports, both my sons gravitated toward athletics. But in camp they were exposed to drama, arts and crafts, and music. I couldn't have anticipated the thrill I felt watching them on stage, singing, dancing, and acting. I felt paternal pride, yes; but it was more than that. I could see in their eyes that *they* were excited, surprised, and proud of their accomplishment. They were taking risks and charting new territory on their paths to adulthood. To this day they are involved in drama as well as sports. This experience brought home for me the value of a balanced and diversified camp program.

Other Key Issues

Enrollment: While some camps close enrollment for their summer sessions as early as January or February, most camps have vacancies into the spring months. It helps to start the decision process early, because you don't want to put a lot of time and effort into finding the perfect camp for your child only to find it's already full. As you get into the spring months, you may run into problems, especially as some camps close enrollment for some age groups once they have a given number of children that age. Even the summer months are not too early to begin thinking about the following summer, especially because some camps offer reduced early registration fees.

Health considerations: The ACA has strict health requirements for those camps it accredits. But since you are entrusting your child to an organization far from home, you should feel personally comfortable with its health facilities and policies. You should be aware of a camp's medical staff, its access to hospitals and specialists, and its overall awareness of health issues and nutrition. Ask for whatever information you need to put your mind at ease.

Camps should be able to accommodate your child's special needs in terms of allergies, weight problems, special diets for specific medical conditions, kosher meals, and vegetarian diets. In recent years, parents frequently ask me about Lyme disease, and whether anyone at my camp has ever contracted it. Fortunately, the answer to that question is no, but the questions and the concerns are legitimate. Poison ivy, insect bites, and allergy conditions are sometimes factors at camp, but these as well as most other minor health problems can be adequately treated by a camp's own medical personnel.

Communication with your child: Most camps have policies about letter writing and phone calls. Since these are your only means of communication with your child while he or she is at camp, you should understand and feel comfortable with the rules. Most camps restrict phone calls between campers and their parents. Phone calls disrupt camp schedules, and, more important, most children react to the voice of a loved one with severe homesickness. Campers who have adjusted beautifully to their new environment can regress after speaking with a parent. Every summer I receive at least one phone call from a distraught parent who wants to know why his or her son or daughter is so miserable that he or she just cried through an entire phone conversation. I try to reassure the parent that all is well. I ask what kind of letters the child has written home. Usually the letters indicate that the child is having a great time; and usually he or she is. But sometimes a child who has not seen or heard from parents in a few days will react very emotionally to the sound of their voices. The child will renew his or her battle with homesickness, and possibly give in to it. Most often, however, the child will be back with friends and counselors within minutes, and the episode will pass. Still, these "crises," however temporary, can be unsettling. Remember that even while phone calls with your child may be limited, you should always have easy access to a camp's director.

The Parent/Director Interview

When you've determined your priorities and preferences among the issues involved in choosing a camp, use this guide to select the three or four that best meet your guidelines. Parents often try to seriously consider as many as a dozen intriguing camps, and they invariably have trouble distinguishing one from another. Once you have narrowed your choices, schedule appointments with the director of each camp. Directors will usually come to your home, meet with you at camp, or arrange a meeting with other interested parents at a mutually convenient location.

If you choose a camp without meeting and interviewing the camp's director, you may be making a mistake. The more you and your child know about the camp (and there is no better single indicator than its director), the more perfect the fit will be. All your questions cannot be answered by brochures or videos. A camp director represents the camp fully—its policies, programs, and philosophy—and he or she should be able to answer your questions.

This interview is your opportunity to discuss your child's special needs. If your child is a bed wetter, the camp personnel should be well prepared to handle the situation in a way that won't embarrass or shame your child. But it is better for them, and for your child, if they are aware of the tendency before they are confronted with an incident, and a crying child, the first night of camp. Be candid about any family crisis—a recent divorce, the illness of a grandparent—as this will trouble a child whether or not he or she is involved at camp. A parent talked to me recently about his son who had just had surgery and now had a noticeable scar across his chest. The parent was concerned about his son swimming and showering, but he also needed reassurance about how the camp would handle his son's embarrassment and self-consciousness.

In order to make the most out of your meeting with a director, you might want to prepare a list of important questions you want answered. The following are suggested discussion topics and questions.

Personnel: Remember, a camp is only as good as the staff it employs. No matter how beautiful and well equipped, a quality camp depends on good personnel. Counselors are responsible for how a child learns activities, how they interact with peers, and how problems are resolved. Counselors should be qualified to teach activities, and they should be warm, sensitive, and intelligent guardians of their campers. It is entirely appropriate for you to ask for whatever information you need for peace of mind.

- How does the camp recruit and train its counselors?
- How many counselors does it have on staff?*

* In the listings the ratio of counselors to campers will not always correspond to the actual number of campers and counselors. Campers stay for shorter or longer sessions, and camps are rarely filled to capacity for the entire summer.

- How many counselors live in each cabin?
- Are background checks of the counselors routinely made?
- What are the required staff certificates and qualifications for teaching risk activities, such as horseback riding, swimming, boating, riflery, archery, or gymnastics?
- How are counselors trained to discipline campers who misbehave?
- Are counselors allowed to drink? to smoke?
- What measures are taken when counselors break the rules?

Health and safety: If your child has special needs, it's essential that you discuss these with the camp director. Find out if and how camp personnel are trained to deal with these problems. And if your child has a chronic health condition, such as asthma, diabetes, or allergies requiring shots, make sure that the camp is equipped to deal with it.

- How many health personnel are employed by the camp?
- How many of the medical staff live and work at the camp?
- What kind of certification do the nurses possess?
- When and how are parents notified about a child's illness?
- What equipment is in the infirmary?
- Does the camp have a night watchman?
- Where is the closest hospital?

Camp policies: A director will exemplify a camp's principles and character, and your interview should give you a much clearer sense of a camp's nature. Your meeting will, one hopes, reassure and inspire you, but you will undoubtedly have specific, miscellaneous questions about policies that may affect your child.

- Are there any four-week programs, and if so, how many campers attend them?
- If I choose not to include my child in an activity for which there is an extra fee, will this decision isolate him or her?
- Is there a camp canteen, and if so, is there a policy about candy and soda purchases?
- Is there a tipping policy?
- Does the camp have a special program to deal with homesickness?
- What is the camp's policy regarding letter writing and phone calls?
- How are campers bunked: by grade, age, or length of stay?
- How does the camp handle requests for special programs (in-

dividual tennis lessons, teaching a camper who is afraid of water to swim, etc.)?
- Who transports the children when they go on trips outside the camp?
- What is the nature of camp security?
- Does the camp provide tutorial services such as remedial reading or math?

A director should respond effectively to your concerns, and he or she should also initiate a relationship with you and your child. This is the foundation of the camping service. This association creates a bond among parent, director, and camper. In the event that you receive a worrisome letter from your child, or some other sign of difficulty, you should feel confident that the problem will be resolved to your satisfaction. The director is responsible for your child's health and happiness.

How do you determine, on the basis of this interview, if the relationship will work? Consider that a youngster leaving the security of home needs a surrogate parent able to provide sensitivity and understanding. Who does he turn to if he can't sleep at night? Or when she falls and scrapes her knee? Kids often turn for support to the caring director who visited, and kept in touch, before camp. The director becomes the anchor a child needs as he or she adjusts to the new environment.

Listen to the director's responses and make sure *you* feel comfortable with them and with the information they provide. Contact other parents whose children attend the camp you are considering. Most likely your decision will come down to a gut feeling that this director will provide a safe, nurturing, learning experience for your child.

Visiting Camps

If possible, you should visit the camp you've chosen when it is in operation. There is no better way to judge it. Most camps are happy to show prospective parents and campers their facilities. Call in advance to make an appointment. Try to visit on a typical day with routine scheduling; avoid special-event days.

Ask to see a cabin your child might live in, and carefully observe the instruction given in various activities. If your child is interested in a specific activity, ask to meet a counselor in charge of that area. You should inspect the dining room, infirmary, and swimming areas. Ask what facilities have been built recently. This will indicate the camp's commitment to, and investment in, its future.

As you walk through the camp, look at the faces of the campers and counselors; their expressions should tell you all you need to know. Smiles, spirit, and enthusiasm are a camp's best endorsements.

NEW ENGLAND

CAMP AWOSTING FOR BOYS
Lakeside, Connecticut ————————————————

Single sex, male (sister camp, Camp Chinqueka for Girls)

Ages: 6–15

Campers: 150

Religious affiliation: None

Fees: $870, 2 weeks / $1,595, 4 weeks / $2,825, 8 weeks

Extra fees: Transportation to and from camp, canteen

Founded: 1900

Program: A structured, noncompetitive program with the opportunity for electives in the afternoons. Campers may specialize in 1 area

Facilities/Activities: *Athletics* 2 baseball fields, 2 soccer fields, 2 basketball courts, 6 hard-surface tennis courts (2 lit), track, volleyball court, fencing, riflery range, archery range, gymnastics area (mats, weights, boxing); *Waterfront* Bantam Lake, swimming, sailing (20 Sunfish, 2 sailboats), 26 canoes, 6 sailboards, 6 water bikes, Fun Bugs, 4 waterski boats, 30 kayaks, 24 rowboats; *Camping* campfire and sleep-out sites; *Creative Arts* indoor and outdoor theaters, wood, metal, and plastic shop, model cars with outdoor track, photography (darkroom), video lab; *Miscellaneous* 10 computers (Tandy, Apple), ropes course, minibikes, go-cart track, horseshoes, Ping-Pong

Boarding: 35 cabins (electricity), showerhouses; dining room (family style), salad bar; laundry done weekly by camp

Counselors: 1 to every 5 campers, 35 counselors total; average age, 21; 30% are foreign

Camp Rules: Parents may call during mealtimes, camper calls permitted only in case of illness; letter required twice a week; no food in cabins

Medical: 2 nurses in camp, waterfront and athletic heads certified EMTs, 50% of staff trained in first aid, 5-bed infirmary, parents telephoned in event of medical emergency; 15 miles from Charlotte Hungerford Hospital

Director: Buzz Ebner
Summer: Litchfield Road, Bantam, CT 06750
  203-567-9678
Winter: Same

Buzz and Barbara Ebner have owned and directed Awosting (and its sister camp, Chinqueka) for more than forty years. Buzz and Barbara have two education degrees and over thirty years of teaching experience between them. Since 1970, the Ebner children have been involved in running the camp as well.

Philosophy: Camp Awosting is one of the oldest private boys camps in continuous operation in the U.S. The emphasis is on the individual. Morning sessions are grouped by age and are run as mini-workshops. The camp philosophy is "learn by doing." As a result, the hands-on method of operation prevails. The athlete and nonathlete function side by side in the same cabin group "so each camper finds his own niche in the camp." There is a scheduled team competition in most sports, but the noncompetitive nature of the program allows all levels to participate freely. Weekly events such as socials and campfires unite Awosting with its sister camp, Chinqueka.

Parent Comment: "As a parent in this day and age, it's very difficult and frightening to try and find a reputable camp into whose hands we place our children. When we came to look over your facility, we still had reservations, but Robert Ebner put our minds at ease. He was so confident everything would be all right that we knew we were making the right choice. When we saw our son last Saturday, we were glad we chose Ebner Camps."

CAMP CHINQUEKA FOR GIRLS
Litchfield, Connecticut

Single sex, female (brother camp, Camp Awosting for Boys)

Ages: 6–15

Campers: 140

Religious affiliation: None

Fees: $870, 2 weeks / $1,595, 4 weeks / $2,825, 8 weeks

Extra fees: Transportation to and from camp, canteen

Founded: 1955

Program: A structured, noncompetitive program with the opportunity for electives in the afternoons. Campers may specialize in 1 area

Facilities/Activities: *Athletics*   2 baseball fields, 2 soccer fields, 2 basketball courts, 6 hard-surface tennis courts (2 lit), track, volleyball court, fencing, riflery range, archery range, gymnastics area (mats, weights, boxing); *Waterfront*   Mt. Tom Lake, swimming, sailing (20 Sunfish, 2 sailboats), 26 canoes, 6 sailboards, 6 water bikes, Fun Bugs, 4 waterski boats, 30 kayaks, 24 rowboats; *Camping*   campfire and sleep-out sites; *Creative Arts*   indoor and outdoor theaters, dance hall, wood, metal, and plastic shop, model cars with outdoor track, photography (darkroom), video lab; *Miscellaneous*   10 computers (Tandy, Apple), ropes course, minibikes, go-cart track, horseshoes, Ping-Pong

Boarding: 35 cabins (electricity), showerhouses; dining room (family style), salad bar; laundry done weekly by camp

Counselors: 1 to every 5 campers, 35 counselors total; average age, 21; 30% are foreign

Camp Rules: Parents may call during mealtimes, camper calls permitted only in case of illness; letter required twice a week; no food in cabins

Medical: 2 nurses in camp, waterfront and athletic heads certified EMTs, 50% of staff trained in first aid, 5-bed infirmary, parents telephoned in event of medical emergency; 15 miles from Charlotte Hungerford Hospital

Director: Barbara Ebner
Summer: Litchfield Road, Bantam, CT 06750
         203-567-9678
Winter: Same

Barbara and Buzz Ebner have owned and directed Chinqueka (and its brother camp, Awosting) for more than thirty years. Barbara and Buzz have two education degrees and over thirty years of teaching experience between them. Since 1970, the Ebner children have been involved in running the camp as well.

Philosophy: At Chinqueka the emphasis is on the individual camper. Morning sessions are grouped by age and are run as mini-workshops. The camp philosophy is "learn by doing," and, as a result, the hands-on method of operation prevails. The athlete and nonathlete function side by side in the same cabin group "so each camper finds her own niche in the camp." There is a scheduled team competition in most sports, but the noncompetitive nature of the program allows all levels to participate freely. Weekly events such as socials and campfires unite Chinqueka with its brother camp, Awosting.

Parent Comment: "Our boy-girl twins have been at the Ebner Camps for five continuous summers. We shopped around for camps by attending camp fairs, asking for recommendations, and by reading. We selected Chinqueka and Awosting for the following reasons: We liked the multigenerational family-run operation and the fact that our children would have contact with European counselors; the camps have fuller programs; and they are affordable. Once our twins spent the first summer at the Ebner Camps, they fell in love with them and have returned till their last eligible year."

KEN-MONT CAMP FOR BOYS
Kent, Connecticut

Single sex, male (sister camp, Ken-Wood Camp for Girls)

Ages: 6–16

Campers: 200

Religious affiliation: None

Fees: $4,200, 8 weeks; $3,500, 6 weeks (international camper option)

Extra fees: Transportation to and from camp, horseback riding, canteen

Founded: 1924

Program: A moderately competitive traditional program of scheduled activities with opportunity for daily camper choices and out-of-camp events

Facilities/Activities: *Athletics* 3 baseball fields (1 lit), 2 softball fields, 2 soccer fields, 12 hard-surface tennis courts, 6 basketball courts, 3 indoor basketball courts (4 lit), indoor street hockey court, riflery range, archery range, 9-hole golf course (par 3), physical fitness room (weights); *Waterfront* lake, swimming in cribs (wooden floor covered with rubber matting), 12 canoes, 12 rowboats, 12 kayaks, 20 sailboats (Sailfish, Phantoms, others), sailboards, 4 motorboats (3 for waterskiing, 1 for patrol), 12-ft. and 9-ft. dinghies; *Camping* campfire and sleep-out sites, nature areas; *Creative Arts* theater, weekly productions, talent shows, arts and crafts, leather crafts, sculpture, painting, macramé, tie-dyeing, weaving, radio station, photography (darkroom), amateur radio center; *Miscellaneous* 4 computers (Tandy) with printers, petting zoo, natural science facility, astronomy, Indian crafts facility, low ropes course, social hall (indoor games, movies)

Boarding: 24 cabins (electricity), 2–4 indoor showers/cabin; dining room (family style), kosher style, salad bar; laundry done weekly by camp

Counselors: 1 to every 3 campers, 70–80 counselors total; minimum age, 25; 30% are foreign

Camp Rules: Phone use depends on individual needs; campers required to write home 3 times per week; food from canteen permitted in cabins, care packages not permitted

Medical: Physician and 4 registered nurses in camp, 24-bed infirmary, parents notified if child spends night in infirmary or is taken out of camp for medical attention; 28 miles from Sharon Hospital

Director: Lloyd A. Albin
Summer: North Spectacle Lake, Kent, CT 06757
    203-927-3042
Winter: 2 Spencer Place, Scarsdale, NY 10583
    914-725-4333

Lloyd Albin has fifty years of experience as camper, counselor, camp director, and owner. A graduate of City College of New York, he lectures at Springfield College, Massachusetts, where he is an adjunct professor in camping. Lloyd has served as president of the Connecticut Camp Directors Association and is a member of the Connecticut Department of Health Camp Advisory Council. He is assisted by his son Michael, a 1988 graduate of Brandeis University.

Philosophy: At Ken-Mont and Ken-Wood Camps, almost four generations of campers have developed a personal philosophy in which ethics, self-esteem, integrity, caring, and sharing are highly valued. "Campers learn how to make decisions based on 'what is right' rather than 'what is legal,' a moral concept that has elevated many to positions of trust and leadership in their chosen careers. The structured program with some specialization continues to be a winning combination."

Parent Comment: "I can't say enough wonderful things about the program. I feel it is the finest camp in every aspect, from the athletics to fulfilling the emotional needs of every individual child."

KEN-WOOD CAMP FOR GIRLS
Kent, Connecticut

Single sex, female (brother camp, Ken-Mont Camp for Boys)

Ages: 6–16

Campers: 200

Religious affiliation: None

Fees: $4,200, 8 weeks; $3,500, 6 weeks (international camper option)

Extra fees: Transportation to and from camp, canteen, horseback riding

Founded: 1924

Program: A moderately competitive traditional program of scheduled activities with opportunity for daily camper choices and out-of-camp events

Facilities/Activities: *Athletics*   softball field, 2 soccer fields, 8 hard-surface tennis courts (4 lit), 2 basketball courts, gymnastics pavilion, riflery range, archery range, 3 volleyball courts, 9-hole golf course (par 3); *Waterfront*   lake, swimming in cribs (wooden floor covered with rubber matting), 12 rowboats, 12 kayaks, 12 canoes, 20 sailboats (Sailfish, Phantoms, others), sailboards, 4 motorboats (3 for waterskiing, 1 for patrol), 9-ft. and 12-ft. dinghies; *Camping*   campfire and sleep-out sites, nature areas; *Creative Arts*   outdoor theater, plays, dance studio, recitals, arts and crafts kilns, jewelry, pottery wheels, sewing machines, other activities, photography (darkroom), radio station; *Miscellaneous*   4 computers (Tandy) with printers, Indian crafts facility, natural science facility, petting zoo, astronomy, social hall (indoor games, movies), low ropes course

Boarding: 24 cabins (electricity), 2–4 indoor showers/cabin; dining room (family style), kosher style, salad bar; laundry done weekly by camp

Counselors: 1 to every 3 campers, 70–80 counselors total; minimum age, 25; 30% are foreign

Camp Rules: Phone use depends on individual needs; campers required to write home 3 times per week; food in cabins permitted, care packages not permitted

Medical: Physician and 4 registered nurses in camp, 24-bed infirmary, parents notified if child spends night in infirmary or is taken out of camp for medical attention; 28 miles from Sharon Hospital

Director: Lloyd A. Albin
Summer: North Spectacle Lake, Kent, CT 06757
203-927-3042
Winter: 2 Spencer Place, Scarsdale, NY 10583
914-725-4333

Lloyd Albin has fifty years of experience as camper, counselor, camp director, and owner. A graduate of City College of New York, he lectures at Springfield College, Massachusetts, where he is an adjunct professor in camping. Lloyd has served as president of the Connecticut Camp Directors Association and is a member of the Connecticut Department of Health Camp Advisory Council. He is assisted by his son Michael, a 1988 graduate of Brandeis University.

Philosophy: At Ken-Mont and Ken-Wood Camps, almost four generations of campers have developed a personal philosophy in which ethics, self-esteem, integrity, caring, and sharing are highly valued. "Campers learn how to make decisions based on 'what is right' rather than 'what is legal,' a moral concept that has elevated many to positions of trust and leadership in their chosen careers. The structured program with some specialization continues to be a winning combination."

Parent Comment: "The camp is wonderful! You and the staff made my daughters feel secure and happy. They both had a terrific summer. The grounds and facilities are beautiful. They are already looking forward to next summer."

NEW ENGLAND EXPERIENCE
Avon, Connecticut ───────────────────────────

Coed

Ages: 7–17

Campers: 300

Religious affiliation: None

Fees: $1,125, 2 weeks / $2,150, 4 weeks / $3,100, 6 weeks / $3,900, 8 weeks

Extra fees: SAT review course

Founded: 1982

Program: A structured, noncompetitive program with an opportunity to select activities as "majors" and "minors"

Facilities/Activities: *Athletics* 3 baseball fields, 2 soccer fields, 8 hard-surface tennis courts, 3 basketball courts (1 indoor), street hockey court, indoor ice skating and hockey rink, gymnastics area, volleyball courts, indoor squash courts, paddle-tennis courts, weight-training area, wrestling, fencing; *Waterfront* pond for paddleboating and sailing, water-skiing on nearby lake, indoor swimming pool; *Camping* campfire and sleep-out sites, nature area; *Creative Arts* dance (ballet, jazz, modern, aerobics), theater production every 2 weeks, arts and crafts, voice instruction, model rocketry, magic; *Miscellaneous* 60 computers (IBM, Macintosh, Apple IIe), ropes course, circus equipment

Boarding: Dormitories (electricity), indoor showers; dining room (cafeteria style), special diets accommodated, salad bar; laundry done weekly by commercial service

Counselors: 1 to every 4 campers, 75 counselors total; average age, 24; 25% are foreign

Camp Rules: Camper calls not permitted during first 5 days of session, permitted afterward during free time; letter writing encouraged; no food in dorms

Medical: Registered nurse in camp, 20-bed infirmary, parents notified immediately if child goes to infirmary; 5 miles from University of Connecticut Children's Hospital

Directors: Judy Schaefer, Gary Kramer
Summer: Avon Old Farms School, Avon, CT 06001
    203-675-4744
Winter: 40 Halley Drive, Pomona, NY 10970
    800-634-1703, 914-354-9267

Judy Schaefer worked for twenty years at the French Woods Festival of the Performing Arts before becoming a director at New England Experience. She has a B.A. in art from the University of Maryland and an M.A. in art education from New York University. When she is not working at camp, Judy is a painter and sculptor.

Gary Kramer worked at several camps before coming to New England Experience. He has a B.A. in health and physical education from Brooklyn College and an M.A. in education from Columbia Teachers College. He has taught health and physical education at the elementary-, junior-high-, and high-school levels, and most recently has worked as an assistant high-school principal. He is currently working toward a doctorate at Columbia Teachers College.

Philosophy: New England Experience promotes a supportive, structured environment. Within this framework the camp tries to encourage individuality and flexibility as well as the development of positive attitudes and self-esteem. Activity groups are small and private instruction is available. "Each camper needs an individual level of structure to make successful decisions."

Camper Comment: "Most of the kids I talked to before I went to camp thought that a camp with classes would be boring. It's not like that at all, at least not at New England Experience. It even has a circus. We got to choose from a lot of different classes and many of us chose circus. That's probably the most unusual choice but we didn't do just that all day. We picked other activities like music, tennis, gym, softball, soccer, squash, dance, computers, debating team, and theater arts. I probably liked the circus and music the most. It wasn't the only thing I loved about camp, but it was the biggest surprise. I felt like I got better at it every day, and when we watched the videotape of the circus show we made, we all felt really proud."

SJ RANCH

Ellington, Connecticut ————————————————————

Single sex, female

Ages: 7–15

Campers: 40

Religious affiliation: None

Fees: $800, 2 weeks / $1,100, 3 weeks / $2,750, 8 weeks

Extra fees: Laundry, canteen

Founded: 1956

Program: An elective, noncompetitive program with emphasis on horsemanship and environmental responsibility

Facilities/Activities: *Athletics* baseball field, hard-surface tennis court; *Waterfront* lake, Red Cross swimming lessons, Water Carnival, canoeing, rowing, Funyaks; *Camping* campfire and sleep-out sites; *Creative Arts* shaded outdoor arts and crafts area; *Miscellaneous* 25 horses, extensive horseback riding facilities (riding trails, barn, tack room, grooming, saddling, bridling, riding rings), recreation hall

Boarding: 8 cabins (no electricity), 2 showerhouses (3 showers/showerhouse); dining room (cafeteria style), vegetarian option; laundry done by camp

Counselors: 1 to every 4 campers, 10 counselors total; most college age; up to 20% are foreign

Camp Rules: No telephone calls between parents and children because of homesickness, parent may talk to director or counselor anytime to find out how child is doing; letters encouraged; food in containers allowed in cabins

Medical: Most staff have advanced first aid training, 2-bed infirmary, camp notifies parent prior to child's visiting hospital unless it's an emergency; 3 miles from Johnson Memorial Hospital

Director: Pat Haines
Summer: 130 Sandy Beach Road, Ellington, CT 06029
        203-872-4742
Winter: 944 Main Street, Newington, CT 06111
        203-225-9539

Pat Haines has an M.A. in recreation from Springfield College and over eighteen years of professional experience in the camping industry. She has been active in the ACA on both a national and regional level, and is an ACA-certified Standards Visitor. She holds Red Cross water safety instructor certification as well as first aid and CPR certification. She is an active member of the Camp Horsemanship Association.

Philosophy: SJ Ranch was begun in 1956 by Mary Haines for her own horse-loving children. It has continued as a family-run camp, with Mary's daughter Pat now acting as director. The camp has remained small, accepting forty girls for each session. This allows campers maximum individual attention, and establishes a home-away-from-home atmosphere. Many of SJ's campers have attended for several summers and continue on as staff.

"Campers have the opportunity to take advantage of a total horsemanship program, with quality instruction, trail rides, and an extensive horse-care program. The riding program is geared to the individual camper's skill and confidence level. Cookout rides, gymkhanas (games on horseback), and other special programs add a change of pace to the regular twice-a-day riding program. Arts and crafts, swimming, and other sports as well as quiet times round out the camper's program, ensuring something special for every camper."

Parent Comment: "Sending my daughter to SJ Ranch is like leaving her with family—I know she'll be in good hands. Thanks to the great training she received at SJ, she is now able to care for her own horses."

CAMP WONPOSET
Litchfield, Connecticut

Single sex, male

Ages: 7–15

Campers: 140

Religious affiliation: None

Fees: $1,320, 3 weeks / $1,584, 4 weeks / $2,673, 7 weeks

Extra fees: Transportation to and from camp, canteen

Founded: 1906

Program: A traditional, general program with a noncompetitive emphasis

Facilities/Activities: *Athletics* 2 baseball fields, soccer field, 2 hard-surface tennis courts, basketball court, 2 tetherball courts, 3 paddle-tennis courts, riflery range, archery range, volleyball courts; *Waterfront* lake, swimming, 19 sailboats, 12 rowboats, 14 canoes, waterski boat; *Camping* campfire and sleep-out sites, nature area; *Creative Arts* extensive wood shop, model rocketry; *Miscellaneous* 4 computers (IBM compatible), recreation room with stage

Boarding: 20 cabins (electricity), 2 showerhouses; dining room (family style); laundry done weekly by commercial service

Counselors: 1 to every 4 campers, 40 counselors total; average age, 25; 10% are foreign

Camp Rules: No telephone calls; letter home required once a week; no food in cabins

Medical: Physician 5 miles from camp, 2 registered nurses in camp, 2 EMTs in support role, 12-bed infirmary, parents notified if child requires medical treatment beyond routine first aid; 10 miles from Charlotte Hungerford Hospital

Director: R. Mark Davis
Summer: P.O. Box 1425, Litchfield, CT 06759
        203-567-9039
Winter: Same

Camp director R. Mark Davis is an internationally known risk-man-
agement trainer. He has served as a program director with the American
Youth Foundation, the Boy Scouts of America, and the Episcopal Di-
ocese of North America. He is a teacher and guidance counselor, has
instructed groups from age five to over age forty, and has conducted
camping programs in sixteen states and six countries.

Philosophy: "Camp Wonposet offers a relaxed but active international
atmosphere in which campers can develop new skills and interests,
improve their self-image, gain a sense of community, and grow to know
themselves better. The camp encourages concern for others, integrity,
the courage to seek self-improvement, curiosity about the natural world,
and civic responsibility. The benefits are professional supervision, broad
skill development, cross-cultural awareness, quality instruction, and resourcefulness."

Parent Comment: "Some of our children's happiest moments have been
those spent at Wonposet. The relaxed atmosphere, the fun, and the
making of lifetime friends have made Camp Wonposet a memorable
part of their lives as well as our own."

ANDROSCOGGIN CAMP FOR BOYS
Wayne, Maine

Single sex, male

Ages: 8–16

Campers: 200

Religious affiliation: None

Fees: $4,250, 8 weeks

Extra fees: Transportation to and from camp, linen service, canteen

Founded: 1907

Program: Structured program with elective periods. Optional extensive day and overnight camping program for campers of all ages

Facilities/Activities: *Athletics* 2 baseball fields, 2 soccer fields, 12 tennis courts (8 hard surface, 4 clay, 4 lit), 2 basketball courts (1 lit), street hockey court, track, riflery range, archery range, volleyball court, lacrosse, weight room; *Waterfront* lake, swimming, canoeing, sailing, sailboarding, kayaking, waterskiing; *Camping* campfire and sleep-out sites, nature area; *Creative Arts* indoor theater, arts and crafts, model rocketry, radio room; *Miscellaneous* recreation room

Boarding: 18 cabins (electricity), 1 indoor showerhouse; dining room (family style), special diets accommodated, salad bar; laundry done weekly by camp, daily towel change

Counselors: 1 to every 3 campers, 65 counselors total; average age, 22; 10% are foreign

Camp Rules: Telephone calls as needed; letter writing twice a week; no food in cabins

Medical: Physician and 2 registered nurses in camp, 9-bed infirmary, parents notified immediately by phone if child is sick; 18 miles from Kennebec Valley Medical Center

Directors: Stan, Peter, and Barbara Hirsch
Summer: Wayne, ME 04284
207-685-4441
Winter: 733 West Street, Harrison, NY 10528
914-835-5800

Stanley and Barbara Hirsch have owned and operated Androscoggin since 1964. Their son, Peter, a camper and counselor for twenty years, joined them as director in 1984. Peter is a graduate of the University of Pennsylvania and Georgetown Law School.

Stanley, a graduate of Yale, was president of the board of directors of Camp Ella Fohs and the East Tremont YMCA. Barbara, a graduate of Endicott and former teacher, is currently president of the board of Surprise Lake Camp. All three Hirsches are members of and Standards Visitors for the ACA.

Philosophy: Androscoggin strives to provide boys with a challenging and supportive environment in which they can learn and grow, experience the give-and-take of group living, and have fun. The daily program is a structured one that encourages campers to participate in every activity.

In addition to the daily program, there is an extensive day and overnight camping program. "The opportunity to expose boys to the out-of-doors and instill in them an appreciation for nature is an exciting and rewarding one. Boys of all ages canoe, hike, bike, and mountain climb in beautiful locations throughout the state. The large majority of Androscoggin's campers and staff return year after year. They come from all across the country and abroad to renew old friendships, form new ones, and share a special summer in Maine."

Parent Comment: "For each of us, Androscoggin is a home away from home. For numerous summers, as camper, counselor, and parent, we have had the opportunity to return to a beautiful, unspoiled area of Maine to rejoin the Andro family. Andro has given us opportunities to grow; to experience new activities (sports, crafts, camping, etc.); to learn sportsmanship, particularly through the intracamp "color war"; and to build long-standing friendships. Andro's environment encourages each camper to learn new skills and develop at his own pace, with outstanding guidance from a caring staff. The Andro spirit is something special and unique . . . it's helping, caring, giving, sharing, learning, teaching, having fun . . . something wonderful to experience but hard to describe."

CAMP ARCADIA
Casco, Maine ─────────────────────────────────

Single sex, female

Ages: 7–17

Campers: 150

Religious affiliation: None

Fees: $1,750, 3½-week program for first-, second-, and third-graders / $2,800, 7 weeks

Extra fees: horseback riding

Founded: 1916

Program: Elective and noncompetitive activities. Every camper participates in swimming, canoeing, and campcraft until an intermediate level

Facilities/Activities: *Athletics* 4 hard-surface tennis courts, gymnastics area, archery range, 2 large fields; *Waterfront* lake, Red Cross swimming certification, synchronized swimming, sailing, canoeing, sailboarding, rowboating; *Camping* campfire and sleep-out sites, campcraft, nature area; *Creative Arts* outdoor theater and drama building, plays for each age group, ceramics, tie-dyeing, batik, weaving, painting, sculpture; *Miscellaneous* recreation room, horseback riding, stable, riding ring, trails

Boarding: 22 cabins (half with electricity), 1 central showerhouse (10 showers); dining room (family style), a few special diets accommodated, salad bar; laundry service

Counselors: 1 to every 4 campers, 58 counselors total; average age, 20; 10% are foreign

Camp Rules: Campers may receive calls if necessary; campers should write home every week; no food in cabins

Medical: Physician on call and nearby, registered nurse in camp, 7-bed infirmary, parents notified if child has to spend night in infirmary; 12 miles from Stephens Memorial Hospital

Directors: Anne H. Fritts, Louise L. Henderson
Summer: Casco, ME 04015
     207-627-4605
Winter: c/o Fritts, Pleasantville Road, New Vernon, NJ 07976
     201-538-5409

Anne Henderson Fritts (A.B., Wellesley College; Sorbonne, Paris; A.M., Columbia University) and Louise L. Henderson (A.B., Wellesley College; M.A., Stanford University) are third-generation camp directors. Anne, a former teacher and mother of four children, is a member of the Maine Youth Camping Association and the ACA. Louise, currently the college guidance counselor at the Chapin School, was the former headmistress of the Sunset Hill School. She is also a member of the Maine Youth Camping Association and the ACA.

Philosophy: Summers full of happiness, fun, friendship, and personal development in the out-of-doors are the goals Arcadia strives for with every girl who comes to camp. "At Arcadia the girls have experiences that sharply contrast with those in cities and suburbs. Through living with other campers and working with an enthusiastic staff in our beautiful Maine woods, fields, and lakes, each girl has the opportunity to develop her personal abilities by participating in our wide-ranging program and by living in a natural environment."

Arcadia believes that campers should be at home in the out-of-doors, so it encourages each girl to participate in campcraft, swimming, canoeing, and boating until she attains the basic levels of proficiency. Arcadia also believes that each girl should plan her own program. In the spring before camp, each girl designs her schedule. And the girls are grouped in their activities by interest and ability rather than by age or living group. There are no intracamp competitive teams.

Parent Comment: "Visiting the camp at the end was most enjoyable. It was a treat to see a group of children who seemed very supportive of each other. It must reflect the teaching and counseling style practiced by the camp. I also really appreciated the importance placed on self-sufficiency. Thank you for the attentive support shown my daughter. I think that with your help she grew in understanding her capabilities."

CAMP CEDAR
Casco, Maine _____

Single sex, male

Ages: 7–15

Campers: 255

Religious affiliation: None

Fees: $4,000, 8 weeks

Extra fees: Transportation to and from camp, medical insurance, canteen, spending money

Founded: 1954

Program: A structured and elective, competitive program offering athletic and nonathletic activities and group and individual activities. Younger campers required to try everything at their own level; individual instruction stressed

Facilities/Activities: *Athletics*   3 baseball fields, 2 soccer fields, 9 hard-surface tennis courts (3 lit), 3 basketball courts (1 lit), street hockey court, track, riflery range, archery range, volleyball court, lacrosse field, indoor basketball court, weight room, wrestling room; *Waterfront*   lake, swimming, sailing (Sunfish), rowboats, canoes, kayaks, sailboards, motorboats, waterski boats; *Camping*   campfire and sleep-out sites, nature area; *Creative Arts*   outdoor and indoor theater, radio room, arts and crafts, model rocketry; *Miscellaneous*   ropes course, climbing wall

Boarding: 20 cabins (electricity), 2 showerhouses; dining room (family style), most eating habits accommodated, salad bar; laundry done in camp every other day

Counselors: 1 to every 4 campers, 75 counselors total; average age, 21; up to 7% are foreign

Camp Rules: Parents may call a reasonable number of times; letters written twice weekly; no food in cabins

Medical: Physician and 3 registered nurses in camp, 11-bed infirmary, parents notified of sick child by calls and letters; 15 miles from Northern Cumberland Memorial Hospital, 25 miles from Maine Medical Center

Directors: Henry M. Hacker, William F. Hacker
Summer: P.O. Box 240, Casco, ME 04015
     207-627-4266
Winter: 1758 Beacon Street, P.O. Box 9, Brookline, MA 02146
     617-277-8080

Henry and Bill Hacker opened Camp Cedar in 1954 and have been active directors every season. Both have graduate degrees in education/ guidance and have been involved in teaching. Bill was a guidance counselor in Westport, Connecticut. Henry owned and directed his own educational center in Brookline, Massachusetts.

Philosophy: Camp Cedar strives to treat each boy as an individual, and to recognize that each camper has his own personality, interests, and abilities. The program is structured, "but flexible enough so that each can achieve up to his potential. We see to it that each camper is treated with care, warmth, and affection, so that every boy knows that he is spending his summer at a camp where respect, responsibility, and love are of supreme importance. We pride ourselves on our staff, and hire counselors who like working with children and have outstanding teaching skills." A large percentage of the staff returns each summer, and many were campers at the camp.

Parent Comment: "Summers at Camp Cedar can best be described as coming home rather than leaving home. The atmosphere is one of camaraderie, friendship, and camp spirit.

"The well-trained staff exposes the campers to many different activities. A great deal of individual and team instruction is given at various skill levels. As the campers mature, they schedule their activities to suit their individual interests. This allows campers to refine their own techniques as well as participate in many team challenges.

"With each season, my son returns a little more self-confident, happy about his accomplishments, and looking forward to the next camp season."

HIDDEN VALLEY CAMP
Freedom, Maine

Coed

Ages: 8–13

Campers: 220

Religious affiliation: None

Fees: $2,095, 4 weeks / $3,495, 8 weeks

Extra fees: Transportation to and from camp, store account

Founded: 1946

Program: A structured and elective, noncompetitive program with emphasis on elective programs in many performing and creative arts

Facilities/Activities: *Athletics* baseball field, soccer field, 2 hard-surface tennis courts, basketball court, street hockey court, gymnastics area (low balance beam, free exercise), volleyball court; *Waterfront* spring-fed lake, swimming, fishing, kayaking, sailboarding, canoeing, boating; *Camping* campfire sites, barns and corrals (llama herd, 40 farm animals), 3 tepees, outdoor kitchen, nature area; *Creative Arts* extensive performing and creative arts building, clowning, mime, juggling, stained glass, pottery, printmaking, fabric arts, photography (2 darkrooms), video lab, 3 dance studios (tap, jazz, modern, ballet), choreography; *Miscellaneous* ropes course, 2 horseback riding rings, outdoor pavilion with hot tub, large-screen television, log cabin

Boarding: 17 cabins (electricity), 1–2 indoor showers/cabin; dining room (family style), vegetarian option; laundry done by camp every 8–9 days

Counselors: 1 to every 3 campers, 75 counselors total; average age, 23; 17.5% are foreign

Camp Rules: 1 telephone call a month under supervision of directors; at least 1 letter per week; no food in cabins

Medical: 4 registered nurses in camp, members of staff trained in first aid and CPR, 8-bed infirmary, parents notified about all problems; 15 miles from Waldo County Hospital

Directors: Peter and Meg Kassen
Summer: Freedom, ME 04941
          800-922-6737, 207-342-5177
Winter: Same

Peter and Meg Kassen have directed summer camps since the mid-1970s. Peter has a master's degree from the Yale School of Management, where he specialized in group dynamics and small business administration. He has trained as a professional counselor and acted as a consultant to a variety of nonprofit organizations. Meg is a registered massage therapist and has a B.A. from the Philadelphia College of Textiles. She has designed camp programs for such activities as crafts, swimming, dance, and farm-animal care.

Philosophy: Hidden Valley focuses on the eight- to thirteen-year-old age group (younger and first-time campers), which helps keep the camp community atmosphere relatively low key. Most campers come to Hidden Valley for four weeks, a healthy stay for those who may be embarking on their first sleep-away experience.

Hidden Valley emphasizes the value of community and encourages children to discover their own interests and strengths. The staff is hired for its professional qualifications (many are teachers, artisans, coaches) as well as "their ability to use humor and insight to create a supportive, nurturing atmosphere. We have a long history of attracting young people from many countries as well as from diverse backgrounds throughout the U.S."

Programs are elective, with guidance provided by staff, directors, and parents. Campers can concentrate in their area of choice.

The directors, who own and live at Hidden Valley year-round, are concerned about the environment, and have incorporated this sensitivity into the camp program. In past years, campers have adopted whales, created recycling projects, and helped turn twenty acres of Brazilian rain forest into a national park.

Parent Comment: "We are pleased that we chose Hidden Valley Camp because the Kassens have created a safe, caring, stimulating community that has enabled our daughter to thrive while she faces the challenge of living away from our family. Each summer she returns home with new interests, lasting friendships, and more self-confidence. We are convinced that we made the right choice when our daughter told us she loved Hidden Valley because 'the people are so nice, you can be yourself, and it's like being at a month-long sleep-over party.' "

CAMP KAWANHEE

Weld, Maine

Single sex, male

Ages: 7–15

Campers: 140

Religious affiliation: None (Christian orientation)

Fees: $2,835, 7 weeks

Extra fees: Transportation to and from camp, trips, incidental expenses

Founded: 1920

Program: A structured and elective, competitive program in both athletic and nonathletic activities. All boys are required to attend activity periods (4 per day) the first 2 weeks of camp; after this 2-week introductory period boys may sign out of the assigned activity and sign in to one of their choice

Facilities/Activities: *Athletics* 4 clay tennis courts, baseball field, soccer field, basketball court, wrestling, archery range, riflery range, volleyball court; *Waterfront* Lake Webb, swimming, fishing, 2 sailboats (Cape Cod knockabouts), 4 dinghies, canoes, rowboats, 12 kayaks, 2 waterski boats; *Camping* campfire and sleep-out sites, campcraft, cookout area, nature area; *Creative Arts* theater, model sailboats, wood shop, metal shop, radio; *Miscellaneous* computers, library, Ping-Pong, outdoor chapel, recreation hall

Boarding: 15 cabins (electricity), 2 showerhouses; dining room (family style), salad bar; laundry done weekly by camp

Counselors: 1 to every 3 campers, 50 counselors total; average age, 28; up to 5% are foreign

Camp Rules: After first 10 days campers may phone home collect or receive calls; letters written once a week; food allowed in cabins

Medical: Registered nurse in camp, 6-bed infirmary, parents telephoned when camper is admitted to infirmary or if hospital is necessary; 14 miles from Franklin Memorial Hospital

Director: Walter W. Estabrook
Summer: Weld, ME 04285
207-585-2210
Winter: 415 South Drexel Avenue, Columbus, OH 43209
614-252-4381

Walter Estabrook has been director of Camp Kawanhee since 1971. A former Kawanhee camper and counselor, he is a graduate of Wesleyan University. He served in World War II as overseas athletic director at a U.S. naval airbase. Following nearly thirty years of sales and purchasing work with the Brown Steel Company of Columbus, Ohio, Walter retired to devote his full time to Kawanhee. The Estabrooks' three sons have been campers and counselors at Kawanhee, and their daughter has also been a Kawanhee counselor. Walter's wife, June, is a graduate of the University of Wisconsin–Stout and works at Kawanhee as an assistant director and bookkeeper.

Philosophy: Founded in 1920 by George and Raymond Frank, Kawanhee strives to maintain its basic mottoes: "fun with purpose"; "learn by doing"; "finish what you start." The aim of the staff is to encourage self-reliance, initiative, and perseverance. "As your son reaches out to capture new goals, he will reach new vision and understanding, returning home in the fall a boy of courage and enhanced power."

Parent Comment: "The Kawanhee experience gave our four sons inner strength and integrity that they will carry with them forever. They grew in confidence and in their eagerness to try new things, all in a relaxed way. They were never happier."

KIPPEWA FOR GIRLS
Winthrop, Maine ───────────────────────────

Single sex, female

Ages: 6½–16

Campers: 180

Religious affiliation: None

Fees: $2,000, 4 weeks / $3,600, 8 weeks

Extra fees: Transportation to and from camp, medical insurance, bedding rental, laundry, horseback riding, canteen

Founded: 1957

Program: An elective program that has each camper design her own activity schedule. Swimming is required and field sports are assigned

Facilities/Activities: *Athletics* baseball field, soccer field, 6 hard-surface tennis courts (4 lit), basketball court, dual-purpose paddle-tennis/basketball court, gymnastics building (Nissen equipment, uneven bars, balance beam, vault, mats), 2 volleyball courts, archery range; *Waterfront* lake (with 44 islands), swimming, 3 sailboards, 12 kayaks, 3 waterski boats, 4 motorboats, 25 canoes, 7 sailboats (2 14-fters, 5 Sunfish); *Camping* campfire and sleep-out sites, nature area; *Creative Arts* theater, plays, scenery design, arts and crafts (3 buildings), ceramics, pottery, sewing, stained glass, painting, silk-screen printing, leather, wood, macramé; *Miscellaneous* Ping-Pong

Boarding: 21 cabins (electricity), 1–2 showers/cabin; dining room (family style), special diets accommodated, kosher style, salad bar; laundry done weekly by camp

Counselors: 1 to every 3 campers, 55 counselors total; average age, 22; up to 20% are foreign

Camp Rules: Campers not permitted to receive or place telephone calls, telephone used for consultations between directors and parents only; letters written twice a week; no food in cabins

Medical: 2 registered nurses in camp, 8-bed infirmary, parents may request to be called and under what circumstances, parents notified if there is an emergency; 12 miles from Kennebec Valley Medical Center

Directors: Marty and Sylvia Silverman, Paul and Trudy Silverman
Summer: RD 1, Box 4150, Winthrop, ME 04364
    207-933-2993
Winter: 60 Mill Street, P.O. Box 307, Westwood, MA 02090
    617-762-8291

Marty and Sylvia Silverman have been involved in camping for more than four decades. Marty has an M.S.W. from Case Western Reserve University. Sylvia is a former elementary-school teacher and outdoor educator. Both are ACA-certified camp directors. Paul Silverman has over twenty years of camp experience and has a master's degree in recreation management. He is a Standards Visitor for the ACA. His wife, Trudy, is a camp administrator.

Philosophy: Kippewa for Girls aims to teach campers new skills and build self-confidence. This is accomplished by an individualized weekly program that is tailored for each girl. Activities include a full range of waterfront activities, as well as media, drama, gymnastics, hiking, and camping. At Kippewa for Girls, "every girl learns with a sense of excitement and anticipation. A full and satisfying camp experience in a caring and nurturing atmosphere is the personal commitment of the Silvermans."

Parent Comment: "I really like Kippewa. It's a special place for my daughter. I believe the reason is that Kippewa allows her to grow in her own particular way. Kippewa has room for many different types of girls and who have a great variety of interests. Most first-time campers come to Kippewa without a friend from home. Girls come to camp from over a hundred different communities and make many new friends. This is a real plus, because there are no cliques from home for a girl to contend with."

CAMP LAUREL

Readfield, Maine ————————————————————————

Coed

Ages: 7–15

Campers: 275

Religious affiliation: None

Fees: $4,275, 8 weeks

Extra fees: Transportation to and from camp, linen service, horseback riding, personal expenses

Founded: 1950

Program: A very structured, moderately competitive program

Facilities/Activities: *Athletics* 3 baseball fields, 2 soccer fields, 8 hard-surface tennis courts, basketball court, gymnastics (balance beam, uneven bars, mats), 2 volleyball courts (lit), archery range; *Waterfront* lake, Red Cross swimming lessons, swim team, water polo, 3 waterski boats, 17 sailboats (Hobies, Sunfish, Javelins, Lazers), 17 sailboards, 18 canoes, 6 rowboats, 5 kayaks; *Camping* campfire and sleep-out sites, nature area; *Creative Arts* outdoor and indoor theaters (12 plays a summer), mime, theater workshops, arts and crafts building, ceramics, photography (darkroom), studio art, crafts, model rocketry, music building, dance studio, radio room; *Miscellaneous* stable and ring for horseback riding, trails, recreation building

Boarding: 46 cabins (electricity), some cabins have showers and others use one of several central showerhouses; dining room (family style), special diets accommodated, kosher and kosher style, salad bar; laundry done weekly by camp

Counselors: 1 to every 3 campers, 90–100 counselors total (30 service staff); average age, 23; up to 10% are foreign

Camp Rules: Parents call office during the day, and that evening their child will call back (4 calls a summer suggested); letter writing every other day; no food permitted in cabins

Medical: 3 registered nurses in camp, several staff certified in first aid and CPR, 12-bed infirmary, parents called if child is seen by doctor, spends night in infirmary, or is injured; 17 miles from hospital

Directors: Ron and Ann Scott
Summer: Readfield, ME 04355
  207-685-4945
Winter: Box 4378, Boca Raton, FL 33429
  800-327-3509, 407-391-1579

Ann Scott's parents started Camp Laurel in 1949, and Ann has spent every summer of her life at Laurel. Ron has been a full-time, year-round director since 1974, and camping has been the sole occupational commitment for the Scott family since then.

As the owners/directors of Laurel, Ann and Ron are both longtime members of the ACA and the Maine Youth Camping Association. Ron has served the ACA as a member of the board of directors of the New York section, ethics chairman of the New York section, and currently serves as a Standards Visitor for the ACA. Ron and Ann are the parents of three children.

Philosophy: Camp Laurel offers a highly structured program with the opportunity to create individualized programs. Laurel is thus able to serve children with a wide variety of interests. Camp Laurel emphasizes its "family atmosphere and friendly environment." Personal improvement and development are stressed, no matter what the inherent ability of each camper may be.

Camp Laurel's staff is committed to quality. "Our staff aims to put our campers' well-being and happiness as our absolute first priority during the camping season. Our staff is mature and superb. Most of all, Camp Laurel is FUN! Our staff and campers are always having what we call fun with a capital F."

Parent Comment: "I just wanted you to know what a wonderful summer my daughter had at Camp Laurel. Once again, she returned home happy, self-confident, and relaxed. She seemed ebullient about her summer and enthusiastic about the friends she made and the new things she tried. Her counselor seemed to have made a particular impression upon her—as a smart, loving, adventurous young woman—a perfect counselor!

"Your camp seems to be a wonderful environment for our child and we are so happy we found you."

MAINE TEEN CAMP
Kezar Falls, Maine ——————————————————————

Coed

Ages: 13–16

Campers: 220

Religious affiliation: None

Fees: $1,950, month (2 sessions) / $3,400, 2 months (full season)

Extra fees: Personal account

Founded: 1984

Program: A structured, progressive program with an emphasis on water sports, tennis, and the creative arts

Facilities/Activities: *Athletics* soccer field, 5 hard-surface tennis courts, tennis pro shop, basketball court, volleyball court; *Waterfront* lake, swimming, sailing, waterskiing, sailboarding, snorkeling, fishing; *Camping* campfire and sleep-out sites (2 sand beaches); *Creative Arts* outdoor theater, dance studio, recording studio, stained glass studio, silversmith studio, music room, photography (2 darkrooms), fine arts center, pottery studio; *Miscellaneous* computers (Tandy, IBM), ropes course, hot tub

Boarding: 20 cabins (electricity), 3 bunkhouses, 30 indoor showers, showerhouses; dining room (family style), vegetarian option, salad bar; laundry done weekly by camp and commercial service

Counselors: 1 to every 4 campers, 65–70 counselors total; most in mid-20s; 25% are foreign

Camp Rules: Campers have access to pay phone; weekly letter home encouraged; food in tight containers permitted in sleeping accommodations

Medical: 3–4 registered nurses in camp, 2–3 EMTs on staff, 10-bed infirmary, parents notified of all medical problems; 2 miles from Sacopee Medical Center, 25 miles from Maine Medical Center

Director: Kris Kamys
Summer: RR 1, Box 39, Kezar Falls, ME 04047
207-625-8581
Winter: Same

Kris Kamys is director and co-founder of Maine Teen Camp. Previously, Kris founded Cony Grant Farm, a coed wilderness program for teens in Bingham, Maine. He has a B.A. and an M.A. from the University of Massachusetts. Kris is an amateur herpetologist and nature photographer.

Philosophy: The goal of the staff at Maine Teen Camp is to create a supportive environment where "fun and growth are part of each day's adventures." Maine Teen Camp offers teens the opportunity to exercise "responsible freedom": campers choose their own program (with two "focus" activities). The 4,000 feet of shorefront means water sports are central at Maine Teen Camp. "Being a part of Maine Teen Camp means joining a group of enthusiastic and happy teens and adults who are having a great time together."

Parent Comment: "We were so happy that our daughter had such a good time at camp this summer. It was her first experience in communal living and I think it was most beneficial and rewarding for her. She returned enthusiastic and keen to go back next year. We find her quite changed—far more open and willing to cooperate and more tolerant of others."

CAMP MANITOU
Oakland, Maine ——————————————————————

Single sex, male (sister camp, Camp Matoaka)

Ages: 7–16

Campers: 195

Religious affiliation: None

Fees: $2,175, 4 weeks / $3,700, 8 weeks

Extra fees: Canteen

Founded: 1947

Program: A structured program with emphasis placed on sports and creative and waterfront activities; personalized teaching program

Facilities/Activities: *Athletics* 3 baseball fields, 7 pitching machines, batting cage, 4 soccer fields, 7 hard-surface tennis courts (5 lit), 5 basketball courts (2 lit), 2 street hockey courts, track, gymnastics area, riflery range, archery range, 3 volleyball courts, 2 football fields, lacrosse field, golf driving range, miniature golf course, fencing, martial arts, indoor gymnasium (basketball, volleyball, street hockey); *Waterfront* lake, swimming, scuba diving, fishing, 12 kayaks, 10 sailboards, 15 sailboats, 3 waterski boats, 10 canoes, 2 patrol boats, 10 rowboats, 4 pedal boats; *Camping* campfire and sleep-out sites, nature area; *Creative Arts* indoor theater, plays, set design, makeup, costuming, lighting, voice, music, radio, arts and crafts, pottery, woodworking, model rocketry, animated film studio, television station; *Miscellaneous* 23 computers (IBM, Apple, Commodore), high and low ropes course, camp museum, astronomy/aquarium building, 2 recreation rooms, library, newspaper room

Boarding: 20 cabins (electricity), 2 showers/cabin; dining room (family style), kosher, vegetarian option, salad bar; laundry done weekly by camp

Counselors: 1 to every 2.5 campers, 83 counselors total; average age, 24; up to 20% are foreign

Camp Rules: Parents can call campers between certain hours; letters written twice a week; no food in cabins

Medical: Physician, 3 registered nurses, and 2 EMTs in camp, 10-bed infirmary, parents called on any hospital visit and if child spends more than 1 day in infirmary; 4.5 miles from Waterville Osteopathic Hospital, 6 miles from Mid Maine Medical Center

Directors: Bob and Amy Marcus
Summer: RFD 2, Oakland, ME 04963
   207-465-2271
Winter: 10 School Master Lane, Dedham, MA 02026
   800-326-1916

Bob Marcus has been at Camp Manitou for forty-three years as camper, counselor, director, and owner. His parents started Manitou. Bob is also a free-lance writer, photographer, basketball coach, and director of a community youth group in his Massachusetts hometown. Amy Marcus has worked as a school psychologist (grades K–12) for fifteen years. She has a master's in education and is completing her Ph.D. in educational administration.

Philosophy: The goal of Camp Manitou is to help boys develop both physically and socially. "We stress learning through participation. Through this method we attempt to impart a sense of belonging and unity that comes from a family atmosphere. We constantly attempt to challenge a boy's mind, as well as his body. Our ultimate goal is to have every camper leave Manitou with the self-confidence to feel good about himself."

Camp Manitou offers teaching programs in forty-three different areas, divided equally between waterfront instruction, land sports, and creative activities.

Parent Comment: "I attended Camp Manitou when I was a child, and went on to become a counselor. The best memories of my youth are my times at Manitou. I met my wife at our sister camp. When my two sons reached camp age, it was my dream that they have the same wonderful camp experience, so I chose Camp Manitou. Both have now spent twelve years at Manitou, and are now counselors. Like me, many of their closest friends are those made at Manitou. Like me, they talk about their camp experiences constantly, and can't wait for the summer. And, like me, they someday look forward to sending their sons to Manitou."

CAMP MATAPONI
Naples, Maine

Single sex, female

Ages: 7–16

Campers: 250

Religious affiliation: None

Fees: $2,250, 4 weeks / $4,000, 8 weeks

Extra fees: Transportation to and from camp, spending account

Founded: 1950

Program: A structured and elective, competitive and noncompetitive program, with schedules dependent upon age and interest of the individual

Facilities/Activities: *Athletics* 2 baseball fields, soccer field, 8 tennis courts (5 clay, 3 hard surface, all lit), basketball court, street hockey court, track, gymnastics (uneven bars, balance beam, floor exercise), archery range, volleyball courts, lacrosse, field hockey, indoor gym; *Waterfront* Sebago Lake, swimming, 10 sailboats (8 Sunfish, 2 Javelins), 14 canoes, 2 waterski boats, 2 sailboards; *Camping* campfire and sleep-out sites, nature area; *Creative Arts* theater, plays, musicals, voice, arts and crafts, fine arts, dance studio; *Miscellaneous* computers (Apple-compatible), recreation hall, library

Boarding: 32 cabins (electricity), 1 shower/cabin; dining room (family style), special diets accommodated, kosher style, salad bar; laundry done weekly by camp

Counselors: 1 to every 3 campers, 108 counselors total; average age, 21; 20% are foreign

Camp Rules: Telephone calls can be made while on a trip; letters written 3 times a week; no food in cabins

Medical: Physician and 2 registered nurses in camp, 5-bed infirmary, parents notified if camper has to spend night in infirmary; 6 miles from Bridgton Memorial Hospital

Director: Richard Shaler
Summer: Naples, ME 04055
207-787-3221
Winter: 10 Old Court Road, Baltimore, MD 21209
301-484-2233

Richard Shaler is a speech therapist for the Baltimore public schools. He has been in camping for thirty years. For twenty years, he was head counselor for a sleep-away camp in West Virginia. Richard has owned and directed Camp Mataponi for seven years. He is married and has three children.

Philosophy: At Mataponi the goal is to provide each camper with a safe, happy, and healthy summer. The Mataponi philosophy is based on "respect and love for the individual young lady." The staff strives to improve campers' skills, permit the blossoming of friendships, and promote a love for the outdoors. Sharing at all levels is also emphasized. As the director puts it: "Every child wants her place in the sun. We are dedicated to finding that place for each of our campers."

Parent Comment: "I would just like to thank you again for helping to make our daughter's camping experience at Mataponi so positive. Once she got over being homesick she had a wonderful time! Thank you for bending the rules and letting her call us that first week. It made all the difference.

"I can't say enough about her counselors; she loved them and they were wonderful with her. They were a perfect match for her.

"On our drive home we heard about all the wonderful events, trips, and daily activities, and also heard some hysterical songs. She made some lasting friendships and all in all the last four weeks were a wonderful experience for her. She's told everyone she loved Mataponi and would recommend it to anyone. I'm sure she'll be back next summer.

"Thanks for everything: your warmth, support, encouragement, and making Mataponi a terrific place to spend four weeks."

CAMP MATOAKA
Oakland, Maine ──────────────────────────

Single sex, female (brother camp, Camp Manitou)

Ages: 7–16

Campers: 185

Religious affiliation: None

Fees: $2,200, 4 weeks / $4,000, 8 weeks

Extra fees: Horseback riding, canteen

Founded: 1951

Program: A combination of structured and elective activities with optional competition. Campers choose their schedules each week with fundamental activities—swimming, tennis, arts and crafts, small craft, and waterskiing—given to every camper

Facilities/Activities: *Athletics*   2 baseball fields, 2 soccer fields, 6 hard-surface tennis courts (all lit), basketball court, street hockey court, archery range, volleyball court, track, indoor gymnastics (bars, beam, vault, floor exercise), playground, golf instruction; *Waterfront*   1,800-acre lake, Red Cross swimming lessons, swim team, paddleboats, 4 waterski boats, sailboarding, kayaking, sailing, canoeing; *Camping*   campfire and sleep-out sites, nature area, barnyard animals; *Creative Arts*   outdoor theater, plays, music, voice, fine arts, general crafts, dance room, photography (darkroom), radio room; *Miscellaneous*   8 computers (IBM, Apple IIe), ropes course, recreation room, 2 horseback riding arenas, stables, paths, Ping-Pong

Boarding: 18 cabins (electricity), 2 showers/cabin; dining room (family style), special diets accommodated, kosher style, salad bar; laundry done weekly by camp

Counselors: 1 to every 3 campers, 82 counselors total; average age, 24; up to 12% are foreign

Camp Rules: Parents can call once a week; letter writing 3 times a week; no food in cabins

Medical: Physician and 3 registered nurses in camp, 8-bed infirmary, parents notified if camper stays in infirmary or is taken to emergency room; 9 miles from Mid Maine Medical Center

Directors: Michael and Paula Nathanson
Summer: RFD 2, Oakland, ME 04963
      207-362-2501
Winter: 8751 Horseshoe Lane, Boca Raton, FL 33496
      800-MATOAKA, 407-488-6363

Second-generation owners and directors Paula and Michael Nathanson have maintained the special qualities and standards of excellence established by Michael's parents, who founded Camp Matoaka in 1951. Michael's sister Susan also plays an integral role in the camp administration. All the Nathansons are certified educators (B.S. in education degrees) and the family has spent almost forty summers at Camp Matoaka.

Philosophy: Matoaka prides itself on its scenic beauty and varied programs, as well as its "family touch and spirit of concern that enables the girls to return home with greater self-confidence and social development." The Nathansons believe that camp must provide each child with an exciting, healthy, and educational summer. Programs are designed to balance individual interests and talents with exposure to a wide variety of experiences in athletics, arts, and social living. In all activities—sports, arts and crafts, communications—each girl receives both small-group and individual instruction, according to her needs. Each camper also receives daily instruction in a number of elective and required courses. These include aquatic and land sports. The Nathansons' belief is that by playing, working, and living with girls of different ages, backgrounds, and places, "each camper gains added social opportunities, new friends, and additional interpersonal skills, as well as valuable insights into living."

Camper Comment: "Basically the Nathansons and Matoaka are family-oriented. The camp is relaxed, balanced, and diversified. It's not too big or small—just right. The individual instruction is outstanding and it's a fun place to be. Matoaka is always in tune with the needs of the campers and counselors and there is always something new and exciting. It's never boring."

MED-O-LARK CAMP
Washington, Maine

Coed

Ages: 11–16

Campers: 200

Religious affiliation: None

Fees: $2,095, 4 weeks / $3,450, 8 weeks

Extra fees: Transportation to and from camp, canteen

Founded: 1946

Program: Combination of structured and elective, noncompetitive activities. Counselors provide assistance choosing electives.

Facilities/Activities: *Athletics* baseball field, soccer field, 2 hard-surface tennis courts, basketball court, fencing area, volleyball court, weight room; *Waterfront* lake, waterskiing, sailing, sailboarding, kayaking, canoeing, fishing, swimming; *Camping* campfire sites, nature area; *Creative Arts* outdoor theater, plays, dance (ballet [not pointe], jazz, folk, African, tap, modern), puppets, improvisation, mime, guitar, arts and crafts, stained glass, clothesmaking, copper work, pottery, jewelry, wood shop, video room; *Miscellaneous* recreation room, ropes course, hot tub, horseshoe pit, barbecue area

Boarding: 24 cabins (electricity), most have indoor showers, there are a couple of showerhouses; dining room (family style), vegetarian option; laundry done weekly by camp

Counselors: 1 to every 3 campers, 70 counselors total; average age, 23; 15% are foreign

Camp Rules: Telephone calls flexible to meet parents' need; letter writing encouraged weekly; no food in cabins

Medical: 4 physicians on call and 5 nurses in camp, 10–12 beds in infirmary, parents notified immediately when child is sick; 20 miles from Pen Bay Medical

Director: Neal Goldberg
Summer: Washington, ME 04574
      207-845-2441
Winter: 334 Beacon Street, Boston, MA 02116
      617-267-3483

Neal Goldberg has owned and operated Med-O-Lark Camp for nineteen years. He received a master's degree in child development and family relations at the University of Connecticut. Before coming to Med-O-Lark, Neal headed a program for retarded children in Philadelphia.

Neal is an active member of, and inspector for, the ACA. He is also a member of the New England Camping Association and the Maine Camp Directors Association. In his free time, Neal, "The Magic Man," puts on benefit magic shows for children.

Philosophy: To encourage "self-motivation and self-expression," the camp offers both structured and free-choice activities. It also seeks to instill a "sense of community responsibility." The staff is responsible, caring, and lighthearted, many of whom are teachers and craftspersons. Many campers come for both sessions.

Med-O-Lark emphasizes human values, self-reliance, and under-standing in an "active yet pressure-free environment." The camp provides individualized attention to first-time campers as well as returning campers, and this creates an atmosphere "where children feel comfortable in trying new activities and broadening their abilities. We are known for our tremendous variety of exciting activities. These are not just words but a representation of our commitment to children and their families."

Parent Comment: "We want to thank you and the staff for everything that made our son's second stay at Med-O-Lark wonderful. We drove up to Maine again and it was great to see the kids happy and fulfilled. Our son was glad to get the tennis instruction. This was very important to us because he not only likes tennis but has never been a kid amenable to any 'lessons.' Again, like last year, he talked on the drive home about the other kids and counselors. He enjoys meeting kids from other countries, and the counselors act as important examples of responsible young adults. We are so glad for the existence of Med-O-Lark, and appreciate the dedication that goes into a place that creates such a warm atmosphere in which kids can learn and grow and laugh."

CAMP O-AT-KA
East Sebago, Maine

Single sex, male

Ages: 8–15

Campers: 150

Religious affiliation: Episcopalian

Fees: $1,595, 4 weeks / $2,795, 8 weeks

Extra fees: Personal account

Founded: 1906

Program: Combination of structured and elective activities. Offers extended overnight canoe and mountain trips for boys 12 and up; boys 14 and older may enroll in the 5-week Maine State–authorized Junior Maine Guide Program, which stresses leadership training

Facilities/Activities: *Athletics* 3 baseball fields, 2 soccer fields, 6 clay tennis courts, basketball court (lit), street hockey court, riflery range, archery range, volleyball court, jogging trail, 2 tetherball courts, weight room; *Waterfront* Sebago Lake, Red Cross swimming lessons, snorkeling, waterskiing, sailboat racing, canoeing, rowboats, 7 sailboats; *Camping* campfire and sleep-out sites, nature trail, nature shed with cages and pens; *Creative Arts* theater, plays, woodworking with power tools, leather shop, drawing and painting, model rocketry, photography (darkroom); *Miscellaneous* chapel, 2 recreation buildings, low ropes course

Boarding: 1 dorm and 20 cabins (electricity), 3 showerhouses; dining room (family style), nonkosher; laundry done weekly by commercial service

Counselors: 1 to every 4 campers, 38 counselors total; average age, 22; 15% are foreign

Camp Rules: No telephone calls to or from campers unless there is an emergency; campers write once a week; no food in cabins

Medical: Physician on call, registered nurse in camp, several counselors have first aid certification, 12-bed infirmary, parent notified by letter or phone depending on seriousness of illness; 15 miles from Northern Cumberland Memorial Hospital

Director: Robert F. Phinney
Summer: East Sebago, ME 04029
　　　　207-787-3401
Winter: 16 Barber Street, Medway, MA 02053
　　　　508-533-2544

Bob Phinney's association with O-At-Ka began in 1967 as a camper. Joining the staff in 1973, he was a cabin counselor for seven summers and headed the campcraft/trips department for ten years. In 1976 he received the Junior Maine Guide Award and in 1980 became a Maine State–certified trip leader instructor. A 1980 graduate of Harvard, during the rest of the year, Bob works at the Dexter School in Brookline, Massachusetts, where he teaches Latin, English, science, and computer literacy. Bob lives in Medway, Massachusetts, with his wife and son.

Philosophy: O-At-Ka is one of the oldest overnight camps in the country. Founded in 1906 by the Reverend Ernest J. Dennen and incorporated in 1942 as a nonprofit educational institution, the camp's focus is on "building character and good citizenship through well-devised programs of wholesome craft and sports activities. Established traditions, a structured program, and a caring staff are O-At-Ka's hallmarks."

Situated on seventy-five acres with over a half-mile of shorefront on Sebago Lake, the campus has over sixty buildings, including the "Bungalow," which contains offices and guest lodging; the "Commons," where the camp family dines; the "Great Hall," for indoor recreational events, meetings, and entertainment; and the screened-in woodland chapel, where the daily "Password" program and Sunday community services are held.

Parent Comment: "Over the past decade, each of our three sons has gone to Camp O-At-Ka, which has been a wonderful experience for them. We have found that the counselors and senior staff show a great deal of interest in each camper as an individual. We have been very pleased with our boys' experience."

CAMP PINECLIFFE

Harrison, Maine ─────────────────────────────

Single sex, female

Ages: 8–15

Campers: 170

Religious affiliation: Jewish

Fees: $4,300, 8 weeks

Extra fees: Transportation to and from camp, health insurance, horseback riding, canteen

Founded: 1917

Program: A structured and elective, noncompetitive program with an emphasis on both sports and creative work

Facilities/Activities: *Athletics* baseball field, soccer field, 6 clay tennis courts, tennis backboard, basketball court, track, gymnastics (uneven bars, mats, beams, horse vault), archery range, 3 volleyball courts; *Waterfront* lake, swimming, waterskiing, canoes, kayaks, Playaks, sailboards, rowboats, sailboats; *Camping* campfire and sleep-out sites, nature area with library, campcraft; *Creative Arts* outdoor theater, musicals, arts and crafts, ceramics (2 wheels, 2 kilns), silver house, dance, cultural activities; *Miscellaneous* recreation room, ropes course, horseback riding, stable, ring

Boarding: 18 cabins (some with electricity), indoor showerhouses (a total of 25 showers); dining room (family style), salad bar; laundry done weekly by camp

Counselors: 1 to every 2 campers, 75 counselors total; average age, 20; up to 17% are foreign

Camp Rules: Campers may receive and make telephone calls at specified times; letters written twice a week; no food in cabins

Medical: Physician lives 5 miles away, 3 registered nurses in camp, waterfront personnel are trained in first aid and CPR, 12-bed infirmary, parents notified immediately when child has a fever; 5 miles from Bridgton Memorial Hospital

Directors: Helen Rosenthal, Susan Lifter
Summer: Harrison, ME 04040
207-583-2201
Winter: 200 East 71 Street, New York, NY 10021
212-988-9666, 614-236-5698

Helen Rosenthal's roots in camping go back to 1919, when she was a camper. Currently the director of Pinecliffe, Rosenthal is listed in *Who's Who in American Women*. Helen has a B.A. from Smith College. She is involved with the New York School of Social Work and she is a board member of the ACA and member of the Maine Camp Directors Association. Helen is also an ACA "Pioneer of American Camping."

Susan Lifter has a B.A. from William Smith College and did her graduate work in guidance at Ohio State University. She started as a camper, at Pinecliffe in 1947. Susan is a member of the ACA and a board member of the Maine Camp Directors Association. She has directed programs for children in crisis in the Columbus city schools.

Philosophy: Through the years, Camp Pinecliffe has tried to create a warm, family atmosphere with many happy, fun-filled educational experiences for its campers. "The basis of the camp's success has been the philosophy that guides it today; teaching campers to live happily and successfully with each other. Nothing is more important than the individual camper. No individual camper, however, is more important than the Pinecliffe family." Encouraging each camper to make her Pinecliffe summer a happy learning experience to remember is Camp Pinecliffe's goal. Helen Rosenthal and Susan Lifter, as second- and third-generation directors, carry on the Pinecliffe family tradition.

Parent Comment: "Thank you for providing my daughter with a wonderful seven summers. The environment at Pinecliffe gave her an opportunity to grow, make wonderful friends, and have memorable experiences which she and we will always cherish. I'm only sorry that we have no more daughters to send you."

PORTANIMICUT: THE SAILING CAMP
Union, Maine

Single sex, male

Ages: 7–16

Campers: 70

Religious affiliation: None

Fees: $1,990, 4 weeks / $3,150, 8 weeks

Extra fees: Transportation to and from camp, personal account

Founded: 1929

Program: A structured and elective, noncompetitive program with emphasis on sailing

Facilities/Activities: *Athletics* baseball field, soccer field, 4 clay tennis courts, basketball court, volleyball court, archery range; *Waterfront* lake, Penobscot Bay, Red Cross swimming lessons, extensive sailing program, sailboards, Sunfish, Lazers, Coronado 15, V-2's, Cape Dory Typhoon, Boothbay Harbor Sloop, double-ended sailing whaleboats with prams (rowboats) and outboards, Cape Cod Mercury, Beetlecats, Hobie 16, Baybirds; *Camping* campfire and sleep-out sites, nature area; *Creative Arts* stage for skits, model sailboats (wood); *Miscellaneous* lodge, Ping-Pong

Boarding: 10 cabins (electricity), 1 showerhouse; dining room (family style), special diets accommodated; laundry done weekly by camp

Counselors: 1 to every 4 campers, 18–20 counselors total; most college age; 12% are foreign

Camp Rules: A couple of telephone calls per month by campers; 1 letter home per week; no food in cabins

Medical: Registered nurse in camp, some staff certified in first aid and CPR, 3-bed infirmary, camp notifies parents following complete assessment of situation; 12 miles from Penobscot Bay Medical Center

Director: Tom Lincoln
Summer: P.O. Box 614, Union, ME 04862
207-785-4949
Winter: P.O. Box 258, South Dennis, MA 02660
508-385-6133

Director Tom Lincoln has been involved in camping for more than thirty years and draws on his experiences as a camper, counselor, and most recently as director of Camp Viking on Cape Cod. He has an extensive knowledge of sailing, seamanship, and racing. Tom, a graduate of the Haverford School and the University of Rochester, is a member of the ACA and the Maine Youth Camping Association.

Philosophy: Portanimicut's small size "fosters a strong family atmosphere, which provides a sensitivity to each boy's needs." The activities, especially sailing, provide exciting, challenging opportunities for each boy to "reach inside himself and discover strengths and resources that he never knew he had. The Portanimicut staff supports each boy as he masters these new challenges, discovers his resourcefulness, gains self-respect, and learns to appreciate others." Portanimicut hopes each camper learns the value of sharing, patience, and helping. Each camper should come to understand that "doing things well is often better than being first."

Parent Comment: "We continue to think of Portanimicut as one of the best experiences our son could have had. All of them weren't pleasant, but they were all things he needed to learn and needed to know he could survive. You did a tremendous amount for him, and we will be glad to tell anyone."

CAMP SKYLEMAR
Naples, Maine ————————————————————

Single sex, male

Ages: 8–15

Campers: 140

Religious affiliation: None

Fees: $4,000, 7 weeks

Extra fees: Transportation to and from camp, laundry and linens, canteen

Founded: 1948

Program: A structured and elective program with emphasis on instruction in all activities; campers polled weekly and their choices build the structured program. Emphasis on tennis as well as golf and lacrosse

Facilities/Activities: *Athletics* 3 baseball fields, 2 soccer fields, 2 lacrosse fields, 8 tennis courts (4 hard surface, 4 Har-Tru, 2 lit), 3 basketball courts (1 lit), street hockey court, riflery range, archery range, volleyball courts, indoor gym (weight training, wrestling, basketball), 6-hole golf course; *Waterfront* lake, waterskiing, swimming, small powerboat, 3 sailboards, 8 canoes, 8 small sailboats, 2 large sailboats; *Camping* campfire and sleep-out sites, nature area, campcraft; *Creative Arts* theater, plays, radio room, arts and crafts, ceramics, oil painting, watercolor, leather, wood, photography (darkroom); *Miscellaneous* computers (IBM), 2 recreation rooms

Boarding: 20 cabins (electricity), 5 with showers, 1 central showerhouse for rest; dining room (family style), kosher style; laundry done weekly by commercial service

Counselors: 1 to every 3.5 campers, 40 counselors total; average age, 22; 10% are foreign

Camp Rules: Parents may call camp at any time, campers are discouraged from calling home; letters written 3 times a week; food allowed in cabins

Medical: Doctor lives 2 miles away, 2 registered nurses in camp, 7-bed infirmary, parents notified if child is kept for a second night in infirmary, or if any X rays prove positive and hospitalization is needed; 8 miles from Northern Cumberland Memorial Hospital

Director: Lee Horowitz
Summer: Naples, ME 04055
207-693-6414
Winter: 7900 Stevenson Road, Baltimore, MD 21208
301-653-2480

After spending a few summers as a camp counselor, Lee Horowitz founded Camp Skylemar in 1948, while a young teacher in Baltimore. Ten years later he became a middle-school principal in Baltimore and a coach at Johns Hopkins University. Later, he accepted the position of principal at a New York high school. Lee was called back to Baltimore as director of secondary education and later joined the Johns Hopkins faculty.

Philosophy: Located twenty-five miles from the Atlantic Ocean on one side and twenty-five miles from the White Mountains of New Hampshire on the other, Camp Skylemar provides "a happy, wholesome experience for boys from all over the United States." Skylemar claims that 90% of the children return each summer. "You don't join Skylemar for a summer, you join for a lifetime. Alumni interest and visitations reflect that."

Four out of five daily periods are structured, with the fifth providing an opportunity for a boy to specialize in the activity of his choice. The sports-oriented program includes a measure of nonathletic pursuits. Extra emphasis is placed on lifetime activities such as tennis, golf, and sailing. Skylemar has a six-hole golf course and also uses the nearby Naples Country Club course.

"Staff selection has been emphasized since the day the camp opened. The staff has played a major role in developing exceptionally warm relationships among campers and between campers and counselors."

Parent Comment: "My two sons claim that at Camp Skylemar they acquired the friendships, skills, attitudes, and other qualities that will last all their lives. They smile and speak of permanent rich memories they say no one can ever take away.

"I agree with the boys. I have watched them grow in physical abilities, in breadth of interest, and in poise. But more important than those more or less tangible results, I have watched the camp produce a huge growth in their ideals, their attitudes, and their relationships.

"Skylemar has brought warmth and depth into the lives of my children."

CAMP TAKAJO
Naples, Maine ───────────────────────

Single sex, male

Ages: 6–16

Campers: 360–80

Religious affiliation: None

Fees: $3,950, 8 weeks

Extra fees: Transportation to and from camp, laundry, canteen

Founded: 1947

Program: A structured and elective (older campers) schedule with competitive and noncompetitive activities

Facilities/Activities: *Athletics* 3 baseball fields, 2 soccer fields, 17 tennis courts (5 clay, 12 hard surface, 6 lit), 4 basketball courts (1 lit), 2 street hockey courts, track, gymnastics area, riflery range, archery range, volleyball courts, indoor gym (basketball, street hockey, volleyball); *Waterfront* lake, swimming, waterskiing, 4 powerboats, 25 sailboats (Sunfish, Javelins, Essex), 2 war canoes, 15 kayaks/Playaks, 20 canoes, scuba gear; *Camping* campfire and sleep-out sites, nature area with animals; *Creative Arts* indoor theater, FM radio station, electronics, photography, music house, arts and crafts, ceramics, woodworking, camp newspaper; *Miscellaneous* movie house, 2 recreation halls, counselor lounge

Boarding: 49 cabins (electricity), 4 showerhouses, indoor shower only in cabin for 16-year-olds; dining room (family style), special diets accommodated, salad bar; laundry done weekly by commercial service

Counselors: 1 to every 3.5 campers, over 100 counselors total; average age, 24; 12% are foreign

Camp Rules: Camper can call home twice a summer; letter writing every other day; no food in cabins

Medical: Physician and 4 registered nurses in camp, 25-bed infirmary, parent is always called if child stays overnight in infirmary; 20 miles from Bridgton, Portland, and Norway hospitals

Director: Jeff Konigsberg
Summer: Long Lake, Naples, ME 04055
     207-693-6675
Winter: 496 LaGuardia Place, Suite 381, New York, NY 10012
     212-979-0606

Jeff Konigsberg was a Takajo camper, counselor, group leader, and associate director before assuming ownership of the camp.

Philosophy: "Good camping, more than any other experience, offers an environment that fosters the development of values." At Takajo, this belief is fundamental and is brought home through sports and games. Integrity, a sense of fair play, appreciation for natural surroundings, compassion—these are vital qualities Takajo hopes to instill in each boy.

Since its beginning in 1947, Takajo has evolved into three distinct groups: Warriors (grades 1–4), Juniors (grades 5–6), and Seniors (grades 7–9). The program for each group is both structured and diversified. The entire camp joins together in certain activities such as campfires, drama productions, talent nights, and weekly barbecues. Most of a camper's daily activities, however, take place within his own group in order to better meet the needs of each individual.

Diversification is the keynote at Takajo. Participation in team sports and tennis is complemented by a wide range of hobbies and skills. As the campers move up in age groups, they receive more and more freedom to choose their hobbies and skills and to specialize in the activities that interest them.

"No description can fully capture the personality of the camp, the spirit of the intimate living relationships, and many of the intangibles that are the essence of Takajo. This is best done in a summer sojourn at Takajo on Long Lake."

Parent Comment: "When I think about Takajo, the first thing that comes to mind is the caring attitude of the people in charge. The director and the group leaders are extremely sensitive to the camper's needs.

"The careful selection of the staff is readily apparent. It is stressed from the very beginning that camp is for the kids and that the counselors are hired to help each child have a positive experience through his relationships with other campers and through the activities in which he participates.

"The facilities at Takajo are exceptional. The way the program is designed and the variety of activities available help each youngster to find his niche and to develop in a way that is both supportive and challenging."

TRIPP LAKE CAMP
Poland, Maine

Single sex, female

Ages: 8–16

Campers: 330

Religious affiliation: None

Fees: $4,200, 8 weeks

Extra fees: Transportation to and from camp, linens, uniforms, store account

Founded: 1911

Program: Combination of structured and elective activities in noncompetitive atmosphere

Facilities/Activities: *Athletics* 2 baseball fields, 2 soccer fields, 18 tennis courts (6 Har-Tru, 12 hard surface, 6 lit), 3 basketball courts (1 lit), archery range, 2 volleyball courts, 2 indoor gyms (gymnastics, floor exercise, vaults, uneven bars, single bar, beam, free weights, exercycles, climbing wall); *Waterfront* lake, swimming, sailing (8 Sunfish, 2 Lazers), 28 aluminum canoes, Hobie Cat, pontoon boat, 4 waterski boats, 6 white-water canoes, 10 kayaks; *Camping* campfire and sleep-out sites, nature area; *Creative Arts* indoor theater (4 shows), 9 separate art shops (pottery, enameling, silver, jewelry, newsletter, photography, arts and crafts, fine arts, video), dance building; *Miscellaneous* 2 horseback riding rings, stable for 12 horses, riding trails, ropes course (22 elements), 2 other rainy-day facilities

Boarding: 49 cabins (electricity), 5 showers/cabin, 2 showerhouses; dining room (family style); laundry done weekly by camp

Counselors: 1 to every 3 campers, 123 counselors total; average age, 25; 15% are foreign

Camp Rules: No telephone calls for new campers during the first 2 weeks, 2 telephone calls per summer; letter writing twice a week; no food in cabins

Medical: Physician and 3 registered nurses in camp, 12-bed infirmary, parents informed by mail if child is in infirmary overnight, parents called by directors if child is in infirmary 3 consecutive nights; 15 miles from Central Maine Medical Center and St. Mary's Hospital

Directors: Bev and Jon Myers
Summer: Box 1000, Tripp Lake Camp Road, Poland, ME 04273
207-998-4347
Winter: 3635 Old Court Road, Baltimore, MD 21208
301-653-3082

Bev and Jon Myers, the owners and directors of Tripp Lake Camp, have been involved with the camp since 1981. Jon has also been president of Londontown Corporation and vice president of its parent company, Interco, Inc. Both Bev and Jon worked as counselors at Camp Takajo in the early years of their marriage, and later sent their three sons to Camp Takajo.

Philosophy: Bev and Jon Myers work toward facilitating positive growth and development in children and young adults. They see the camping experience as an environment that supports that goal. Each Tripp Lake camper is encouraged to take charge of her life and to develop her unique potential with "reason, imagination, and human concern."

The program at Tripp Lake Camp has been designed to provide each camper with an opportunity to experience success in her own special abilities. Whether in athletics, the arts, or other activities, each girl is encouraged to improve her skills so that at the end of the summer, she can take home a sense of accomplishment.

Each day's schedule is prepared one day in advance and includes choices made by the campers.

"The proof of the success of Tripp Lake's unique approach can be found in the fact that many of our campers are second-, third-, and even fourth-generation Tripp Lakers."

Parent Comment: "A challenging, fun, high-spirited, and loving environment are just a few of the adjectives to describe Tripp Lake Camp. The girls are taught terrific athletic skills, including swimming, tennis, and many field sports. The adventurous overnight trips have made my daughter more responsible, confident, and independent.

"Friendships and camaraderie are the keys to Tripp Lake Camp. These relationships blossom and endure over the years because the girls respect and admire each other.

"Jon and Bev Myers care about the girls in absolutely everything they do. They guide the girls with a gentleness and caring that make Tripp Lake special! *Most* important, my daughter has had a great time."

CAMP VEGA
Kents Hill, Maine

Single sex, female

Ages: 8–15

Campers: 300

Religious affiliation: None

Fees: $4,325, 8 weeks

Extra fees: Transportation to and from camp, canteen

Founded: 1936

Program: A structured and elective, competitive program in which campers may choose areas of interest

Facilities/Activities: *Athletics* 2 baseball fields, pitching machine, 2 soccer fields with underground irrigation, 10 hard-surface tennis courts, 2 basketball courts, track and field course, archery range, fencing area, 2 volleyball courts, gymnastics building (springboard floor, 3 beams, 2 unevens, vault box, mini-trampolines, harness), fencing, golf range area with golf net, softball, dugouts, weight-lifting building (Nautilus, bike, rowing machine); *Waterfront* Echo Lake, swimming, fishing, water-skiing (4 Ski Nautiques), 25 sailboats (Sunfish, Hobies, others), 12 sail-boards, 2 4-man sculls, 12 canoes, 4 kayaks; *Camping* campfire and sleep-out sites, campcraft, nature building; *Creative Arts* 400-seat indoor theater, plays, drama workshop, lighting and sound room, voice and singing, videotaping, arts and crafts, ceramics, jewelry, macramé, clay modeling, stained glass, painting, sketching, woodworking, 2 dance buildings (tap and jazz/ballet); *Miscellaneous* horseback riding, 2 stables, tack room, 2 rings, trails, 20-station ropes course, zip line to lake, outdoor art pavilion, cheerleading area, recreation rooms (2 12-ft.-wide screens)

Boarding: 27 cabins (electricity), showers in cabins and showerhouses; dining room (family style), salad bar; laundry done weekly by camp

Counselors: 1 to every 3 campers, 110 counselors total; average age, 21; no foreign counselors

Camp Rules: 1 telephone call per camper (extra for birthday); letter writing encouraged, 2 letters mandatory per week; no food in cabins

Medical: Physician, 4 registered nurses, and athletic trainer (trained in athletic injuries) in camp, 14-bed infirmary, parents notified if child is sick; 17 miles from Kennebec Valley Medical Center

Directors: Dick and Linda Courtiss
Summer: Kents Hill, ME 04349
      207-685-3707
Winter: Box 1771, Duxbury, MA 02332
      617-934-6536

Dick Courtiss began his career in camping as a camper and loved it so much he became a counselor, unit head, waterfront director, and associate director. He and his wife, Linda, have been owners and directors of Vega since 1975. Dick played football and lacrosse at Syracuse University and has a degree in physical education. His extensive involvement in athletics as a participant and as a coach has contributed to the athletic emphasis at Camp Vega. Prior to his full-time involvement at Vega, Dick owned and operated Rhodes Enterprises, producers of home and flower shows throughout New England for ten years. Linda has a business background in personnel management and has assisted in the operation of the camp since 1975.

Philosophy: Vega is a camp that strives for "character building through sports." Vega has many goals for its campers. The first is that each camper discover her potential in camp, which Vega feels can extend through adult life. "Expectations are achieved through personalized instruction by professionals, who work closely with the counselors." Another goal is to have each girl benefit from the "moral and ethical tone emphasized in everyday living. We teach our campers to be gracious with their accomplishments by helping others and being fair." Also, Camp Vega strives for a democratic atmosphere so campers can learn decisionmaking and community participation. This is accomplished through the "camper council" in which elected older girls meet regularly with the director to discuss camp issues. Vega hopes that the acquisition of these skills will extend itself "civically and globally as our youth come face-to-face with global environmental and political issues."

Parent Comment: "Vega is to summer camps what the Ivy League is to education. The idyllic waterfront of Echo Lake and the camp's facilities offer numerous activities. But the best part of Vega is the staff. The counselors not only have an expertise in one of the activity areas, they are well trained to work with the campers. At Vega, each girl is encouraged to reach her potential in a supportive atmosphere. The girls are warm and gracious to each other. There's not a dry eye at the final banquet and your daughter will make friendships that just might last a lifetime."

CAMP WAGANAKI
East Waterford, Maine

Single sex, male

Ages: 8–16

Campers: 60

Religious affiliation: None

Fees: $700, 2 weeks / $1,175, 4 weeks / $1,700, 6 weeks

Extra fees: Transportation to and from camp, laundry, canteen

Founded: 1919

Program: A structured and elective program with competitive and non-competitive activities; emphasis in soccer, waterskiing, and an extensive camping and hiking program

Facilities/Activities: *Athletics* 3 baseball fields, soccer field, 3 hard-surface tennis courts, basketball court, street hockey court, riflery range, archery range, volleyball court; *Waterfront* lake, swimming, waterskiing, sailing, canoeing; *Camping* campfire and sleep-out sites, nature area; *Creative Arts* outdoor theater, arts and crafts; *Miscellaneous* recreation room

Boarding: 14 cabins (electricity), 1 showerhouse (6 showers); dining room (family style), special diets accommodated, salad bar; laundry done weekly by camp

Counselors: 1 to every 5 campers, 12 counselors total; average age, 21; up to 10% are foreign

Camp Rules: Telephone calls made when necessary; letters written at least once a week; food allowed in cabins

Medical: Registered nurse in camp, some EMT and several advanced first aid personnel in camp, 6-bed infirmary, parents notified immediately regardless of how sick child is; 10 miles from Stephens Memorial Hospital

Director: Dana E. Johnson
Summer: East Waterford, ME 04233
207-583-4402
Winter: 18 Reed Street, Westbrook, ME 04092
207-797-5345

Dana E. Johnson is a public-school teacher. Dana has taught swimming since age seventeen and was a waterfront director at a large Maine camp for five years. In 1984 Dana bought Waganaki and became its director.

Philosophy: Waganaki prides itself on its small size (sixty campers). "We are uncrowded. Here a camper can get to know each person in camp and each boy does not have to compete for simple things such as counselor time or use of equipment." Waganaki believes in building youth through solid sports activities—soccer and waterskiing in particular—and through an extensive outdoor camping and hiking program. This combination of fun and skill building in a group environment promotes a happy, satisfying summer. Director Johnson claims that since 1984 when he bought the camp, "Waganaki has not produced one single unhappy camper or parent."

Parent Comment: "My son grew up at Camp Waganaki. He learned to take care of himself and to get along with others. His self-confidence grew and he wasn't allowed to get down on himself. He had a great summer."

CAMP WALDEN
Denmark, Maine ——————————————————————————

Single sex, female

Ages: 9–15

Campers: 150

Religious affiliation: None

Fees: $4,075, 8 weeks

Extra fees: Transportation to and from camp, health insurance, linen rental, intensive riding, white-water rafting, Mount Washington trip, camper allowance

Founded: 1916

Program: A structured and elective program with individual scheduling to accommodate special requests such as intensive tennis, riding, and gymnastics. Honor system used. Girls help run several phases of camp

Facilities/Activities: *Athletics* baseball field, soccer field, 7 tennis courts (4 clay, 3 hard surface, 2 lit), basketball court (lit), gymnastics, 2 volleyball courts, archery range, indoor gym; *Waterfront* lake, swimming, beach area, sailing, 13 canoes, 3 kayaks, 4 sailboards, 2 waterski boats, chase boat; *Camping* campfire and sleep-out sites; *Creative Arts* theater, drama, arts and crafts, pottery, enamel, silver, painting, drawing; *Miscellaneous* 4 computers (Apple IIe), horseback riding (2 rings, stable, ring and field jumping), recreation room, air hockey, bumper pool, Ping-Pong

Boarding: 15 cabins (no electricity), 2 showerhouses (15 stalls); dining room (family style), special diets accommodated, salad bar; laundry done weekly by camp

Counselors: 1 to every 3 campers, 55 counselors total; average age, 21; 20% are foreign

Camp Rules: One pay phone for campers to use, parents can telephone camp at any reasonable hour; letter writing encouraged, cabin counselors write parents of all new campers and younger campers; food allowed in cabins if consumed within 48 hours

Medical: Registered nurses in camp, many staff members certified in first aid and CPR, also part-time EMT in camp, 4-bed infirmary, parents notified if child's temperature is over 100 or daughter has accident that requires medical attention; 8 miles from Northern Cumberland Memorial Hospital

Directors: Helen Herz Cohen, Wendy S. Cohen
Summer: Route 1, Box 129, Denmark, ME 04022
            207-452-2901
Winter: P.O. Box 3427, Charlottesville, VA 22903
            804-293-3730

Helen Herz Cohen has directed Camp Walden for over forty years. She has a master's degree in guidance. She is dedicated to the notion that camping aids a young woman's growth. Her daughter Wendy has a bachelor's degree in physical education and twenty years of Walden experience.

Philosophy: Camp Walden defines itself "by option, possibilities, and relationships." Campers have the option to try new activities; there are the limitless possibilities when exploring the Appalachian Mountains and Maine rivers; and mostly, there are the relationships formed when young women are learning about themselves.

Walden's honor system seeks to teach campers to trust and respect each other without enforcing stringent rules and regulations. "Friendships are formed through the sharing of thoughts, ideas, and an occasional ice cream cone. Whether it is two fourteen-year-olds discussing their goals for the future while sitting on top of a rock, or a dining room that resounds with raucous singing, Walden is the spirit of the people who call it home for eight weeks each summer."

Camper Comment: "A few years ago, I was asked to identify several monumental experiences in my life. Camp Walden headed the list. I cannot think of a time in which I experienced such invaluable growth while forming friendships that have stayed with me throughout adulthood (including a weekly indoor tennis game composed solely of former Walden campers). Walden taught me about values and about the importance of trying new things while holding on to past accomplishments. It introduced me to the wonders of the wilderness and the excitement of hearing my name cheered when I hit a home run. I often think of Camp Walden, and when I do, I smile."

CAMP WAZIYATAH
Harrison, Maine

Coed

Ages: 7–15

Campers: 200

Religious affiliation: None

Fees: $2,150, first 4 weeks / $1,875, second 4 weeks / $3,600, 8 weeks

Extra fees: Transportation to and from camp, medical insurance, laundry, white-water rafting (senior trip), canteen

Founded: 1926

Program: A structured and elective, competitive and noncompetitive program

Facilities/Activities: *Athletics* 2 baseball fields, 2 soccer fields, 10 hard-surface tennis courts (2 lit), 3 basketball courts (2 lit), riflery range, archery range, volleyball court, indoor gym, gymnastics (parallel bars, horse vault, springboard, balance beams); *Waterfront* lake (2,000-ft. shoreline), swimming, canoeing, sailing, snorkeling, water polo, water slide, diving board, inboard waterski boat, outboard waterski boat, rowboats, 2 small motorboats, sailboards; *Camping* campfire and sleep-out sites, nature area; *Creative Arts* outdoor theater, plays, stage design, scriptwriting, lighting, directing, dance, photography (darkroom), video studio, makeup, arts and crafts, ceramics, drawing, jewelry, leather, wood, pottery, sculpture, weaving, silk-screen printing, model rocketry; *Miscellaneous* horseback riding (2 rings, trails, stable), recreation room

Boarding: 24 cabins (electricity), 3 showerhouses (18 individual stalls); dining room (family style), special diets accommodated, salad bar; laundry done weekly by camp (shower towels and sheets provided daily by camp)

Counselors: 1 to every 3 campers, 75 counselors total; average age, 21; up to 20% are foreign

Camp Rules: Parents may arrange telephone calls after first week, 1 call per week; 1 letter a week required; no food in cabins

Medical: Camp pediatrician is 15 minutes away, 2 registered nurses in camp, waterfront staff and many counselors have CPR, 12-bed infirmary, parents notified when child has been in infirmary overnight or in case of accident or serious illness; 8 miles from Stephens Memorial Hospital

Directors: Tom and Nancy Armstrong
Summer: RR 2, Box 465, Harrison, ME 04040
      207-583-6781
Winter: P.O. Box 86569, Madeira Beach, FL 33738
      813-391-0022

Tom and Nancy have been involved with children through education, camping, and community work for over forty years. Tom was developer, owner, and director of Glenmere Country Day Camp, in Norton, Massachusetts, for sixteen years. He has a B.S. and an Ed.M. and has worked for thirty-two years as a mathematics teacher. Nancy was busy with family, community activities, and teaching in elementary school for thirteen years. Both are active members of the ACA, participating in seminars and workshops to keep abreast of current trends and advancements in programs.

Philosophy: At Waziyatah the aim is "to provide a fun, safe summer." Campers may choose their own program from a large range of competitive and noncompetitive activities. Competition is offered through intercamp games with an emphasis placed on participation and good sportsmanship. Individual sports, theater, arts and crafts, riding, waterfront activities, and trip programs offer alternatives to those who do not want a competitive program.

Meals, special events, and evening programs "help foster friendship and provide the opportunity to work as a team. Twilight, rest period, and bedtime are also special cabin times."

Waziyatah's goals are to develop independence, self-esteem, good moral attitudes, and respect for others. Waziyatah also tries to develop an awareness and appreciation for the environment through good daily living practices.

Parent Comment: "Having had children at Waziyatah for five years, we cannot say enough about its special atmosphere and spirit which have allowed our son and daughter to grow in confidence, self-esteem, and independence. Each summer our children have had wonderful experiences, participating in a tremendous variety of activities that are both fun and creative, and making lasting friendships with young people from all over the country."

CAMP WEKEELA
Canton, Maine

Coed

Ages: 6–16

Campers: 320

Religious affiliation: None

Fees: $2,450, 4 weeks / $4,175, 8 weeks

Extra fees: Transportation to and from camp, canteen

Founded: 1981

Program: A structured, moderately competitive program offering over 65 activities

Facilities/Activities: *Athletics*   2 softball fields, soccer field, 6 hard-surface tennis courts, basketball court, street hockey court, gymnastics, track, archery range, volleyball court, indoor gym, Universal weight machine; *Waterfront*   lake, Red Cross swimming lessons, competitive swimming, sailing, waterskiing, canoeing, snorkeling, water polo, scuba diving, fishing, kayaks, Funyaks, rowboats, sailboards; *Camping* campfire and sleep-out sites, nature area; *Creative Arts*   outdoor theater (shows every 10 days), theater crafts, radio station, arts and crafts, photography (darkroom); *Miscellaneous*   high and low ropes course, recreation room

Boarding: 20 cabins (electricity), number of showers in cabins varies; dining room (family style), special diets accommodated, kosher available, salad bar; laundry done every other day by camp

Counselors: 1 to every 3 campers, 90 counselors total; average age, 21; up to 3% are foreign

Camp Rules: Telephone calls can be received by children at mealtimes after the first week; letters written twice a week; no food in cabins

Medical: Physician on call, 2 registered nurses in camp, 10-bed infirmary, parents notified if child is sick; 18 miles from Central Maine Medical Center

Directors: Eric and Lauren Scoblionko
Summer: RFD 1, P.O. Box 275, Route 219, Canton, ME 04221
　　　207-224-7878
Winter: 130 South Merkle Road, Columbus, OH 43209
　　　614-235-3177

Eric Scoblionko has a B.A. and an M.A. from the University of Pennsylvania. He was a teacher for several years and has been in camping all his life. Lauren Scoblionko has a B.A. from Brandeis University and an M.B.A. from Boston University. The Scoblionkos have three children. Camp Wekeela has received the highest certification from the ACA.

Philosophy: Wekeela stresses comfortable interaction during learning and development of skills. The camp's philosophy is: "Self-esteem and a yearning for self-fulfillment are keystones to a successful life."

Wekeela places an emphasis on the individual camper with individual tutoring in activities. There is also the added stimulation of group and team competition. When handled properly, Wekeela believes, competition helps campers learn to manage success and disappointment. The camp staff strives to maintain a healthy equilibrium between competition and cooperation. "Wekeela means drawing on one's inner resources, acquiring new skills, and doing all this in a relaxed, non-threatening, supportive atmosphere."

Parent Comment: "My daughter seems from letters and phone calls to have had the most incredible summer experience. I have never heard her so excited and thrilled about her summer before. She actually asked to stay for the next four weeks. No doubt, she will be with you eight weeks next year. I just wanted to thank you for your caring and concerned way with campers. You are obviously doing everything right."

CAMP WIGWAM
Harrison, Maine ————————————————————————

Single sex, male

Ages: 6–16

Campers: 135

Religious affiliation: None

Fees: $2,650, 5 weeks / $3,500, 7 weeks

Extra fees: Transportation to and from camp, uniform, canteen

Founded: 1910

Program: An elective, noncompetitive program with emphasis on tennis and golf. Intercamp sports

Facilities/Activities: *Athletics*   2 baseball fields, soccer field, 7 hard-surface tennis courts, 2 basketball courts, midget basketball court, street hockey court, golf, riflery range, archery range, volleyball courts, miniature golf, tetherball; *Waterfront*   lake, swimming, rowboating, canoeing, sailboarding, sailing, motorboating, waterskiing, snorkeling, fishing; *Camping*   campfire and sleep-out sites, nature area; *Creative Arts*   outdoor theater, mime, glee club, stagecraft, music, plays, arts and crafts, ceramics, woodworking, model rocketry, photography, newspaper, video club, radio room; *Miscellaneous*   computers (Tandy, Macintosh), horseshoes, recreation room, shuffleboard, chess club

Boarding: 22 cabins (electricity), 12 tents, showerhouses; dining room (cafeteria style), special diets accommodated, salad bar; laundry done weekly by commercial service

Counselors: 1 to every 3 campers, 46 counselors total; average age, 22; 5% are foreign

Camp Rules: Telephone calls can be made or received by campers; letters written twice a week; food allowed, within limits, in cabins and tents

Medical: Physician in camp part-time, 2 registered nurses, 2 CPR-certified counselors, and 1 EMT-certified counselor in camp, 12-bed infirmary, parents notified immediately when child is sick; 6 miles from Northern Cumberland Memorial Hospital

Director: Robert W. Strauss
Summer: Harrison, ME 04040
207-583-2300
Winter: Same

Robert Strauss, owner and director of Camp Wigwam, took over own-ership and operation of the camp in 1978. Ned and Helen Strauss, Robert's parents, owned the camp since 1965. Robert received a B.S. from Lake Forest College in 1974, majoring in psychology, and then worked toward a graduate degree in abnormal psychology at Florida Atlantic University from 1975 to 1976. He has been a member of the ACA since 1978.

Philosophy: Camp Wigwam is a traditional camp located in the foothills of the White Mountain National Forest in southwestern Maine. The entire property is cradled in a huge pine grove on the natural white sand beach of Bear Lake. Wigwam emphasizes its waterfront, tennis, and golf programs. With four campers and a counselor in each cabin, the young men at Camp Wigwam are encouraged to select the activities in which they wish to participate, and their daily program is structured to include these areas. Though sports are an integral part of Wigwam, the camp philosophy stresses participation rather than strict competi-tion. "A caring and relaxed environment, Camp Wigwam enables a young man to thrive in a community of his peers."

Camper Comment: "I have been affiliated with Camp Wigwam since the third grade, when I started as a camper. I am now graduating from college. I have seen every angle of the Wigwam experience over the years from camper to counselor. In the simplest terms, Wigwam is a summer home for a youngster. We are nurtured by the Wigwam staff just as our parents would, but given the valuable opportunity to ex-perience the independence of summer camp life. We grow in so many ways over the course of the summer and hold memories of Wigwam deep in our hearts through every day of our lives."

CAMP WILDWOOD
Bridgton, Maine

Single sex, male

Ages: 7–15

Campers: 190

Religious affiliation: None

Fees: $3,800, 8 weeks

Extra fees: Canteen

Founded: 1953

Program: A structured and elective program with competitive and non-competitive activities

Facilities/Activities: *Athletics* 3 baseball fields, soccer field, 11 Har-Tru tennis courts (3 indoor, 7 lit), 4 basketball courts (3 lit), street hockey court, touch football, riflery range, archery range, volleyball courts, 25,000-sq.-ft. indoor gym (3 full courts for basketball); *Waterfront* lake, swimming, sailing, sailboards, waterskiing, inner tubing, canoes, kayaks; *Camping* campfire and sleep-out sites, nature area; *Creative Arts* radio room, arts and crafts, outdoor theater; *Miscellaneous* 4 computers (Apple IIe), printers, recreation room, BMX bicycles

Boarding: 30 cabins (electricity), showerhouse; dining room (cafeteria style), special diets accommodated, salad bar; laundry done weekly by commercial service

Counselors: 1 to every 3 campers, 60 counselors total; average age, 20; 10% are foreign

Camp Rules: Director calls all new parents on the second or third night of camp, parents can then call once a week; letters written at least twice a week; no food in cabins

Medical: 2 registered nurses in camp, 2–5 beds in infirmary, 2 isolation beds, parents notified if child is ill more than 24 hours and if there is any kind of serious problem; 2 miles from Northern Cumberland Memorial Hospital, 20 miles from Norway Hospital, 38 miles from Maine Medical Center

Director: Mark Meyer
Summer: Bridgton, ME 04009
      207-647-8864
Winter: 838 West End Avenue, New York, NY 10025
      212-316-1419

Mark Meyer has been with Wildwood for twenty-five years. He started as a counselor, then became group leader. He has been director for the last ten years. Mark graduated from City College. He works with kids all year round and is involved with an after-school sports club, the Astros.

Philosophy: Wildwood is known for its facilities and staff. There are private instructors in every activity area.

Campers must take daily swimming and tennis lessons. The rest of the day (three periods) is filled with activities of the campers' choosing. "Because of our involvement with children all year round, we feel our campers receive a fantastic camping experience."

Camper Comment: "Returning to Wildwood is like going back to your family. The fresh air and beautiful surroundings make it an ideal place to be. You make wonderful friends and everyone has a good time."

CAMP WINNEBAGO

Kents Hill, Maine ───────────────

Single sex, male

Ages: 8–15

Campers: 140

Religious affiliation: None

Fees: $2,425, 4 weeks / $4,350, 8 weeks

Extra fees: Transportation to and from camp, medical insurance, photos, canteen

Founded: 1919

Program: A structured and elective, competitive program

Facilities/Activities: *Athletics* 2 baseball fields, soccer field, 7 Har-Tru tennis courts, basketball court, street hockey court, riflery range, archery range, volleyball courts, tetherball courts, Universal weight machine; *Waterfront* 1,100-acre lake, swimming, canoeing, sailing, kayaking, sailboarding, waterskiing; *Camping* campfire and sleep-out sites, nature area, campcraft; *Creative Arts* outdoor theater, plays, radio room, arts and crafts; *Miscellaneous* 3 recreation rooms, ropes course, Ping-Pong, library

Boarding: 31 cabins (no electricity), 2 showerhouses; dining room (family style), salad bar; laundry done weekly by camp

Counselors: 1 to every 3 campers, 48 counselors total; average age, 24; 18% are foreign

Camp Rules: Telephone calls by campers are discouraged; letters written 3 times a week; no food in cabins

Medical: Physician and registered nurses in camp, 6-bed infirmary, parents notified if child is seriously injured, hospitalized, or spends the night in infirmary; 17 miles from Kennebec Valley Medical Center

Director: Phillip Lilienthal
Summer: Kents Hill, ME 04349
207-685-4918
Winter: 1606 Washington Plaza, Reston, VA 22090
703-471-1705

Director and owner Phil Lilienthal has been involved in camping since his father became associated with Winnebago when Phil was two. A camper and counselor at Winnebago, Phil became director in 1974. Previously, he worked as a counselor at a Fresh Air Fund camp, and, in the Peace Corps, he organized and established Ethiopia's first residential camp program. More recently, Phil has been on the board of the Maine Youth Camping Association, acted as program chair of the private independent camp segment of the International Camping Conference in Washington, D.C., and was a member of the board of directors of the ACA.

Philosophy: Camp Winnebago seeks to expose each boy to as many experiences as his interests may direct, so that he can develop the tools to make mature decisions. The camp's guiding principles are to instill in every camper an appreciation for group living, foster native abilities, and develop and strengthen character so that each individual can become a self-fulfilling and contributing member of society. Winnebago offers "more experiences than any one camper can possibly enjoy, but we encourage each boy to try, to experiment, and to participate. We accept each boy for what he has to offer and seek to make each feel comfortable at his own level of skills and interests."

Programs are designed for personal involvement, with the choice of activities left to each camper. Winnebago considers this "directed freedom," in which the staff members maintain the supervision and control they believe necessary for a meaningful camp experience.

In all sports and activities, a boy's full use of his capacity matters more to Winnebago than winning. "We stress effort, improvement, and, of course, achievement. We do this through staff encouragement, expert instruction and rewards for accomplishment."

Parent Comment: "What a very nice boy you returned to me! What did you do to activate his consideration and even temper so well? He is a joy to be with. Says he had a great time, too!"

BELVOIR TERRACE
Lenox, Massachusetts

Single sex, female

Ages: 9–17

Campers: 165

Religious affiliation: None

Fees: $4,400, 8 weeks

Extra fees: Transportation to and from camp, studio art course, refundable canteen

Founded: 1954

Program: An individually structured teaching program; professional instruction and graded classes in all programs. Campers can major in any one area or combine program choices to develop a broad-based plan

Facilities/Activities: *Athletics* playing fields, 6 Har-Tru tennis courts (4 lit), basketball court, gymnastics, indoor gym with Nissen equipment (mats, beams, vault, trampoline), fencing, 2 volleyball courts; *Waterfront* 2 swimming pools (1 lit, heated, Olympic size); *Camping* campfire sites; *Creative Arts* 3 theaters (includes black box, proscenium, Shakespeare space), acting technique, musical theater, Shakespearean acting, mime, directing, video acting, art studios (drawing, painting, printmaking, sculpture, ceramics, weaving, crafts, jewelry), photography, 3 dance studios, 2 music buildings, 16 private music studios, filmmaking; *Miscellaneous* computers

Boarding: Mansion, 4 modern dorms (electricity, air cooling), modern tile baths with showers in all living areas; dining room (family style), kosher and vegetarian requests accommodated, salad bar; laundry done weekly by camp

Counselors: 1 to every 3 campers, 65 counselors total; average age, 25; 10% are foreign

Camp Rules: Telephone calls can be made weekly by campers (must be scheduled with staff); letters encouraged; no food in dorms

Medical: Contract with local pediatrician, 2 registered nurses in camp, 6-bed infirmary, camp notifies parents if children taken to physician or sleep overnight in infirmary; 4 miles from Berkshire Medical Center

Director: Nancy S. Goldberg
Summer: Lenox, MA 01240
        413-637-0555
Winter: 145 Central Park West, New York, NY 10023
        212-580-3398

Nancy Goldberg joined the Belvoir staff in 1954, the camp's first summer. At Belvoir, Nancy was a sports counselor, head of the sports department, and for the past fifteen years has been the program director responsible for organizing the program, hiring and supervising staff, and developing the site.

Nancy attended Bryn Mawr College, majoring in English. While teaching English in the Newton public schools, Nancy did graduate work in education at Harvard. She has directed after-school arts programs for youth in New York City at the Hebrew Arts School and is currently at Steps. Nancy is a board member of the New York ACA and an ACA Camp Standards Visitor.

Philosophy: Belvoir Terrace is an individually structured teaching camp for art, dance, music, theater, and individual sports. Belvoir seeks to provide a community where young women are nurtured, make friends, and develop skills and interests.

Each camper works out her own individual schedule, choosing from more than forty class options. Campers can develop a strong major, a dual major, or can choose a wide range of classes from art through sports. Skill is an expected outcome and not a prerequisite for the program, but the staff can challenge even the most advanced high-school students. In class, learning is stressed but the girls may enjoy the result of their hard work in art openings, music recitals, theatrical performances, and intercamp sports events. The program is augmented by guest artists and frequent trips to cultural events in the Berkshires.

Parent Comment: "Surprise . . . ! Our daughter has had this enrollment contract completed since the day your letter arrived. She has indeed become 'her own person' and perhaps survived another rite of adolescence, peer pressure.

"We are all looking forward to another great (and sadly a last) summer at your exceptional camp. The experience has given our daughter self-confidence and excellent skills in so many areas."

CAPE COD SEA CAMPS
Brewster, Massachusetts —————————————————————

Coed

Ages: 7–17

Campers: 340

Religious affiliation: None

Fees: $1,025, 10-day Camp-O-Rama for ages 7–9 / $2,185, 3½ weeks / $3,945, 7 weeks

Extra fees: Transportation to and from camp, optional trips to scenic areas

Founded: 1922

Program: An elective program in which campers choose activities on a weekly basis; emphasis on swimming and sailing

Facilities/Activities: *Athletics*   2 baseball fields, 2 soccer fields, 9 hard-surface tennis courts, 3 basketball courts, street hockey court, gymnastic pavilion (parallel bars, beam, vault, floor exercise), 2 riflery ranges, 2 archery ranges, 3 volleyball courts, lacrosse field, football field, track; *Waterfront*   swimming pool, Long Pond (1,000-ft. beachfront), 6 canoes, 8 sailboards, waterskiing, rowing (dinghies), sailing (24 Mercury 15's, 12 Sunfish); *Camping*   campfire and sleep-out sites, nature center; *Creative Arts*   outdoor theater, woodworking shop, arts and crafts center (pottery, jewelry, drawing), photography (darkroom), video instruction; *Miscellaneous*   ropes course (10 elements), indoor Ping-Pong

Boarding: 29 cabins (electricity), junior counselor girls have 2 showers/cabin, others share 5 showerhouses (averaging 10 showers each); dining room (cafeteria style), kosher style, salad bar; laundry done weekly by camp

Counselors: 1 to every 5 campers, 72 counselors total; average age, 20; 6% are foreign

Camp Rules: Calls discouraged the first 10 days, after which parents urged to set up a time to call; campers encouraged to write home weekly; care packages allowed in cabins

Medical: Pediatrician in camp daily, 9–12, 4 nurses in camp, 20-bed infirmary, parents notified when a child is seen by the doctor or spends night in the infirmary; 18 miles from Cape Cod Hospital, 5 miles from Medicenter

Directors: Mrs. Berry D. Richardson (Executive Director), David L. Peterson, Sherry A. Mernick (Directors, Resident Programs)
Summer: Cape Cod Sea Camps, P.O. Box B, Brewster, MA 02631
          508-896-3451, 508-896-3626
Winter: Same

Mrs. Berry D. Richardson, executive director, is the daughter of the camp's founder and has been associated with the camps as a camper, counselor, director, and now executive director. A graduate of Skidmore College, she has served on the ACA New England section board and was secretary of the Cape Cod Association of Children's Camps.

Sherry A. Mernick, a director of the resident program, began working at Cape Cod Sea Camps in 1968. She received her B.S. from Skidmore College and an M.Ed. from Northeastern University. She is an active member of the ACA, acting as secretary for the 1990 ACA national convention.

David L. Peterson, the other director of resident programs, began working at Cape Cod Sea Camps in 1970. He is a graduate of Southern Connecticut State University and has teaching certification in Massachusetts and New South Wales, Australia. An ACA-certified camp director, David currently serves on the national board of the ACA and is vice president of the New England section of the ACA.

Philosophy: Cape Cod Sea Camps' strong emphasis on education can be seen in its sailing program. From basic instruction through racing, campers can choose to follow a recreational or competitive approach to the sport. Campers who choose sailing do so for the entire morning or afternoon.

Campers are encouraged to accept responsibility and display a commitment to others in "a supportive environment filled with fun and friendship."

Parent Comment: "Every story our son has told us of his experience has been delightful. The athletic program was perfect. But it goes beyond that, somehow. Your staff members created a happy environment and were truly fine role models. Our son hopes to stay in touch with his new 'global' collection of friends.

"Our initial reluctance to have our son away for seven weeks was quickly replaced with the feeling that your camp was the right place at the right time with the right people.

"We are certain you are very proud of your camp but felt the need to let you know how much your hard work and dedication meant to one young man and his parents. To quote our son, 'It was the best summer of my life.' Now that is a difficult task to accomplish!"

CRANE LAKE CAMP
West Stockbridge, Massachusetts ——————————————

Coed

Ages: 6–15

Campers: 280

Religious affiliation: None

Fees: $3,450, 8 weeks

Extra fees: Trips to cultural events, canteen

Founded: 1954

Program: Campers can specialize in tennis, gymnastics, sports, performing arts, and swim team. Noncompetitive and competitive activities

Facilities/Activities: *Athletics*   2 baseball fields, 2 soccer fields, 6 hardsurface tennis courts (3 lit), 3 basketball courts (2 lit), 2 street hockey courts, track, riflery range, archery range, 2 volleyball courts, indoor gym (basketball, hockey), gymnastics pavilion; *Waterfront*   swimming pool, lake, waterskiing, canoeing, sailboarding, rowboating, sailing, paddleboating; *Camping*   campfire and sleep-out sites, pioneering, nature area, farm area; *Creative Arts*   outdoor theater, drama, dance, arts and crafts, woodworking, model rocketry; *Miscellaneous*   4 computers (IBM), recreation and game room, ropes course

Boarding: 36 cabins (electricity), 3–4 showers/cabin; dining room (family style), special diets accommodated, kosher style; laundry done by commercial service every 5 days

Counselors: 1 to every 3 campers, 120 counselors total; average age, 21; 15% are foreign

Camp Rules: Campers can make telephone calls once a week, parents call according to the schedule made; campers write home 3 times a week; no food in cabins

Medical: Local doctor comes in every day, 3 registered nurses in camp, all waterfront people qualified in CPR, 8-bed infirmary, parents notified when child is in infirmary; 10 miles from Berkshire Medical Center

Directors: Ed and Barbara Ulanoff
Summer: West Stockbridge, MA 01266
      413-232-4257
Winter: 10 West 66 Street, New York, NY 10023
      212-549-8930

Owner and director of Crane Lake Camp, Edwin S. Ulanoff has a B.S. in physical education from Penn State University and played varsity football and tennis. He has an M.S. in camping education from NYU. He was a teacher in the New York City school system for twenty-five years and coached basketball and track. He has been with Crane Lake for thirty-six years.

Philosophy: Crane Lake seeks to allow each child his or her individuality while becoming an integral part of the camp community. A balance is sought that "helps a camper understand responsibility, build long-lasting friendships, and have a fun-filled summer."

Crane Lake emphasizes land sports, with group and individual coaching clinics, as well as a waterfront program highlighted by the new swimming pool and our own private lake. Campers visit many of the cultural attractions located nearby, including Tanglewood, the Jacob's Pillow Dance Theater, and the Berkshire Theater Arts Festival. "Crane Lake is a place where first-time campers, as well as seasoned campers, have the time of their life."

Parent Comment: "Suzanne had an absolutely marvelous summer at Crane Lake. Your camp has more of everything for a fun-filled experience. Her memories of summer 1989 are the best! She speaks with such enthusiasm about her new friends, the staff, the camp spirit, and all she shared with everyone at Crane Lake.

"As a parent and as a previous camper, I am so happy that she spent the summer of 1989 at such a well-organized camp. Thanks for a wonderful summer. We will always speak highly of Crane Lake."

CAMP GREYLOCK FOR BOYS
Becket, Massachusetts —————————————————————————

Single sex, male (sister camp, Camp Romaca for Girls)

Ages: 6–16

Campers: 330

Religious affiliation: None

Fees: $4,250, 54 days

Extra fees: Transportation to and from camp, health/accident insurance, canteen

Founded: 1916

Program: Emphasis on physical and emotional growth

Facilities/Activities: *Athletics* 6 baseball fields (1 lit), 6 soccer fields, 17 hard-surface tennis courts (7 lit), 6 basketball courts (4 lit), 2 street hockey courts, track, archery range, 3 volleyball courts (1 lit), lacrosse field, cross-country track, 4-hole golf course, indoor gym, weights; *Waterfront* lake, Red Cross swimming lessons, rowboating, canoeing, sailing, kayaking, waterskiing, sailboarding, water polo, water basketball; *Camping* campfire and sleep-out sites, nature area; *Creative Arts* outdoor and indoor theaters-in-the-round, arts and crafts, woodworking, sculpture, oil painting, photography lab, ceramics; *Miscellaneous* computers (Tandy), ropes course, vegetable farm, tree farm, Ping-Pong, recreation hall (video theater), staff room, farmhouse (fireplace)

Boarding: 63 cabins (electricity), showers in cabins, 3 showerhouses; dining room (cafeteria style: breakfast and lunch; family style: dinner), special diets accommodated, salad bar; laundry done weekly by commercial service

Counselors: 1 to every 3 campers, 100 counselors total; average age, 22; 15% are foreign

Camp Rules: Telephone calls can be made by either campers or parents; letter writing twice a week; food in cabins discouraged

Medical: Physician and 3 registered nurses in camp, 3 EMTs on staff, 14-bed infirmary, parents notified upon injury and illness; 20 miles from Berkshire Medical Center

Director: Bert Margolis
Summer: Route 8, Becket, MA 01223
　　　　413-623-8921, fax: 413-623-5049
Winter: 200 West 57 Street, Suite 307, New York, NY 10019
　　　　212-582-1042, fax: 212-765-8177

Bert Margolis began his association with Greylock at age nine. After being a camper, he became a counselor and then head counselor. After graduating from Johns Hopkins University he did graduate work in psychology at Columbia University. A lecturer and writer for the Association of Private Camps and the ACA conferences, Bert is also co-owner of and adviser to Greylock's sister camp, Camp Romaca.

Philosophy: Camp Greylock operates with a credo that stands against physical bullying and verbal putdowns and guides older campers to take care of younger campers. "Games participation, fun, and laughter" are all encouraged. Campers "play fairly, play by the rules," and are instructed to treat their opponents with courtesy and respect.

"The Renaissance man: this is our dream. We want our campers to enter manhood strong of body, strong of mind, emotionally mature, knowledgeable in the fields of music, literature, art, history, and philosophy. We want them to be protectors of the weak. We want them to stand up and not be silent when such silence gives affirmation to any evil in this world. Such a man has much chance for happiness; such a man has much chance to love and be loved."

Parent Comment: "When we think of summer our thoughts are about our sons at Camp Greylock. The counselor staff is composed of role models accomplished in academics, the arts, and athletics. These individuals instruct and direct our boys toward healthy lifetime goals. They learn to play the game according to the rules and are encouraged to do their best to reach their full potential. Greylock represents a place for a unique combination of physical and mental growth. As parents we focus on how much our sons are growing by being a part of Greylock, its environment, its people, its future."

CAMP LENOX
Lee, Massachusetts

Coed

Ages: 7–16

Campers: 205

Religious affiliation: None

Fees: $4,000, 8 weeks

Extra fees: Round-trip bus, canteen

Founded: 1918

Program: A competitive, sports-oriented program with heavy emphasis on skill development in tennis, basketball, baseball, soccer, and all water sports. Campers may select 2 specialties per week and spend up to 3 hours a day on each specialty

Facilities/Activities: *Athletics* 3 baseball fields, batting cage, soccer field, 15 tennis courts (10 hard surface, 5 Har-Tru, 5 lit), 4 basketball courts (2 lit), golf driving range, street hockey court, track, gymnastics area (8 Universal stations, trampoline, balance beam, even and uneven parallel bars, horse), archery range, volleyball court; *Waterfront* spring-fed lake, Red Cross swimming lessons, competitive swimming, sailing (6 Sunfish, 6 Phantoms, 14-ft. Hobie Cat, 14-ft. Echo sloop, 12-ft. Zuma sloop), sailboarding, scuba diving, waterskiing; *Camping* campfire and sleep-out sites; *Creative Arts* outdoor amphitheater, radio room, model rocketry, arts and crafts; *Miscellaneous* 6 computers (Apple), ropes course

Boarding: 28 cabins (electricity), showers in many cabins, 3 shower-houses; dining room (family style), salad bar; laundry done weekly by commercial service

Counselors: 1 to every 3 campers, 65 counselors total; average age, 21; 10% are foreign

Camp Rules: No calls allowed the first 2 weeks, then parents allowed to leave messages for campers and campers return calls at appointed time; letters written 3 times a week; no food in cabins

Medical: Physician and registered nurse in camp, 10-bed infirmary, parents notified upon camper admission to infirmary; 18 miles from Berkshire Medical Center

Directors: Monty Moss, Richard Moss
Summer: Route 8, Lee, MA 01238
          413-243-2223
Winter: 270-80 Grand Central Parkway, Floral Park, NY 11005
          718-225-9076

Monty Moss has taught and coached physical education for twenty-eight years in the Great Neck, New York, school system. He holds an M.A. in health, physical education, and recreation from Columbia University, where he played varsity basketball and baseball.

Richard Moss has been associated with Camp Lenox for twenty years, beginning as a camper, then counselor, program director, and most recently as associate director. He has a B.A. in education and an M.A. in humanistic psychology from the University of Vermont, where he played varsity basketball.

Philosophy: Camp Lenox's goal is for each child to have fun, improve skills, and develop greater self-confidence. The directors believe that camp should support the efforts of parents in developing a child who is physically and emotionally secure in today's world. Lenox does this by offering a "highly spirited and focused summer camp with programs in sports, arts, and outdoor camping. All our campers are helped to find their niche through a mixture of elective and preassigned scheduling and an emphasis on a happy and caring bunk life."

Parent Comment: "Lenox has been a special place for our two sons. They both attended from when they were nine to when they were sixteen. Both of our sons are good athletes but the sustenance they received at camp in the areas of social and emotional development was a great addition to the things we did with them at home. We thank Lenox for their help in the growth of our children. We have a third son who will be attending soon."

CAMP ROMACA FOR GIRLS
Hinsdale, Massachusetts

Single sex, female (brother camp, Camp Greylock for Boys)

Ages: 7–15

Campers: 170

Religious affiliation: None

Fees: $4,000, 8 weeks (grades 1–6) / $4,200, 8 weeks (grades 7–9)

Extra fees: Transportation to and from camp, medical insurance, canteen

Founded: 1930

Program: A structured, noncompetitive program for the younger campers. An elective program in the morning for older campers. Competitive activities available in swimming and tennis

Facilities/Activities: *Athletics* baseball field, 2 soccer fields, 9 tennis courts (6 hard surface, 3 clay, 4 lit), basketball court, gymnastics area (2 balance beams, vault, uneven bars, climbing ropes), indoor gym, archery range, volleyball courts; *Waterfront* lake, swimming, rowboating, canoeing, sailboating, sailboarding; *Camping* campfire and sleep-out sites; *Creative Arts* theater, plays, production classes, arts and crafts, pottery, silver, wheels, dance; *Miscellaneous* recreation building

Boarding: 23 cabins (electricity), showers in cabins; dining room (family style); laundry done weekly by commercial service

Counselors: 1 to every 3 campers, 80 counselors total; average age, 20; 30% are foreign

Camp Rules: Telephone calls can come in to campers; letters written 3 times a week; no food in cabins

Medical: Physician and registered nurse in camp, 9-bed infirmary, camp notifies parents if child stays overnight in infirmary; 13 miles from Berkshire Medical Center

Directors: Karen and Arnold Lent
Summer: Longview Avenue, Hinsdale, MA 01235
413-655-2715
Winter: 1685 Grand Avenue, Suite 200B, Baldwin, NY 11510
516-867-0217

In 1970 Bert Margolis and Irv Schwartz, who had been directors of Camp Greylock for almost four decades, bought Camp Romaca. In 1973, Arnold and Karen Lent assumed the directorship. The Lents brought to Romaca a wealth of camping experience and outstanding camping reputations gathered during more than two decades of working with children, primarily at Greylock and Romaca.

Philosophy: At Romaca they believe that the security that comes from an inner sense of femininity must develop during the childhood years if the adult years are to become years of happiness and satisfaction. Therefore, they feel that the camping experience should be dynamic and full of fun.

The directors describe their camp as a "dynamic, many-faceted program, led by enthusiastic, skilled women and men who have a positive, forward-looking approach to daily life." Believing that camp is a wonderful place to learn, Romaca programs campers for instruction on an individual and small-group basis in order to improve skills and feelings of adequacy. Romaca wants its campers to "become independent, constructive, confident citizens."

"In the final essence, a good camping experience is based upon freedom . . . freedom gained from self-discipline, from a good feeling of self, from intelligent adult guidance. Romaca firmly believes that a good camp will help the child take another step along her way toward becoming a competent citizen of the adult world—enabling her to face the realities of life, to handle success, to take and understand failure, and to have a positive, healthy approach to daily life."

Camper Comment: "Camp Romaca is the best. You make wonderful friends. It teaches you so much about life, and the counselors are always there for you. It is my summer home."

SHIRE VILLAGE CAMP
Cummington, Massachusetts ────────────────────

Coed

Ages: 7–14

Campers: 100

Religious affiliation: None

Fees: $1,075, 3 weeks / $1,550, 4 weeks / $2,500, 7 weeks

Extra fees: Transportation to and from camp

Founded: 1972

Program: A noncompetitive environment with focus on skill development

Facilities/Activities: *Athletics* baseball field, soccer field, hard-surface tennis court, basketball court, street hockey court, archery range, volleyball courts; *Waterfront* swimming pool, pond, rowboats, canoes; *Camping* campfire and sleep-out sites, nature and animal barn, garden pasture; *Creative Arts* theater, arts and crafts, woodworking, photography (darkroom); *Miscellaneous* horseback riding, rings, trails, stables, rock climbing, backpacking, canoe trips, cultural day trips, recreation room

Boarding: 6 cabins (electricity), 4 dorms, indoor showers; dining room (family style), vegetarian option; laundry done weekly by commercial service

Counselors: 1 to every 5 campers, 10 specialists, 22 counselors total; average age, 21; 10% are foreign

Camp Rules: Telephone calls permitted; parents encouraged to write, no policy for children; no food in cabins

Medical: Physician on 24-hour call, registered nurse and assistant nurse in camp, staff trained in first aid and CPR, 11-bed infirmary, parents notified if child stays overnight in infirmary; 18 miles from Cooley Dickinson Hospital

Director: Beth Schneider
Summer: Mellor Road, Cummington, MA 01026
      413-634-2281
Winter: 17 Old Orchard Road, New Rochelle, NY 10804
      914-636-3672

Beth Schneider has had extensive experience with Shire Village. She was a camper when the camp was founded and later served as camper-worker, counselor, group counselor, and assistant director. Beth holds a B.A. in education and is a graduate student in educational administration at Teachers College, New York. She belongs to the ACA and the Association of Teachers of Independent Schools.

Philosophy: Shire Village is a small, nonprofit camp that encourages campers to try new experiences and to develop skills and relationships at their own pace. It believes that creative expression flourishes in a relaxed, nonsexist, interracial, noncompetitive atmosphere. "The most important thing we can offer children is the opportunity to appreciate their own uniqueness and the uniqueness of others, while experiencing the rewards and responsibilities of community living."

Parent Comment: "All three of our children have spent their middle years at Shire Village. Although the camp is small and our children have very distinctive interests, their summers have been full and productive. Doing everything from crafts and drama to tennis and canoeing, our children have been able to hone their skills in a friendly, noncompetitive atmosphere. As a parent, it's wonderful to know that your child will always be treated as an individual in a caring manner by a devoted and experienced staff."

CAMP CODY FOR BOYS
Freedom, New Hampshire —————————————————————

Single sex, male

Ages: 7–16

Campers: 160

Religious affiliation: None

Fees: $2,000, 4 weeks / $3,500, 8 weeks

Extra fees: Transportation to and from camp, medical insurance, canteen

Founded: 1926

Program: A moderately competitive program with at least 2 daily electives.

Facilities/Activities: *Athletics* 2 baseball fields, soccer field, 5 hard-surface tennis courts (all lit), 2 full-court and 4 half-court basketball courts, 2 street hockey courts, riflery range, archery range, 2 volleyball courts, tetherball, indoor gym, weight and exercise room, skateboard ramps, sports field house; *Waterfront* Ossipee Lake, swimming, fishing, waterskiing, sailing (15 boats), 24 kayaks, 24 canoes, 12 sailboards, 4 rowboats, Zodiac patrol boats, boathouse; *Camping* campfire and sleep-out sites, nature area; *Creative Arts* theater (plays, skits, talent shows), AM radio station, ham radio operation, wood shop with power tools; *Miscellaneous* computers (IBM, Apple), ropes course, horseshoes, Ping-Pong, recreation room

Boarding: 26 cabins (electricity), indoor showers; dining room (family), special diets accommodated, kosher style, salad bar; laundry done weekly by camp

Counselors: 1 to every 3 campers, 65 counselors total; most in early 20s; 15% are foreign

Camp Rules: Campers may accept calls during regular hours; campers required to write home twice a week; no food in cabins

Medical: 2 registered nurses in camp, several staff are EMTs, all staff have basic first aid and CPR training, 7-bed infirmary, parents notified in case of medical emergency; 20 miles from Huggins Hospital

Directors: Alan J. Stolz, Maryann and Philip Ross
Summer: Ossipee Lake Road, Freedom, NH 03836
603-539-4997
Winter: Five Lockwood Circle, Westport, CT 06880
203-226-4389, 203-226-3932

Camp Cody has been owned and directed for over thirty years by Alan J. Stolz, his daughter Maryann, and her husband, Philip Ross. Alan is a national consultant on camp/child health and safety and an ACA Standards Visitor.

Philosophy: Camp Cody's goal is to create a warm family atmosphere. Camp Cody strives to give campers fun, adventure, learning, and friendships in a program that is busy, varied, and exciting. To honor each camper's accomplishments, instructors attempt to eliminate overt competition between campers. "We are proud of our sports coaching staff, our adventure trip instructors, our arts/sciences staff, and our support staff for helping make campers' summers the best summer of their lives."

Parent Comment: "I sent my son to Camp Cody not only to learn to become independent but also to develop new skills and have fun. He did this and made many new friends too. A mature, fun, and caring young man has emerged as a result of his six summers at Camp Cody and the terrific influence of its staff and leadership."

KINGSWOOD CAMP FOR BOYS
Pike, New Hampshire ────────────────────────────

Single sex, male

Ages: 7–15

Campers: 125

Religious affiliation: None

Fees: $1,850, 4 weeks / $3,000, 8 weeks

Extra fees: Transportation to and from camp, spending allowance

Founded: 1945

Program: Competitive sports played on a daily but elective basis, with hiking and canoe trips offered as alternatives

Facilities/Activities: *Athletics*   2 baseball fields, soccer field, 4 clay tennis courts, 2 basketball courts (lit), street hockey court, riflery range, archery range, volleyball court, indoor gym, wrestling, weight room; *Waterfront*   Lake Tarleton, swimming, sailing, waterskiing, sailboarding, boating, canoeing, Playaks; *Camping*   campfire and sleep-out sites, nature area; *Creative Arts*   theater, short skits, short acts, arts and crafts, photography (darkroom); *Miscellaneous*   recreation room

Boarding: 13 cabins (electricity), 1 large showerhouse; dining room (family style), special diets accommodated, salad bar; laundry done weekly by camp

Counselors: 1 to every 4 campers, 30 counselors total; most are 18–22; 5% are foreign

Camp Rules: Parents may telephone during meals; letter writing once a week; food permitted in cabins during designated times and under counselor supervision

Medical: Registered nurse in camp, several staff have taken first aid, CPR, and lifesaving training, 10-bed infirmary, parent notified if child becomes ill; 32 miles from Dartmouth Hitchcock Medical Center

Directors: Robert and Alice Wipfler
Summer: Pike, NH 03780
603-989-5556
Winter: 7101 Clarden Road, Bethesda, MD 20814
301-656-8406

Kingswood is owned and directed by Bob and Alice Wipfler. Bob's commitment to camping runs deep; he has spent thirty-six of his forty-two summers at boys camps in the White Mountain region—as camper, counselor, and director. When Alice married Bob in 1971, she developed an interest in the business side of camping. The couple's two boys are Kingswood's most spirited campers. After teaching seventh-grade history at Landon School in Bethesda, Maryland, for nineteen years, Bob now devotes his full attention to directing Kingswood. Alice remains just as busy running the winter camp office while attempting to keep track of their three children.

Philosophy: Kingswood believes that a happy camp environment results from counselors' encouraging campers to be confident about trying new activities. During each time block, Kingswood campers select an area of interest. Instructional periods, the most structured part of the day, have a "relaxed, nonthreatening tone. Yet the pace is brisk, and the day is filled with one adventurous and challenging event after another. Perhaps this is why a Kingswood boy is so loyal to the camp."

Parent Comment: "I really enjoyed my visit to Kingswood. Even though it was short, it was enough for me to understand why our son felt so comfortable there. Bits and pieces of his experience are coming out and it is quite clear that he truly felt like he was part of a family. Running a camp that fits individual needs so well is an enormous task, but one that you obviously do well. We see such growth in our son even in the short time he has been away, but more than that, we picked up a boy who was really happy!"

CAMP MARLYN
Andover, New Hampshire —————————————————

Single sex, female

Ages: 6–16

Campers: 75

Religious affiliation: None

Fees: $885, 2 weeks / $1,670, 4 weeks / $2,450, 6 weeks / $3,250, 8 weeks

Extra fees: Canteen

Founded: 1931

Program: A structured and elective, noncompetitive program with an emphasis on English riding

Facilities/Activities: *Athletics* 3 hard-surface tennis courts (1 indoor), archery range, volleyball court; *Waterfront* lake, Red Cross swimming lessons, canoeing, sailing, sailboarding; *Camping* campfire and sleep-out sites, nature area; *Creative Arts* outdoor theater, arts and crafts; *Miscellaneous* horseback riding with emphasis on English riding, trails, rings, arena, recreation room, chapel, barn, farmyard animals, library

Boarding: 10 cabins (no electricity), showers in cabins; dining room (family style), vegetarian option; laundry done weekly by commercial service

Counselors: 1 to every 3 campers, 21 counselors total; average age, 21; 90% are foreign

Camp Rules: Parents may call director in the evening, no telephone calls to campers; letter writing is encouraged (must write on Sunday); no food in cabins

Medical: Registered nurse in camp, 2-bed infirmary, parents notified if child is sick or has had an injury; 8 miles from New London Hospital

Directors: Leona and Bill Jenkins
Summer: P.O. Box 59, Bradley Lake, Andover, NH 03216–0059
      603-735-5159
Winter: Same

Leona and Bill Jenkins have both had several years in camping, including many years at Marlyn. They have three children of their own and have worked locally in schools and adult education.

Philosophy: Marlyn's directors believe its success as a camp lies in the quality and commitment of its staff and council. "Professional educators and young college women who all share a zest for life, beauty, and nature make up the Marlyn staff. Enrichment of life is not a scheduled activity; it happens and is made possible by emotionally mature, socially adjusted leadership. A warm trust exists among those staff who accept the challenge and find gratification in living and working with young people. From a pat on the head to a reassuring hug, we at Marlyn intend to care for your child."

Marlyn's facilities are simple and rustic. The camp property includes a mile of frontage on Bradley Lake and a view of Mt. Kearsarge.

Parent Comment: "This summer will be our daughter's fourth stay at Camp Marlyn. She likes the community feeling of a camp where she gets to know nearly everyone. Some friendships made there have extended beyond the camp season. As parents, we like the philosophy that encourages each girl to fulfill her own potential. Every summer our daughter indulges her love of animals by riding horses and caring for the farmyard babies. However, the variety of activities has encouraged her to try new skills like sailboarding and archery.

"Camp Marlyn has been a year-round experience. Newsletters from the Marlyn Owl and the winter ski reunion all make her feel that she is part of a special club. This spring, as always, she is eagerly scanning the newsletter to learn which friends are returning and which countries her counselors call home. We all anticipate that she will have a wonderful time again this year."

CAMP MERRIMAC
Contoocook, New Hampshire ————————————————

Coed

Ages: 6–16

Campers: 240

Religious affiliation: None

Fees: $3,100, 8 weeks

Extra fees: Ice hockey, figure skating, canteen

Founded: 1919

Program: An elective and structured, mostly noncompetitive program that allows campers to specialize in ice hockey, figure skating, tennis, and gymnastics

Facilities/Activities: *Athletics* 4 baseball fields, 2 soccer fields, 8 tennis courts (4 hard surface, 4 Har-Tru, 4 lit), 2 basketball courts, street hockey court, gymnastics (rings, pommel horse, parallel bar, balance beam), riflery range, archery range, 3 volleyball courts, 9-hole miniature golf course, golf driving range, fencing, badminton, indoor gym; *Waterfront* spring-fed lake, swimming, waterskiing, sailing, kayaks, canoes, rowboats; *Camping* campfire and sleep-out sites; *Creative Arts* theater, drama workshops, radio room, fine arts, arts and crafts, model rocketry; *Miscellaneous* computers (Commodore 64), 2 recreation rooms, arena for ice skating and indoor tennis 10 miles away

Boarding: 28 cabins (electricity), 3–4 showers/cabin; dining room (family style), special diets accommodated, kosher; laundry done weekly by camp

Counselors: 1 to every 4 campers, 60 counselors total; average age, 21; percentage of foreign counselors varies each year

Camp Rules: Campers may make telephone calls after 2 weeks but only when called by parent; letters written 3 times a week; food allowed in cabins

Medical: Physician and 2 registered nurses in camp, 10-bed infirmary, parents informed if child stays more than 1 night in infirmary; 10 miles from Concord Hospital

Director: Werner Rothschild
Summer: Route 2, Contoocook, NH 03229
603-746-3195
Winter: 14 Joyce Lane, Woodbury, NY 11797
516-364-8050

Werner Rothschild has spent nearly four decades in camping and education for children of all ages. He has been an elementary-school teacher, soccer coach for elementary-, high-school, and college students, waterfront director, and director of Camp Merrimac for over thirty years.

Philosophy: Camp Merrimac aims to provide children with a happy, safe, and rewarding summer. Its philosophy for attaining this goal focuses on guiding each child's physical, emotional, and social growth during the summer months. "We endeavor to make this goal a reality for every camper by utilizing to the utmost our diverse backgrounds in camping and education, and by utilizing the capabilities of our professional staff. Our varied program promotes the development of each child's skills through individualized instruction in all land and water sports and creative activities."

Parent Comment: "Having both had extensive camping experience in our youth, we began the selection process for our own children's camp placement with preconceived criteria. We were aware of our children's needs, as well as our own.

"Physical facilities were an important consideration, but our requirements also stressed the need for a diversified program that would meet the growing interests of our children, a caring professional staff, 'involved' owners and directors, and a safe environment.

"Our children 'grew up' at Camp Merrimac. They developed social and athletic skills that have become necessary requirements for success as young professional adults. We do not hesitate to highly recommend the 'Camp Merrimac experience.' "

CAMP MERRIWOOD FOR GIRLS
Orford, New Hampshire —————————————————————

Single sex, female (brother camp, Camp Moosilauke for Boys)

Ages: 8–15

Campers: 115

Religious affiliation: None

Fees: $1,550, 3 weeks / $1,900, 4 weeks / $2,950, 7 weeks

Extra fees: Trips, horseback riding

Founded: 1949

Program: A structured program with daily electives; opportunity for concentration in area of choice

Facilities/Activities: *Athletics* 6 tennis courts (2 hard surface, 4 clay, several lit), 3 tennis backboards, gymnastics pavilion (high and low beam, uneven parallel bars, vault, springboard, mats), soccer field, softball field, basketball court, archery range, tetherball; *Waterfront* lake, Red Cross swimming lessons, sailing, canoeing, waterskiing, fishing, sailboarding, rowboats, Playaks; *Camping* campfire and sleep-out sites, nature area; *Creative Arts* drama theater, 2 pianos, arts and crafts (ceramics, jewelrymaking), photography (darkroom); *Miscellaneous* horseback riding, Ping-Pong, bicycles

Boarding: 12 cabins (electricity), showerhouse; dining room (family style), special diets and vegetarians accommodated; laundry done weekly by commercial service

Counselors: 1 to every 3.5 campers, 32 counselors total; average age, 21; 5% are foreign

Camp Rules: No telephone calls first 2 weeks of camp, afterward campers can receive calls, and make calls on camp outings; letter writing required twice a week (letter used as meal ticket); no food in cabins

Medical: Doctor on call, nurse in camp, all waterfront counselors certified in water safety instruction, 6-bed infirmary, parents notified if child is ill overnight or has an injury; 25 miles from Dartmouth Hitchcock Medical Center

Directors: Gary and Judy Miller
Summer: Camp Merriwood, Upper Baker Pond Road, Orford, NH 03777
603-353-9882
Winter: 7 Field Road, Riverside, CT 06878
203-637-4674

For more than forty years, the Miller family has operated both Camp Merriwood and its brother camp, Camp Moosilauke. Merriwood is now directed by Gary and Judy Miller, second-generation family directors. Both Gary and Judy are trained educators and have been operating the camp for nearly thirty years. During the rest of the year Gary is director of admissions and dean of students at the Horace Mann School in Riverdale, New York. Gary and Judy have three children, who also assist in the running of the camp.

Philosophy: The purpose of Merriwood is to develop a young girl's self-confidence. This is accomplished through activity, campfires, and programs that develop self-esteem. Also incorporated in the instructional activities is an intercamp competitive schedule for those girls who wish to compete. The directors and owners find it very important to be involved personally with the girls on a daily basis. They are often found teaching or supporting the girls in their activities. "With 115 girls in the camp, it is special the way everyone gets to know one another quickly."

Camper Comment: "I consider my days at Merriwood my most memorable and fun childhood memories. The atmosphere at Merriwood was one in which friendship and sensitivity were stressed, and that showed in everyone—the counselors, the campers, and especially the Millers. Campfires every Sunday night and 'friendship night' were special times for everyone. I really appreciated the excellent instruction and individualized attention I received in tennis.

"Merriwood was a place to nurture and develop friendships that would hopefully be long-lasting. Given the fact that it's been almost ten years since I've left Merriwood and my best friend is the same person I slept next to in Cabin 1 as a nine-year-old, I'd say that the Merriwood experience is still definitely a part of my life."

CAMP MOOSILAUKE FOR BOYS
Orford, New Hampshire —————————————————————

Single sex, male (sister camp, Camp Merriwood for Girls)

Ages: 7–16

Campers: 100

Religious affiliation: None

Fees: $3,400, 7 weeks (3- and 4-week options available)

Extra fees: Horseback riding

Founded: 1904

Program: A structured program with daily electives; opportunity for concentration in area of choice available for older campers. Emphasis on trips program and sports achievement

Facilities/Activities: *Athletics* 2 baseball fields, 2 soccer fields, 7 clay tennis courts, tennis backboard, 2 basketball courts (lit), lacrosse field, football field, archery range, tetherball; *Waterfront* lake, Red Cross swimming lessons, fishing, waterskiing, sailing, canoeing, Playaks, kayaks, sailboards, rowboats; *Camping* campfire and sleep-out sites, nature area; *Creative Arts* arts and crafts area, photography (darkroom), piano; *Miscellaneous* recreation room, Ping-Pong, horseback riding, strong trips program (bicycling, backpacking, canoeing, white-water rafting)

Boarding: 18 cabins (electricity), 2 showerhouses; dining room (family style), special diets and vegetarians accommodated; laundry done weekly by commercial service

Counselors: 1 to every 4 campers, 25 counselors total; average age, 21; 8–10% are foreign

Camp Rules: No telephone calls first 2 weeks of camp, afterward campers can receive calls, and make calls on camp outings; letter writing required twice a week; no food in cabins

Medical: Doctor on call, nurse in camp, all waterfront counselors certified in water safety instruction, 8-bed infirmary, parents notified if child sees doctor; 25 miles from Dartmouth Hitchcock Medical Center

Directors: Port and Heidi Miller, Bill and Sabina McMahon
Summer: Camp Moosilauke, Orford, NH 03777
      603-353-4545
Winter: P.O. Box E, Orford, NH 03777
      603-353-4754

For the past fifty-two years, the Millers have run Camp Moosilauke. Moosilauke is now directed by Port and Heidi Miller, second-generation family directors, and their daughter Sabina and her husband, Bill, third-generation directors. Port took over the camp twenty-five years ago. He attended Horace Mann, Colgate, and received his doctorate from Columbia University. During the rest of the year Port has his own management consulting firm. Bill and Sabina also attended Colgate and Columbia. Bill received his M.B.A. from Columbia, and Sabina received a master's in education. During the rest of the year Bill works in advertising.

Philosophy: The purpose of Moosilauke is to develop a young boy's self-confidence. This is accomplished through activity, specifically the extensive trips program. Incorporated in the instructional activities is an intercamp competitive schedule as well as an extensive intramural schedule for those boys who wish to compete. The directors/owners interact with the boys daily.

Parent Comment: "Moosilauke provides a summer of fun with a purpose. The instruction is excellent, as is the stress on sportsmanship. The range of activities in which the boys participate is incredibly wide. My son came home being able to do things he never thought he could do. Thank you, from both of us."

NEW ENGLAND HOCKEY AND FIGURE SKATING CAMP   *Contoocook, New Hampshire* —————

New England Hockey Camp (N.E.H.C.)—Single sex, male
New England Figure Skating Camp (N.E.F.S.)—Single sex, female

Ages: 6–16

Campers: 100

Religious affiliation: None

Fees: N.E.H.C.: $800, 2 weeks / $1,600, 4 weeks / $2,400, 6 weeks / $3,200, 8 weeks

N.E.F.S.: $1,100, 2 weeks / $2,200, 4 weeks / $3,300, 6 weeks / $4,400 / 8 weeks

Extra fees: None

Founded: 1968

Program: Both competitive and noncompetitive skating programs offered

Facilities/Activities: *Athletics* intensive hockey and ice skating instruction on ice rink (190 ft. by 85 ft.), 4 baseball fields, 2 soccer fields, 4 hard-surface tennis courts (2 lit), 2 basketball courts (1 lit), gymnastics area, riflery range, archery range, 2 volleyball courts, golf driving range, miniature golf course, street and roller hockey court, weight lifting; *Waterfront* lake, swimming, sailing, canoeing, kayaking, waterskiing; *Creative Arts* dramatics; *Miscellaneous* computers (Commodores), ropes course

Boarding: 10 cabins (electricity), indoor showers; dining room (family style), special diets accommodated; laundry done once every 5 days by camp

Counselors: 1 to every 2 campers, 100 counselors total; average age, 20; 25% are foreign

Camp Rules: Phone calls permitted after the first week at camp; letter writing 3 times a week; food permitted in cabins

Medical: Physician and nurse in camp, 10-bed infirmary, parents notified by phone after child spends 2 nights in infirmary; 11 miles from Concord Hospital

Director: Werner Rothschild
Summer: Route 2, Contoocook, NH 03229
603-746-3195
Winter: 14 Joyce Lane, Woodbury, NY 11797
516-364-8099

Werner Rothschild has spent over forty years in camping. He has also taught elementary school, coached high-school soccer, and been a camp waterfront director. He directs Camp Merrimac in New Hampshire.

Philosophy: The aim of the New England Hockey and Figure Skating Camp is to provide each camper, whether a beginner or an advanced skater, with a program that will allow him or her to develop into a mature and confident skater. The camp director and counselors believe that this aim can be most effectively met by maintaining a small counselor-to-camper ratio and by providing each camper with individualized and group instruction.

Parent Comment: "Our daughter attended this year's figure skating camp and had a marvelous time. She can't stop talking about it. The counselors and instructors were excellent. Since you were so good to provide us with parents for references last spring, I thought I should volunteer to be one of those parents. Please feel free to give our name to any family considering sending their child to your camp."

CAMP ROBINDEL FOR GIRLS
Centre Harbor, New Hampshire ─────────────

Single sex, female

Ages: 7–15

Campers: 250

Religious affiliation: None

Fees: $4,250, 8 weeks

Extra fees: Transportation to and from camp, canteen

Founded: 1951

Program: A moderately structured program in a moderately competitive environment

Facilities/Activities: *Athletics* baseball field, 2 soccer fields, 10 tennis courts (2 clay, 5 hard surface, 3 Har-Tru, 3 lit), basketball court, roller skating, gymnastics area (3 beams, 2 uneven bars, mats, vault and runner, 2 springboards), 2 volleyball courts, archery range; *Waterfront* Lake Winnipesaukee (700-ft. beach), swimming, sailing (8 Phantoms, 2 catamarans), waterskiing, 10 canoes, 5 rowboats, 15 sailboards, 6 Playaks; *Camping* campfire and sleep-out sites; *Creative Arts* outdoor and indoor theaters (4 musicals each summer), arts and crafts building (2 floors), dance studio, photography, yearbook; *Miscellaneous* horseback riding (14 horses), trails, 2 rings, recreation hall, lodge

Boarding: 15 cabins (electricity), 2–4 showers/cabin; dining room (family style), kosher style, salad bar; laundry done weekly by camp

Counselors: 1 to every 3 campers, 100 counselors total; average age, 23; 15% are foreign

Camp Rules: No calls the first 3 weeks, then 1 call per week permitted; campers required to write home 3 times a week; no food in cabins

Medical: Physician and 3 registered nurses in camp, 10-bed infirmary, parents notified if child spends more than 1 night in infirmary or in case of medical emergency; 25 miles from Lakes Region General Hospital

Directors: Ann and Nat Greenfield
Summer: Lake Winnipesaukee, Geneva Point Road, Centre Harbor,
      NH 03226
      603-253-9271
Winter: 1271 Mill Road, Meadowbrook, PA 19046
      215-884-3326

Ann Greenfield is a mother and educator who has taught in public and private schools. She has an M.A. in education and was a camper and counselor before becoming co-owner and co-director of Robindel. In 1979 she was appointed president of Golden Slipper Women, a Philadelphia philanthropic camping organization.

Nat Greenfield is a nonpracticing attorney and has been a camp director since 1974. He has spent eighteen consecutive summers as a camper and counselor.

Philosophy: Camp Robindel attempts to create a warm, friendly atmosphere for the girls. The camp's main goal is for each camper to leave feeling better about herself. The director believes in "healthy competition" and the idea that cabin living promotes "cooperation, sharing, and consideration for the needs and rights of others." Activities are generally athletic and the focus of the athletics is to improve each camper's skills at her own pace, thereby maximizing a child's enjoyment.

Parent Comment: "Nat and Ann know all the kids and when you call they don't just 'yes' you. They take care of any problems immediately. Our daughter is allergic to nuts and the cook made a special batch of brownies for her without the nuts. There are many nice touches, like the Big Sister program, which is for all new campers. This is our daughter's third summer at Robindel and each time she comes home she is extremely happy and can't wait to go back."

SUNAPEE ARTS CAMP
Georges Mills, New Hampshire ————————————

Coed

Ages: 7–15

Campers: 80

Religious affiliation: None

Fees: $365 per week (3-, 5-, or 8-week program)

Extra fees: None

Founded: 1928

Program: An elective, noncompetitive program with an emphasis on the arts

Facilities/Activities: *Athletics* large field, 2 hard-surface tennis courts, basketball court, archery range; *Waterfront* lake, swimming, rowboats, canoes, sailboats, kayaks; *Camping* campfire sites; *Creative Arts* large theater, improvisation, plays, musical productions, voice instruction, flute class, piano, guitar, woodwinds, horns, strings, arts and crafts, woodworking, photography, pottery, fabrics, drawing, design class

Boarding: 12 cabins (electricity), 2 showerhouses; dining room (family style), special diets accommodated, salad bar; laundry done weekly by camp

Counselors: 1 to every 4 campers, 20 counselors total; average age, 25; 5% are foreign

Camp Rules: Telephone calls allowed after first 10 days; letters written twice a week; no food in cabins

Medical: Registered nurses in camp, several staff have first aid certification, 8-bed infirmary, nurses decide when to notify parents about sick children; 7 miles from New London Hospital

Directors: Bruce and Helen Charpentier
Summer: Box 177, Georges Mills, NH 03751
603-763-5111
Winter: 19 Myrtle Street, #817, Boston, MA 02114
617-742-6781

Bruce and Helen Charpentier have master's degrees in education and psychology. Both have been teachers. They have been owners and directors of Sunapee Arts Camp for thirty years.

Philosophy: Sunapee Arts Camp emphasizes creative activities, such as drama, pottery, music, art, and woodworking. Campers select their own program and follow the same morning pattern for about ten days so they can experience growth in skills. In the afternoons, campers choose daily from a variety of imaginative counselor offerings, as well as traditional waterfront and sports activities. "Sensitive staff members help each camper to gain a sense of belonging and involvement."

The camp believes that music and the creative arts are important for healthy individual development and that creativity is nourished in the natural camp setting.

Camper Comment:

Camp Sunapee's the only camp for me
There's none other where I'd like to be
You get up at the wake-up bell, and
The counselors treat us fairly well
Even if they yell

Every Friday Night is dance night, ya' know
So you better brush up on your do-si-do
We do lots of folk dance until we drop
Then we get some good old rock and pop
I wish the music never stops!

Carnival comes up at the end of three weeks
We have fortune-tellers and mysterious sheiks
Along with traveling clowns with rosy cheeks

Just some of the reasons I come back each year
As long as Sunapee's around, I'll be here.

KINIYA
Colchester, Vermont ——————————————————————————

Single sex, female

Ages: 7–17

Campers: 125

Religious affiliation: None

Fees: $1,900, 4 weeks / $3,150, 8 weeks

Extra fees: Laundry, canteen

Founded: 1919

Program: Traditional structured activities with the opportunity for individually designed programs; emphasis on sailing and the arts

Facilities/Activities: *Athletics* 5 tennis courts (2 hard surface, 3 clay), gymnastics building, volleyball courts, archery range; *Waterfront* Lake Champlain, swimming, sailing (5 Lazers, 5 Tanzers, 32-ft. O'Day ketch, international 110), waterskiing (Ski Nautique), 6 canoes, 4 rowboats; *Camping* campfire and sleep-out sites, tenting and scouting skills, Indian tepee; *Creative Arts* dance building, large theater (plays each week), separate arts and crafts building (full program); *Miscellaneous* horseback riding, stable (30 horses), 10-acre hunt course, 1½-mile cross-country course, dressage ring, stadium jumping ring, 3 teaching rings, trails

Boarding: 25 cabins (electricity), indoor showers and showerhouses; dining room (family style), vegetarian option, salad bar; laundry done weekly by commercial service

Counselors: 1 to every 3 campers, 40 counselors total; average age, 26; 30% are foreign

Camp Rules: Telephone calls permitted after first 10 days; letter home required once a week; no food in cabins

Medical: 3 registered nurses in camp, 5-bed infirmary, parents notified if child stays overnight in infirmary; 12 miles from Medical Center of Vermont

Directors: Marilyn and John Williams
Summer: 77 Camp Kiniya Road, Colchester, VT 05446
802-893-7849
Winter: Same

Marilyn Williams has a B.A. from Pennsylvania State University and has been a substitute teacher for fifteen years in Vermont. She is a past president and a current board member of the Vermont Camping Association. John Williams has a B.A. from St. Lawrence University in New York. He purchased Camp Kiniya and spent his first summer there in 1952. John serves on a board of the ACA.

Philosophy: Kiniya tries to provide campers with a secure, cooperative atmosphere. Girls develop initiative and self-esteem through accomplishments in programs in sports and the arts. Each girl has an opportunity to design her own program, and each is asked to explore at least one new area. Cabin groups learn basic scouting skills and go on at least one mountain overnight. Each cabin group learns basic sailing skills and shares musical, dance, or acting talents during a theater night.

Parent Comment: "Our daughter's summer was a complete success . . . She gained in confidence, learned new skills, and, as an only child, made a start in learning how important it is, if one wants friends, to consider others, to share, and to compromise; she is looking forward to being with you again."

LOCHEARN CAMP FOR GIRLS

Post Mills, Vermont

Single sex, female

Ages: 7–16

Campers: 155

Religious affiliation: None

Fees: $1,850, 4 weeks / $3,400, 8 weeks

Extra fees: Transportation to and from camp, horseback riding, canteen

Founded: 1916

Program: A noncompetitive program with a combination of structured and elective activities

Facilities/Activities: *Athletics* comprehensive game field for soccer, lacrosse, archery, field hockey, softball, and volleyball, 3 clay tennis courts, indoor gymnastics (high and low beams, uneven parallel bars, springboard, floor mats); *Waterfront* lake, Red Cross swimming lessons, diving, canoeing, sailing (10 Sunfish), waterskiing, snorkeling, Playaks; *Camping* campfire and sleep-out sites, outdoor classroom in the pines, nature areas; *Creative Arts* indoor theater (musical drama, improvisation), dance studio, arts and crafts, pottery, weaving, basket weaving, art through nature; *Miscellaneous* horseback riding (16 stalls, 2 rings, trails), hiking, freshwater pond, Ping-Pong, recreation room

Boarding: 28 cabins (electricity), showerhouses; dining room (family style), vegetarian option; laundry done weekly by camp

Counselors: 1 to every 3 campers, 65–70 counselors total; average age, 22; 25% are foreign

Camp Rules: Parents may call directors to discuss campers' progress; letter writing encouraged; no food in cabins

Medical: Registered nurse in camp, staff certified in first aid and CPR, 5-bed infirmary, parents notified if child requires overnight stay in infirmary or a visit to physician; 16 miles from Dartmouth Hitchcock Medical Center

Directors: Rich and Ginny Maxson
Summer: Post Mills, VT 05058
        802-333-4211
Winter: Same

Rich and Ginny Maxson bring to Lochearn over twenty-five years of experience in human service, including counseling, youth development, leadership training, and summer camping. Rich has degrees in law and in counseling. He is currently continuing his studies at the doctoral level at Harvard University. In addition to providing individual and group counseling, Ginny has worked with several national corporations to build effective and supportive management teams.

Philosophy: Lochearn is situated on Lake Fairlee in rural Vermont. Lochearn offers an environment of mutual respect, caring, and cooperation. "With over twenty-five different creative arts and athletic activities to choose from, girls participate in a diversified program that combines individual attention, fun, achievement, and a high level of safety. Campers find their summer filled with smiles, strong values, and warm memories."

Parent Comment: "Thank you for the wonderful experience our daughter had again this year at Lochearn. She came back in glowing health, full of enthusiasm for returning next year . . . Though always quite independent and self-reliant, she has come home with a very strong sense of confidence and a deep satisfaction with her accomplishments."

CAMP WYODA
Fairlee, Vermont

Single sex, female

Ages: 7–16

Campers: 80

Religious affiliation: None

Fees: $1,145, 3 weeks / $1,760, 4 weeks / $2,750, 7 weeks

Extra fees: Transportation to and from camp, horseback riding, canteen

Founded: 1916

Program: A general program with a combination of structured and elective activities

Facilities/Activities: *Athletics* 2 baseball fields, 2 soccer fields, 2 clay tennis courts, gymnastics area (mats, balance beam), archery range, volleyball courts; *Waterfront* lake, swimming, diving, rowing, canoeing, sailing, sailboarding, waterskiing; *Camping* campfire and sleep-out sites, nature cabin, small animals (chickens, ducks, geese, sheep); *Creative Arts* theater (all-camp musical), woodcraft circle, lessons and ensemble instruction (violin, viola, cello), arts and crafts (weaving, pottery, copper enameling); *Miscellaneous* buildings with fireplaces and areas for rainy-day activities

Boarding: 18 cabins (electricity), indoor showers; dining room (family style); laundry done weekly by camp

Counselors: 1 to every 3 campers, 27 counselors total; average age, 21; 25% are foreign

Camp Rules: Parents may phone at mealtimes after first week; letter home required once a week; no food in cabins

Medical: Registered nurse in camp, 5-bed infirmary, parents notified if child requires medical treatment; 18 miles from Dartmouth Hitchcock Medical Center

Director: Mary Kay Binder
Summer: RR 1, Box 284, Lake Fairlee, Fairlee, VT 05045
       802-333-4310
Winter: 11 DeWolf Road, Old Tappan, NJ 07675
       201-768-0371

Mary Kay Binder, director of Camp Wyoda for the past twenty years, grew up in camping. Mary's grandparents, both educators, started Wyoda. Mary has attended Wyoda as a camper and counselor, teaching nature, hiking, and music. She also worked as a counselor-in-training and a waterfront counselor at two other New England camps. Robert, Mary's husband, assists in the operation of the camp.

Philosophy: Camp Wyoda is "committed to providing a healthy, happy, and rewarding summer" for the campers who attend. Individual accomplishment in activities is stressed, and there are many opportunities to receive recognition for newly developed skills. Competitiveness is not emphasized, however. "The great variety of new experiences in Wyoda's nurturing environment appeals to each camper's particular interests and contributes to improved self-confidence and maturity."

Parent Comment: "We'd like to express our hearty thanks to you for what was obviously a great camp experience for our daughter this summer. 'I love camp' was the theme of most all her letters home, and the proof of the pudding was what we saw and heard when we picked her up . . . What a happy kid came running to greet us! The good-byes between campers and counselors were slow and reluctant, with a lot of obvious affection. We wish to compliment you on a job well done."

MID-ATLANTIC STATES

ECHO HILL CAMP
Worton, Maryland

Coed

Ages: 7–16

Campers: 138

Religious affiliation: None

Fees: $710, 2 weeks / $1,375, 4 weeks / $2,250, 8 weeks

Extra fees: Transportation to and from camp, medical and accident insurance, horseback riding, canteen

Founded: 1917

Program: A structured, noncompetitive program with camper choice of activities

Facilities/Activities: *Athletics* softball field, soccer field, hard-surface tennis court, basketball court, riflery range, archery range, tetherball, lacrosse; *Waterfront* Chesapeake Bay, swimming, waterskiing, sea sledding, crabbing, fishing, sailing (Sunfish, Hobie Cats, Lazer, 2 larger boats), sailboards, canoes, trimaran canoe; *Camping* campfire and sleep-out sites, wildlife preserve, Indian village; *Creative Arts* arts and crafts; *Miscellaneous* ropes course with zip line and Alpine tower, horseback riding (barn, field, ring), garden, recreation room, lodge

Boarding: 3 cabins (1/electricity), 2 showerhouses; dining room (family style), special diets accommodated, vegetarian option, salad bar; laundry done weekly by camp

Counselors: 1 to every 4 campers, 40 counselors total; average age, 21; 20% are foreign

Camp Rules: Telephone calls not permitted by campers except in emergencies; letter writing encouraged; no food in cabins

Medical: Registered nurse and 2 EMTs in camp, staff certified in first aid and CPR, 5-bed infirmary, parents notified by phone if child spends night in infirmary; 13 miles from Kent and Queen Anne's Hospital

Director: Peter P. Price, Jr.
Summer: Worton, Maryland 21678
        301-348-5303
Winter: Same

Peter has over twenty-five years of experience in both camping and education. After earning his B.S. in psychology at Michigan State University, he founded Echo Hill and later founded the Echo Hill Outdoor School, an environmental school accredited by the State of Maryland Board of Education. Peter is an active member of the ACA.

Philosophy: Echo Hill seeks to provide an atmosphere conducive to the creative expression of each individual camper, and to foster his or her appreciation and respect for the environment. Echo Hill also seeks to foster the physical and artistic potential of each of its campers. The director and counselors believe that this can best be achieved by encouraging the campers to become actively involved in the camp's sports and extracurricular activities.

Parent Comment: "This is the first camp our son liked. I think the counselors related well to the children as well as to each other. Our son liked the freedom of choice and we liked the fact that there was some structure. The staff seemed friendly, involved, and available. They are good listeners for the children and the parents. Best of all, our son had a great time."

APPEL FARM ARTS AND MUSIC CENTER
Elmer, New Jersey ——————————————————————

Coed

Ages: 9–17

Campers: 174

Religious affiliation: None

Fees: $2,500, 4 weeks / $4,200, 8 weeks

Extra fees: None

Founded: 1960

Program: An elective and noncompetitive program with emphasis on arts and music

Facilities/Activities: *Athletics* baseball field, soccer field, 2 hard-surface tennis courts, basketball court, 2 volleyball courts; *Waterfront* 2 swimming pools; *Camping* campfire site, nature area; *Creative Arts* outdoor theater, plays, stage combat, improvisation, technical theater, radio room, film animation, weaving, ceramics, sculpture, painting, drawing, metalwork, woodwork, fiber arts, costume shop, jewelry, dance studio, percussion and rock studios, electronic music studio, video room, 3 photography labs, music house, music practice rooms; *Miscellaneous* 2-acre organic garden

Boarding: 23 cabins (electricity), 1 shower/cabin; dining room (cafeteria style), vegetarian option, salad bar; laundry done weekly by camp

Counselors: 1 to every 2 campers, 90 counselors total; average age, 29; 20% are foreign

Camp Rules: Campers may not make or receive phone calls but parents may relay messages through staff; letter writing encouraged; no food in cabins

Medical: Daily physician visit, 2 registered nurses in camp, 6-bed infirmary, medical staff contacts parent if child requires medical treatment; 1 mile from Elmer Community Hospital

Director: Rena Levitt
Summer: P.O. Box 770, Elmer, NJ 08318–0770
       609-358-2472
Winter: Same

Camp director Rena Levitt has been responsible for the administration of Appel Farm since 1988. She was assistant camp director in 1987 and program coordinator from 1985 to 1986. A sculptor, Rena Levitt came to Appel Farm in 1981 to teach sculpture and welding. During the summers, Rena continues to teach workshops.

Philosophy: Appel Farm Arts and Music Center is a not-for-profit organization located on a 176-acre farm in southern New Jersey. Appel Farm's summer arts program offers instruction in theater, music, dance, the fine arts, and the media arts, as well as sports and swimming. "We provide a warm, supportive, and culturally rich environment in which children feel good about expressing their creativity, regardless of their skill level. Although children at Appel Farm produce wonderful plays, music, and art work, we are far more interested in the *process* of learning than in the *product*. Our main concern is for the children to have a joyous and positive experience with the arts as a means of learning more about themselves."

Parent Comment: "I don't know which is the most impressive—the artistic resources, or the warm, supportive climate you create. Perhaps some wonderful mixture of both."

CAMP BACO
Minerva, New York ─────────────────────────

Single sex, male (sister camp, Camp Che-Na-Wah)

Ages: 6–16

Campers: 190

Religious affiliation: None

Fees: $3,400, 8 weeks

Extra fees: Personal spending

Founded: 1951

Program: A structured program with electives; competitive and non-competitive activities

Facilities/Activities: *Athletics* 3 baseball fields, soccer field, 8 hard-surface tennis courts, 3 basketball courts, street hockey court, track, archery range, 2 volleyball courts, hockey rink, lacrosse field, play-ground, indoor gym (basketball court), physical fitness room; *Waterfront* lake, swimming, waterskiing, fishing, rowboats, canoes, sailboats, kay-aks, sailboards; *Camping* campfire and sleep-out sites, nature area; *Creative Arts* indoor and outdoor theaters, drama, voice, music, arts and crafts, photography room, radio room; *Miscellaneous* computers, recreation room

Boarding: 20 cabins (electricity), 1–3 showers/cabin, 1 showerhouse; dining room (family style), kosher style, salad bar; laundry done weekly by commercial service

Counselors: 1 to every 3 campers, 60 counselors total; average age, 20; 5%–10% are foreign

Camp Rules: Parents can call their children and campers can call out at set times; letter writing at least 3 times a week; limited food in cabins

Medical: Physician and nurse in camp, some staff with first aid certi-fication, 16-bed infirmary, parents notified by telephone of illness; 45 miles from Glens Falls Hospital, 13 miles from North Creek Health Center

Directors: Mel Wortman, Robert Wortman, Jerrold Wortman
Summer: Route 28 North, Minerva, NY 12851
518-251-2919
Winter: 80 Neptune Avenue, Woodmere, NY 11598
516-374-7757

Mel Wortman has been a schoolteacher and principal. He is a past president of the Association of Independent Camps and a member of the Resident Independent Camp Committee, New York section, ACA. Mel has been a camp director for thirty-six years.

Bob Wortman is also a schoolteacher. Bob's camping experience includes being head counselor and director for fifteen years.

Jerrold Wortman has been a camp director for five years.

Philosophy: Camp Baco is a family business, owned and directed by the Wortman family. Their programs "encourage optimum skills and leadership development." Boys have many opportunities for coed socialization with the girls of Camp Che-Na-Wah. "Over the years, generations of campers return again and again to spend their summers at Baco, developing a love of the outdoors and nature, making friendships that last a lifetime."

Baco strives for a balanced program through a variety of individual, social, and creative activities. "Good feelings are built by trying new things, meeting people, making friends, and learning to care for yourself and for others."

Parent Comment: "We had such a wonderful weekend at camp that we had to write. Visiting Day was very special for us. Our visit at Baco turned out to be the highlight of the summer. The great memories of summers at Baco returned as we shared the day with our son.

"Nothing could make us happier than to see him thrive as a confident and happy camper at Baco. All of the programs, especially tennis and the waterfront, as well as his counselors, are first-rate.

"We look forward to spending many more special summers with you at Baco."

BRANT LAKE CAMP
Brant Lake, New York ─────────────────────

Single sex, male

Ages: 7–16

Campers: 340

Religious affiliation: None

Fees: $4,050, 8 weeks

Extra fees: Transportation to and from camp, senior trips

Founded: 1917

Program: A structured and elective, competitive and noncompetitive program; emphasis on tennis, water sports, basketball, baseball, and soccer. Program is graded and progressive by age groups

Facilities/Activities: *Athletics* 4 baseball fields, 4 soccer fields, 15 clay tennis courts (1 lit), 7 basketball courts (4 lit), 2 street hockey courts, 2 tracks, archery range, 2 volleyball courts, gymnastics (beams, rings, mats, chin bar, springboard, horse), indoor gym; *Waterfront* lake, swimming, fishing, 10 rowboats, 12 canoes, 2 waterski boats, 3 patrol boats, 12 sailboats, 6 kayaks; *Camping* campfire and sleep-out sites, nature area; *Creative Arts* outdoor theater (2 shows per week), radio room, ceramics, art, woodwork, jewelry, sculpture; *Miscellaneous* 6 computers (Apple), recreation room, game room

Boarding: 48 cabins (electricity), 4 large showerhouses and 6 individual showers (2 showers at lake); dining room (cafeteria style: junior camp; family style: senior camp), special diets accommodated, kosher style, salad bar; laundry done as needed by camp

Counselors: 1 to every 3 campers, 110 counselors total; average age, 23½; 25% are foreign

Camp Rules: No telephone calls first 10 days, then allowed weekly; letters written 3 times a week; no food in cabins

Medical: Physician and 3 registered nurses in camp, many paramedics on staff, many staff members trained in first aid and CPR, 11-bed infirmary, parents notified if child stays overnight in infirmary; 32 miles from Glens Falls Hospital, 25 miles from Ticonderoga Hospital

Director: Robert S. Gersten
Summer: Brant Lake, NY 12815
518-494-2406
Winter: 84 Leamington Street, Lido Beach, NY 11561
516-432-1555

Robert Gersten has been in camping for sixty years, all of which have been at Brant Lake Camp. Over a forty-year period, Robert has gone from camper, counselor, group head, head counselor to his present position as director. Robert's son has been at Brant Lake all his life and is director of programs and the senior camp. The administrative director, Robert Gersten's cousin, has been a director for twenty-five years.

Robert has been a teacher, coach, dean of students, and a member and president of his board of education for forty years. Robert's son is also a teacher and a coach.

Philosophy: The ideal at Brant Lake is to provide a child with a dynamic, healthy, diverse environment in which to develop athletic and interpersonal skills of lifelong value. Brant Lake believes that camp "is an incomparably rich source of fun and wholesome adventure, an institution unique in its capacity to guide and develop each individual camper's interests, personality, and abilities."

The camp's philosophy has been developed over the years based on the knowledge that camp can be an integral part of a child's learning experience. At Brant Lake self-confidence and personal integrity are fostered through group living experiences, playing cooperatively on teams, learning new skills, and associating with counselors who serve as role models. Campers major and minor in their favorite activities, and athletic and other skills are developed through "an extensive activities program and the expert, sensitive instruction of our staff. Brant Lake is proud of its more than seventy-year history of unparalleled success—a deep source of wisdom and experience."

Parent Comment: "We love Brant Lake Camp for its caring, warm, friendly attitude. The directors and counselors (many return every year) are fine, vital, enthusiastic people who are involved closely with every camper and activity.

"The camp is also on a beautiful lake and has great facilities. Their tennis program is as good as any specialty camp, as are most of their programs. My son wants to return forever! We send him back each year because it is one of the most positive experiences of his life."

CAMP CHE-NA-WAH
Minerva, New York ────────────────────────

Single sex, female (brother camp, Camp Baco)

Ages: 6–16

Campers: 160

Religious affiliation: None

Fees: $3,400, 8 weeks

Extra fees: Personal spending

Founded: 1923

Program: A structured program with electives; competitive and non-competitive activities

Facilities/Activities: *Athletics* basketball court, 2 baseball fields, soccer field, 6 hard-surface tennis courts (1 lit), track, gymnastics area, archery range, 2 volleyball courts, lacrosse field, play area; *Waterfront* lake, swimming, fishing, waterskiing, sailing, canoes, rowboats, kayaks, sailboards; *Camping* campfire and sleep-out sites, nature area; *Creative Arts* outdoor and indoor theaters (drama, vocal music, dance), arts and crafts, radio room, photography room; *Miscellaneous* 3 computers, library, recreation room

Boarding: 15 cabins (electricity), 1–2 showers/cabin; dining room (family style), kosher style, salad bar; laundry done weekly by commercial service

Counselors: 1 to every 3 campers, 50 counselors total; average age, 20; 5%–10% are foreign

Camp Rules: Parents can call their children and campers can call out at set times; letter writing at least 3 times a week; limited food allowed in cabins

Medical: Physician and nurse in camp, some staff with first aid certification, 12-bed infirmary, parents notified by telephone of illness; 13 miles from North Creek Health Center, 45 miles from Glens Falls Hospital

Directors: Ruth Wortman, Anita Wortman
Summer: Minerva, NY 12851
   518-251-3129
Winter: 80 Neptune Avenue, Woodmere, NY 11598
  516-374-7757

Ruth Wortman has been a schoolteacher and guidance counselor. She is a past president of the New York State Camp Directors Association and a former board member of the New York section of the ACA. She was a head waterfront counselor and has been a director for thirty-six years.

Anita Wortman is a social worker. Before becoming a director she was program director.

Philosophy: Camp Che-Na-Wah is a family business, owned and directed by the Wortman family. They have many years of experience in the fields of education and camping.

Che-Na-Wah and its brother camp, Camp Baco, believe they offer the best of both worlds: separate activity programs for boys and girls to encourage optimum skills and leadership development, as well as many opportunities for coed socialization and friendship.

Parent Comment: "Camps Che-Na-Wah and Baco have always been a tradition in our family. We both attended as children and later met as counselors. When it came time to choose a camp for our daughters, the only choice was Che-Na-Wah. Our daughters have truly loved every moment of their camp experience. Beautiful summer memories of warmth, spirit, and friendships found at Che-Na-Wah will remain with them always. Year after year, from the time they board the bus in June until they tearfully arrive home, each summer is the 'best ever.' "

DIANA-DALMAQUA
Glen Spey, New York ————————————————

Coed

Ages: 6–16

Campers: 250

Religious affiliation: None

Fees: $3,650, 8 weeks

Extra fees: Trips, canteen

Founded: 1928

Program: A structured, moderately competitive program with some elective activities

Facilities/Activities: *Athletics* 3 baseball fields, 3 soccer fields, 6 hard-surface courts (4 lit), 3 basketball courts (1 lit), street hockey court, 3 volleyball courts, lacrosse field, indoor gym, archery range; *Waterfront* swimming pool, lake, waterskiing, sailing, swimming, kayaking, canoeing, pedal-boating; *Camping* campfire and sleep-out sites, nature area; *Creative Arts* radio station, theater (4 musicals a summer), craft studio, wood shop, fine arts studio, pottery shop, photography room, video studio, guest artists; *Miscellaneous* 12 computers (Commodore), recreation room, go-carts

Boarding: 32 cabins (electricity), 2 showers/cabin; dining room (family style), special diets accommodated with advance notice, kosher style, salad bar; laundry done weekly by camp

Counselors: 1 to every 4 campers, 64 counselors total; average age, 19–20; 15% are foreign

Camp Rules: After the first 10 days campers may receive telephone calls at prearranged times; minimum of 3 letters home per week; food in cabins discouraged

Medical: Physician and 2 registered nurses in camp, 20-bed infirmary, parents notified in medical emergencies; 11 miles from Mercy Community Hospital

Directors: Sy and Judy Alter, Ellis and Jean Marmor
Summer: White Road, Glen Spey, NY 12737
            914-856-1432
Winter: 2236 East 57 Place, Brooklyn, NY 11234
          718-241-1388

Sy and Judy Alter have been involved in summer camping for more than thirty years; Jean and Ellis Marmor for more than forty years. The two couples have worked together at Diana-Dalmaqua for twenty-two years. Sy is the athletic director at Canarsie High School in Brooklyn. Ellis is a theater arts teacher and a Standards Visitor for the ACA, as well as treasurer of the New York chapter of the ACA.

Philosophy: Nestled in the Catskill region of Sullivan County along the Delaware River, Diana-Dalmaqua prides itself on a relaxed, warm, and friendly atmosphere which has been our distinguishing characteristic. Campers are divided into groups of about twenty-four children, usually by age. Activities are planned around camper interests and skill levels. Emphasis at Diana-Dalmaqua is always on instruction and improvement, though the program does contain some competition.

Parent Comment: "Diana-Dalmaqua is an outstanding camp. I felt my children were well supervised. The counselors were warm and caring and everyone seemed to know each other. It has a family feeling and a healthy concern with the campers' safety."

CAMP EAGLE HILL
Elizaville, New York —————————————————

Coed

Ages: 6–16

Campers: 250

Religious affiliation: None

Fees: $1,900, first 4 weeks / $1,600, second 4 weeks / $3,300, 8 weeks

Extra fees: Canteen

Founded: 1963

Program: A structured, competitive program with emphasis on sports, waterfront activities, and creative arts

Facilities/Activities: *Athletics* 4 baseball fields, 2 soccer fields, 4 hard-surface tennis courts, 2 basketball courts (lit), street hockey court, archery range, 2 volleyball courts, handball, paddleball, indoor gym (basketball); *Waterfront* swimming pool, lake, fishing, rowing, canoeing, paddleboats, kayaks, sailboards; *Camping* campfire and sleep-out sites, nature area; *Creative Arts* indoor theater, woodwork, ceramics, printing, art, guitar, photography, model rocketry; *Miscellaneous* recreation room

Boarding: 18 cabins (electricity), 2 showers/cabin; dining room (cafeteria style), special diets accommodated, kosher style, salad bar; laundry done weekly by camp

Counselors: 1 to every 3 campers (ages 6–12), 1 to every 7 for older campers, 50 counselors total; average age, 19; 20% are foreign

Camp Rules: Parents and children can call in the evening; letter writing 3 times a week; food allowed in cabins

Medical: Registered nurse and nurse's assistant in camp, 10-bed infirmary, parents notified if camper stays in infirmary 2 days; 11 miles from Columbia Greene Hospital

Director: Murray Scherer
Summer: White Oak Road, Elizaville, NY 12523
914-756-2426
Winter: 11 Wagon Wheel Drive, New City, NY 10956
914-638-0427

Murray Scherer has been involved with children all of his adult life. As a teacher, assistant principal, and principal in the New York City public-school system for thirty-three years, he has devoted his professional life to sharing with children the fun and beauty of the educational process. As founder, owner, and director of Camp Eagle Hill, Murray continues to use his forty years of camp experience in providing children with summers of safe, recreational fun. Lillian Scherer, his wife, is also involved in running the camp.

Philosophy: Camp Eagle Hill believes that camp should be an adventure. Campers are thus urged to discover new and exciting activities and enjoy those activities already known. Camp Eagle Hill wants its campers to become independent, and see what it is like to "make it on their own."

"Our program is filled with fun, interesting, and worthwhile activities. Our adult staff brings our fun-filled program to life every day. We believe that a camper who is involved at activity and learning is bound to have a great time at camp. Above all else, we encourage the enjoyment of a camp experience filled with lasting friendships and values which form the foundation for a lifetime of happiness and pleasure."

Parent Comment: "I am immensely pleased with your camp. My daughter had a wonderful time and still talks about it. I think it did her a world of good to be away and involved in so many worthwhile activities. She is very proud of her many accomplishments there."

INDIAN SPRINGS CAMP
Pine Bush, New York ———————————————————

Coed

Ages: 7–15

Campers: 65

Religious affiliation: None

Fees: $1,900, 4 weeks / $3,400, 8 weeks

Extra fees: Transportation to and from camp, medical insurance, canteen

Founded: 1958

Program: A structured and elective, noncompetitive program with emphasis on English and Western riding, dance and art programs

Facilities/Activities: *Athletics*   baseball field, soccer field, 2 hard-surface tennis courts, basketball court, archery range, volleyball court, boccie, golf, football, bowling, shuffleboard; *Waterfront*   swimming pool, lake, fishing, canoes, rowboat, paddleboat, water slide; *Camping* campfire and sleep-out sites, hiking trails, nature area; *Creative Arts* dance, playwriting, drama, puppetry, arts and crafts, pottery, ceramics, batik, jewelry; *Miscellaneous*   recreation room, outdoor pavilion, 2 horseback riding rings, animal care, gardening, Ping-Pong

Boarding: 5 cabins (electricity), 2 showers/cabin, 2 dorms; dining room (family style), special diets accommodated, salad bar; laundry done weekly by camp

Counselors: 1 to every 5 campers, 16 counselors total; average age, 21; 12% are foreign

Camp Rules: Telephone calls made on special family occasions; letter writing encouraged weekly; no food in sleeping accommodations

Medical: Registered nurse in camp, some counselors certified in first aid and CPR, 5-bed infirmary, parents notified if child is ill, injured, or taken to physician or hospital (called after visit to an outside facility); 12 miles from Ellenville Community Hospital, 16 miles from Horton Memorial Hospital

Director: Acelia Spadola
Summer: Box 300, RD 2, Pine Bush, NY 12566
914-744-2676 (fax same number)
Winter: Same

Acelia Spadola is the parent of five children and has taught public school and college for twenty years. A camp director for thirty-two years, Acelia has an M.S. in education, a B.S. in nursing education, and is a certified nurse.

Philosophy: Indian Springs focuses on building camper character through its extensive horsemanship program. With a supplemental Red Cross swimming program and arts and dance activities, the camp promotes the feeling that it is "a little world unto itself." Indian Springs strives to make the community an international one, with campers from at least ten countries each season. As a result, the director feels that campers "learn that we share many similarities as well as differences."

Camper Comment: "I attended Indian Springs for seven years as a camper and two years as a counselor. As a result, I feel I have developed emotionally and socially more than would have been possible in other situations. I have just completed a tour of Europe, where I was able to visit with five families that I had met at camp.

"Our cultural experiences both in camp and out of camp will stay in my memory. There was a 'feeling' of camaraderie that lasted well after the actual camp experience."

KUTSHER'S SPORTS ACADEMY
Monticello, New York

Coed

Ages: 7–17

Campers: 525

Religious affiliation: None

Fees: $2,145, 4 weeks / $3,945, 8 weeks

Extra fees: Canteen

Founded: 1968

Program: A structured and elective, competitive and noncompetitive program with emphasis on sports instruction

Facilities/Activities: *Athletics* 3 baseball fields, 3 soccer fields, 17 hard-surface tennis courts (lit), 9 basketball courts (6 lit), street hockey court, track, gymnastics, volleyball courts, physical fitness center, indoor gym (3 tennis courts, 3 basketball courts), karate, judo, wrestling, weight training; *Waterfront* swimming pool, lake, waterskiing, 14 sailboats, rowboats, canoes; *Creative Arts* theater for movies, talent show, dances, and evening activities

Boarding: 44 cabins (electricity), 2–3 showers/cabin, 34 dorms; dining room (cafeteria style), special diets accommodated, kosher style, salad bar; laundry done weekly by camp

Counselors: 1 to every 5 campers, 115 counselors total, 30 coaches; average age, 20–21; 35% are foreign

Camp Rules: Telephone calls can be received or made after first week of camp; letters written twice a week; no perishable food in sleeping accommodations

Medical: Physician, 5 registered nurses, and 2 athletic trainers (knowledgeable about athletic injuries) in camp, 20-bed infirmary, parents notified if child stays overnight in infirmary; 10 miles from Harris Community Hospital

Director: Robert Trupin
Summer: Monticello, NY 12701
      914-794-5400
Winter: 3 Snowflake Lane, Westport, CT 06880
      203-454-4991

Robert Trupin has a B.A. in American studies from Yale University, an M.B.A. in management and behavioral sciences from New York University, and an M.S. in guidance and counseling from Fordham University. He was the director of Camp Trupin in Connecticut for seven years and has been the executive director of Kutsher's Sports Academy for the past fourteen years. He has also directed the Oscar Robertson basketball camp and Rising Star basketball camp as well as several cheerleading camps. Robert taught in the New York City school system for two years and was the athletic director and basketball coach at Friends Seminary in New York City for four years.

Philosophy: The Kutsher's Sports Academy program aims at building skills and techniques, while ensuring an enjoyable summer for campers. "Our carefully selected staff provides individual attention and positive learning experiences which in turn foster a high degree of self-esteem within each individual." While sports are used as the vehicle for learning about life, the atmosphere is not overly competitive. As the boys and girls progress, it is hoped that they obtain a greater understanding of themselves and others.

Under Kutsher's elective program all campers select the scope of their own activities, choosing those they are most interested in. The program permits a wide range of interests and establishes freedom of choice and independence for the camper. Guidance in selecting activities is provided if needed. Campers also play in a league of their choice.

All sports are directed by high-school and college coaches. The coaches are assisted by college athletes who also serve as bunk counselors. Group leaders, who organize the nonsports aspects of the camp, along with the counselors "foster a strong group feeling."

Parent Comment: "Our son and daughter are excited to be returning to Kutsher's Sports Academy this year for their fourth summer. Kutsher's has provided our children with individualized attention to their athletic development in the sports they choose. In addition to daily instruction, children receive a wonderful feeling of warmth from the mature and caring staff. The sharing of experiences with bunkmates and counselors develops a camaraderie that grows from year to year."

CAMP LINCOLN FOR BOYS
Keeseville, New York

Single sex, male (sister camp, Camp Whippoorwill for Girls)

Ages: 8–15

Campers: 80

Religious affiliation: None

Fees: $2,300, 5 weeks / $2,700, 7 weeks

Extra fees: Transportation to and from camp, canteen

Founded: 1920

Program: An elective, noncompetitive program governed by individual choice

Facilities/Activities: *Athletics* large multipurpose field for baseball, soccer, softball, touch football, and low-organization games, 3 clay tennis courts, half-court basketball court, archery range, 3 tetherball courts, volleyball court; *Waterfront* lake, swimming, fishing, 22 sailboats, 12 sailboards, 38 canoes, 24 rowboats, 6 kayaks; *Camping* campfire and sleep-out sites, nature center; *Creative Arts* theater, plays, concerts, talent shows, songfests, social events, woodworking, art shop, photography (darkroom); *Miscellaneous* high and low ropes course, horseback riding and rings, several recreation rooms, animal shelter, Ping-Pong

Boarding: 17 cabins (electricity), 2 showerhouses; dining room (family style), special diets accommodated, salad bar; laundry done weekly by commercial service

Counselors: 1 to every 4 campers, 20 counselors total; minimum age, 18, majority in their 20s; 5% are foreign

Camp Rules: Campers may receive calls at mealtimes and may place calls with permission of the staff, families urged to use the phone sparingly; weekly letter required; no food in cabins

Medical: Physician on call, registered nurse in camp, EMT on staff, all counselors certified in first aid and CPR, 4-bed infirmary, parents notified in event of medical emergency, if child spends night in infirmary, or visits doctor; 17 miles from Champlain Valley Physicians Hospital

Director: Peter L. Gucker
Summer: RR1, Box 188, Keeseville, NY 12944
518-834-5151
Winter: 36 Wellwood Road, Demarest, NJ 07627
201-768-6198

Peter L. Gucker grew up at Camp Lincoln, the camp founded by his father. He has an A.B. from the University of Rochester and an M.A. from Columbia University. He has served in the navy as an officer and taught English for thirty-seven years at the Horace Mann School in New York. He has been camp director since 1957.

Philosophy: "We wish to offer children and their counselors an extended opportunity to live together simply in the outdoors; to provide them with safe, healthy, and at the same time challenging surroundings. Because resourcefulness and confidence grow through willing effort, work experience is offered to all campers. We are eager to sharpen children's awareness of the wilderness environment and to work with them in finding sensible ways to preserve it. And we wish to encourage interest in sports and activities that will last a lifetime, backed up by good health and nutrition. From such opportunity children can experience comradeship, the exhilaration of accomplishment, a sense of their own worth, and the beginning of appreciation for the beauty and vitality of our natural world."

Parent Comment: "Both of my children find your camp a wonderful experience. I believe it is because they have found the kids and the counselors very kind, fun, and easy to get to know. They love the activities because they can make their own choices and determine their own pace. They certainly experience self-motivation and being responsible for themselves. Above all, they relax—a very important thing for urban children."

CAMP OQUAGO
Andes, New York

Coed

Ages: 6–16

Campers: 200

Religious affiliation: None

Fees: $1,995, 4 weeks / $3,495, 8 weeks; $2,895, 8 weeks (tenth- and eleventh-graders)

Extra fees: Trip fund

Founded: 1930

Program: A structured and elective, competitive and noncompetitive program

Facilities/Activities: *Athletics* 3 baseball fields, 2 soccer fields, 4 hard-surface tennis courts (lit), 3 outdoor basketball courts (1 lit), indoor basketball court, street hockey court, gymnastics, archery range, 3 volleyball courts (sand court); *Waterfront* spring-fed lake, rowboats, kayaks, canoes, paddleboats, sailboats, sailboards, waterskiing; *Camping* campfire and sleep-out sites, nature area; *Creative Arts* indoor theater, drama, arts and crafts, pottery, woodworking, model rocketry, photography, radio room; *Miscellaneous* 5 computers (Apple IIe), recreation room, animal farm, bicycles, Ping-Pong, video games, ropes course

Boarding: 28 cabins (electricity), 2 showers/cabin; dining room (family style), special diets accommodated, kosher style, salad bar; laundry done weekly by camp

Counselors: 1 to every 2 children, 100 counselors total; 55 college age, 45 adults; 5% are foreign

Camp Rules: Campers must ask to make telephone calls; letters written twice a week; food strongly discouraged in cabins

Medical: Local doctor sees campers daily, 2 registered nurses in camp, 8-bed infirmary, another 2 for isolation, parents notified if child is in infirmary overnight, visits emergency room, or makes any visit to specialist; 10 miles from Margaretville Memorial Hospital

Directors: Laura and Stuart Chase
Summer: Perch Lake, Andes, NY 13731
        914-676-3131
Winter: 143 Overlook Terrace, East Hills, NY 11577
        516-621-5088

Laura and Stuart Chase have been involved in camping for most of their lives. They have been campers, counselors, head counselors, and, since 1977, the owners and directors of Camp Oquago. Both Laura and Stuart were teachers before becoming camp directors. Stuart is on the board of directors of the New York section of the ACA and the New York State Camp Directors Association. He also coaches a local youth basketball team. The Chases have two children who are campers at Oquago. Camp Oquago is a full-time profession for Laura and Stuart, who spend twelve months a year involved in camp-related activities.

Philosophy: Camp Oquago strives to build character and provide campers with an exciting, fun, healthy summer. "We understand that not every child is an exceptional athlete and not every child is an exceptional artist, but every child wants and deserves to have fun."

Camp Oquago emphasizes relationships, and aims at having its campers be accepting of one another. "Our campers learn to care about each other in terms of who they are and not for who they are not." Activities are organized for the purpose of developing confidence, self-esteem, and getting to know each other. By summer's end, the Chases say that everyone knows everyone in camp.

Parent Comment: "Our two boys have been at Oquago since 1978. Our eldest is now a counselor. Our feelings about it could best be summed up by comparing it to an extended family. There's an instant warmth about the camp that you feel as soon as you drive in.

"Our children have made friends who seem closer to them than those at home. Their athletic and social skills were influenced to a great extent at Camp Oquago. We guess the most important thing is that they look forward to going to camp, they're happy when they're there, and they start counting the days to the next summer after they come home."

POINT O'PINES CAMP FOR GIRLS

Brant Lake, New York

Single sex, female

Ages: 6–16

Campers: 235

Religious affiliation: None

Fees: $4,050, 8 weeks

Extra fees: Transportation to and from camp, canteen

Founded: 1957

Program: A structured and elective, noncompetitive program. Younger children are in structured program; older children have combined program

Facilities/Activities: *Athletics* 2 baseball fields, 2 soccer fields, 12 tennis courts (8 clay, 4 hard surface, 4 lit), basketball court, indoor basketball court, track, gymnastics, archery range, volleyball courts; *Waterfront* lake, swimming, canoeing, rowboating, sailing, sailboarding, kayaking, waterskiing; *Camping* campfire and sleep-out sites, 500-acre farm, nature area; *Creative Arts* theater, plays, new fine arts center, radio room; *Miscellaneous* horseback riding, recreation rooms

Boarding: 38 cabins (electricity), 2 showers/cabin; dining room (family style), special diets accommodated, kosher style, salad bar; laundry done weekly by camp

Counselors: 1 to every 2.5 children, 128 counselors total; average age, 20; 15% are foreign

Camp Rules: 3 or 4 telephone calls a summer for children (extra calls for birthdays or illness); 3 letters written a week; no food in cabins

Medical: Physician and registered nurse in camp, 6-bed infirmary, parents always notified if child is sick; 45 miles from Glens Falls Hospital

Directors: Sue and Jim Himoff
Summer: Brant Lake, NY 12815
        518-494-3213
Winter: 40 East 78 Street, New York, NY 10021
        212-288-0246

Sue and Jim Himoff have been owners and directors of Point O'Pines since 1984. Jim has served as president of an international merchant banking organization. Sue has worked with children and as an independent artist. Both Sue and Jim were campers and counselors for many years. Their love for children and their longtime relationship with Brant Lake Camp were the primary reasons they decided to enter camping.

Philosophy: At Point O'Pines the directors believe that the best way to ensure a successful camp experience is to provide an active, structured environment in which the camper has the opportunity to gain self-confidence and independence through a wide range of activities. The social experience of learning to live, work, and play with others is equally important. "At Point O'Pines, campers enjoy themselves while participating to the fullest. They make lifelong friends with other campers and counselors and develop a true appreciation of the outdoors."

Point O'Pines is a traditional camp: the program is structured, campers are in uniform, and there is "reasonable discipline." While there is a wide range of activities, there is particular emphasis on water sports and tennis. The younger campers are scheduled to participate in almost every activity that is offered, whereas the older girls are allowed to be more selective in their programming. According to the directors, "we are noted for our fine facilities, the excellence of our supervision, the high level of our instruction, and the strong feeling of family which pervades our camp."

Parent Comment: "My daughter had the best summer of her life. She loves Point O'Pines and expects to go back. You must be doing something right. Keep the great job up. With you as the new owners, Point O'Pines has developed an outstanding reputation. Good luck."

POK-O-MACCREADY

Willsboro, New York ————————————————————————

Brother/sister

Ages: 7–16

Campers: 250

Religious affiliation: None

Fees: $1,175, 4 weeks / $2,275, 6 weeks

Extra fees: Transportation to and from camp, laundry and blanket

Founded: 1905

Program: Individuals arrange own schedule on a major/minor basis; major activities are held every day and minor every other day

Facilities/Activities: *Athletics* 2 baseball fields, 2 soccer fields, 5 hard-surface tennis courts (4 lit), basketball court, street hockey court, gymnastics area, riflery range, archery range, volleyball court, weight lifting; *Waterfront* lake, swimming, 20 rowboats, 22 kayaks, 25 canoes, 10 sailboards, 16 sailboats; *Camping* campfire and sleep-out sites, campcraft, nature area; *Creative Arts* outdoor theater, drama, arts and crafts, Indian crafts, spinning and weaving, pottery, model rocketry, wood shop, blacksmithing; *Miscellaneous* 5 computers (Commodore, IBM), horseback riding, 3 barns, riding rings, trails, low ropes course, rock-climbing tower, 6 recreation rooms

Boarding: 42 cabins (some with electricity and showers), 2 shower-houses, 2 dorms; dining room (family style), salad bar; laundry done weekly by commercial service

Counselors: 1 to every 4 campers, 60 counselors total; average age, 22; 12% are foreign

Camp Rules: No calls for the first 10 days; letter writing once a week; no food in sleeping accommodations

Medical: Registered nurse in camp, EMT on staff, several counselors have first aid training, 15-bed infirmary, parents called if camper goes to hospital or stays overnight in infirmary; 20 miles from Champlain Valley Physicians Hospital

Director: Jack Swan
Summer: Mountain Road, Box 290, Willsboro, NY 12996
     518-963-8366
Winter: P.O. Box 5016, Brookfield, CT 06804
     203-775-9865

Jack Swan has been a history teacher and admissions counselor for Westminster College. Founder of the Pok-O-MacCready outdoor education center and trustee of the Adirondack Scholarship Foundation, he is an avid hiker, canoer, member of the Adirondack Mountain Club, and Adirondack 46er Club (climbing over forty-six mountains over four thousand feet in the Adirondacks). Pok-O-MacCready was founded by Jack's grandfather in 1905; Jack is a third-generation camp director. He and his wife became owners of the camp in 1963. Jack, who is a member of the ACA standards committee, has a B.A. from Westminster College and an M.A. from Syracuse University.

Philosophy: At Pok-O-MacCready each camper arranges his or her own schedule. The camp has a large horseback riding program, which includes daily riding and weekly trips to horse shows outside of camp. In the "horsemaster program," campers have the opportunity to take care of the horses.

In addition to the riding program, the camp has a full range of activities including team competition with other camps and local teams in soccer, tennis, volleyball, baseball, and sailing.

Pok-O-MacCready also boasts a working farm from the 1830s, which houses a pig, sheep, chickens, and oxen. Campers can also learn gardening, blacksmithing, shinglemaking, and Colonial cooking, which are taught in the facility.

Parent Comment: "I have had three children at Pok-O-MacCready Camps and their passionate commitment to the place says far more than I could about its special qualities. The oldest, a boy who loves the wilderness and mountain climbing, started there at age fourteen, and now at nineteen is a counselor. My second son has applied to be a counselor and my daughter will spend her fifth summer there this year.

"The physical setting of the camp, in the northern Adirondacks, is marvelous. But the best thing about the camp is the spirit of the place— the relationships, the great affection that develops between staff and youngsters, and the enduring friendships that form between campers.

"The family that runs Pok-O-MacCready (eighty years or so), the Swans, are quite remarkable in their love for their work, love of the place, and their enduring commitment to the 'Pok-O Spirit.' "

CAMP REGIS–APPLE JACK

Paul Smiths, New York ——————————————————

Coed

Ages: 6–16

Campers: 180

Religious affiliation: None

Fees: $1,800, 4 weeks / $3,150, 8 weeks

Extra fees: Transportation to and from camp, spending money

Founded: 1946

Program: A structured and elective, noncompetitive program; optional sports program

Facilities/Activities: *Athletics* 2 baseball fields, 2 soccer fields, 7 hard-surface tennis courts, basketball court, street hockey court, cross-country running, gymnastics, archery range, 2 volleyball courts, indoor gym at college 2 miles away; *Waterfront* freshwater lake, swimming, 14 sailboats, 10 Funyaks, 12 rowboats, 14 canoes, 4 motorboats, 6 sailboards; *Camping* campfire and sleep-out sites, farm area with animals, nature area; *Creative Arts* outdoor theater, indoor playhouse, plays, talent shows, dance, arts and crafts; *Miscellaneous* recreation room, ropes course

Boarding: 14 cabins (electricity), indoor showerhouses; dining room (family style), special diets accommodated, salad bar; laundry done weekly by camp

Counselors: 1 to every 3.5 campers, 55 counselors total; average age, 23; 8% are foreign

Camp Rules: Parents can phone once a week; children write parents once a week; food allowed in cabins

Medical: 2 registered nurses in camp, many counselors have first aid and CPR training, 20-bed infirmary, parents notified if child sees camp doctor or stays overnight in infirmary; 12 miles from Saranac Lake General Hospital

Directors: Michael Humes, Pauline Humes
Summer: P.O. Box 245, Paul Smiths, NY 12970
518-327-3117
Winter: 107 Robinhood Road, White Plains, NY 10605
914-997-7039

Camp Regis–Apple Jack was founded by Earl B. Humes and Pauline L. Humes in 1946. Mr. Humes was an assistant dean of students at City College of New York and was head of development for New College, Sarasota, Florida. His summers were spent working with children in the camping field. Mrs. Humes was a teacher at several private schools in New York City (Little Red Schoolhouse and Downtown Community). She was involved in student-teacher supervision and her summers were spent in children's camping. Their son, Michael, grew up in Camp Regis. After receiving his teacher's degree from Pace University and working as a teacher, he became the director of Camp Regis–Apple Jack in 1980. Pauline continues to remain active as co-director.

Philosophy: Since Camp Regis–Apple Jack was founded, it has had staff and children from countries around the world. Camp Regis–Apple Jack has always believed that "camping is education, and education is community as well as the learning of skills." For this reason, the staff encourages children to take part in group workshops in all areas of instruction. Campers are allowed to choose their primary activities. The program is "group-centered." Boys and girls reside in cabins of twelve to sixteen boys or girls of the same age group. Group counselors participate in all activities with their group. They also help campers plan special group activities and trips. "Camp should be a place for fun and learning new skills, but the center of the camp experience should be a growing sense of independence, confidence, and individuality coupled with a realization of the need to work together."

Parent Comment: "Camp Regis–Apple Jack has been unique to my family for several reasons. For the past eight years, camp has been able to provide a safe, warm, and accepting environment to my son and daughter. Over the years, the counselors have been mature, competent, and aware of the children's needs in relationship to their ages.

"My children have developed friendships, which I'm sure will be lifelong. The rich source of cultures and backgrounds has also been a major asset. Camp has also contributed to my children's development of self-esteem.

"The philosophy and values at Regis–Apple Jack lead to a positive learning experience similar to those I experienced when I attended as a camper some years ago."

CAMP SCATICO
Elizaville, New York ————————————————————

Brother/sister

Ages: 7–16

Campers: 260

Religious affiliation: None

Fees: $3,550, 54 days

Extra fees: Transportation to and from camp, trips for 15-year-old group, expense account

Founded: 1921

Program: A structured environment for younger children; older children select half of their program

Facilities/Activities: *Athletics* 8 baseball fields, 3 soccer fields, 11 hard-surface tennis courts (10 lit), 6 basketball courts (2 lit), 2 street hockey courts (1 lit), gymnastics area (enclosed building), 2 riflery ranges, 2 archery ranges, 3 volleyball courts, golf driving range, putting green, indoor basketball gym, weight-training center, indoor soccer facility; *Waterfront* spring-fed lake, swimming (sand and clay crib bottoms), fishing, sailing, canoeing, kayaking, sailboarding, rowboating, Fun Bugs, paddleboards, no motorboats; *Camping* campfire and sleep-out sites, hiking trails, 2 nature areas; *Creative Arts* theater, dramatics, plays, talent shows, set design, lighting, music, dance studio, arts and crafts, ceramics, photography, radio room; *Miscellaneous* areas for indoor activities, Ping-Pong, films, tapes

Boarding: 30 cabins (electricity, attic fans), showers in all cabins, 3 showerhouses; dining room (family style), kosher style, salad bar; laundry done weekly by commercial service

Counselors: 1 to every 3.5 campers, 80 counselors total; college age; 20% are foreign

Camp Rules: After first week telephone calls accepted for campers at nonactivity times, director always available between 10:30 p.m. and midnight; letters written 3 times a week; some food allowed in cabins

Medical: Physician and 3 registered nurses in camp, 15-bed infirmary, parents notified if child goes to hospital or spends a second night in infirmary, consultation on long-standing medical problems; 15 miles away from Northern Dutchess Hospital

Directors: Ruth and Irwin Fleischner, David Fleischner
Summer: Elizaville, NY 12523
     914-756-2444
Winter: 25 Fenimore Road, New Rochelle, NY 10804
     914-632-7791

Irwin Fleischner was a teacher and principal at James Monroe High School in New York City. He was the boys head counselor at Scatico and is a past president of the Association of Independent Camps and the New York State Camp Directors Association. Ruth Fleischner was a teacher. Their son, David, has a bachelor's degree from Columbia and graduate degrees in business and journalism from NYU. The Fleischners bought Camp Scatico in 1964 and have been involved with camping for many years.

Philosophy: At Camp Scatico the aim is to further the development of the individual by providing an enjoyable experience in group living while achieving competence in skills. To implement these goals Scatico has a wide variety of activities, all of which emphasize participation and improvement. The key element in this combination is the counselor, and Scatico tries to attract mature people with an understanding of youngsters.

Parent Comment: "The fact that Camp Scatico is considered to be a cut above the rest is not because of its well-maintained athletic fields or its varied program complete with art and drama or, of course, the beautiful lake, but rather because of the relationships between the campers and their counselors.

"My association with Camp Scatico began almost forty years ago with my brother, when we were campers in 1952. In 1977 my own daughters, ages six and eight, began their Scatico experience. The first visiting day confirmed that the mystique was still there when the girls were greeted by name by the much older campers as if they were old friends. Over and over again, I hear of friends made at Scatico lasting a lifetime through college into adulthood. This has been true for me and my daughters, who are now in college and living with former bunkmates.

"Often I have asked myself about this special ingredient Scatico adds to its camping experience. It is this special ingredient that makes the campers resent missing a summer. Even when exciting alternatives are offered, the campers feel sad when the years are finally over."

CAMP SOMERHILL
Athol, New York ————————————————————————

Coed

Ages: 7–14

Campers: 160

Religious affiliation: None

Fees: $600, 1 week / $3,500, 8 weeks

Extra fees: Transportation to and from camp, baggage

Founded: 1960

Program: Campers plan their own program

Facilities/Activities: *Athletics* 2 baseball fields, 2 soccer fields, 6 hard-surface tennis courts (all lit), 3 basketball courts (all lit), 2 volleyball courts, cross-country track, gymnastics area, riflery range, archery range, street hockey court; *Waterfront* 2 swimming pools, lake (canoeing, fishing, nature study), second lake (waterskiing, sailing, sailboarding, scuba diving); *Camping* campfire and sleep-out sites, nature area; *Creative Arts* outdoor theater, plays, voice and instruments, radio station, model rocketry, electronics, ceramics, drawing, glassblowing, wood, leather, batik, silk screening, dance room, photography; *Miscellaneous* 6 computers (Commodore 64, IBM, Apple II), horseback riding, stable

Boarding: 5 dorms (electricity), showers in each dorm; dining room (cafeteria style), special diets accommodated, salad bar; laundry done weekly by camp

Counselors: 1 for every 4 campers, 40 counselors total; average age, 24; 10% are foreign

Camp Rules: Parents may call anytime to speak with director, may call their child once a week; letter writing twice a week; no food in dorms

Medical: Physician on call, registered nurse, and certified first aid and CPR personnel in camp, 7-bed infirmary, parents notified if child spends night in infirmary or visits hospital; 8 miles from Warrensburg Medical Center, 20 miles from Glens Falls Hospital

Directors: Larry and Dr. Lynn Singer
Summer: High Street, Athol, NY 12810
      518-623-3890
Winter: 20 Huntley Road, Box 295, East Chester, NY 10709
      914-793-1303

Lynn Singer has a Ph.D. in psychology, and a B.S. and M.A. in health and physical education. She is an assistant professor at Long Island University and Mercy College. Lynn has her own private therapy practice and writes for professional journals. Larry Singer is a retired teacher from the New York City school system. He has been director and owner of Camp Somerhill since 1960. He currently teaches counseling and health on the college level.

Philosophy: Camp Somerhill seeks to promote creativity and self-reliance through freedom of choice and responsibility of action. Campers choose their activities daily from a large number of choices. There is instruction, adventure, fun, and personal development. What counts for Somerhill is that each camper has a rewarding experience.

All areas of camp life are enjoyed in small groups, with emphasis placed on cooperation and the development of each individual camper.

Parent Comment: "We were impressed by the concern you and your staff showed toward our son. I want you to know how grateful we feel to you and the many other dedicated people who make Somerhill possible. You have given of yourselves so that children may grow in achievement and learn to understand themselves and others in a beautiful atmosphere of responsibility, freedom, and creativity."

CAMP SUMMIT

Summitville, New York ———————————————

Coed

Ages: 6–16

Campers: 300

Religious affiliation: None

Fees: $3,750, 8 weeks

Extra fees: Shipping trunk, horseback riding

Founded: 1961

Program: A structured program with opportunities for choice in activities; time for extra instruction

Facilities/Activities: *Athletics* 4 baseball fields, 4 soccer fields, 6 hard-surface tennis courts (4 lit), street hockey court, 2 basketball courts, track, gymnastics, archery range, 4 volleyball courts, indoor gym; *Waterfront* swimming pool, spring-fed lake, canoeing, sailing, waterskiing, kayaking, rowboats, paddleboats, sailboards; *Camping* campfire and sleep-out sites, nature area; *Creative Arts* outdoor theater, drama, radio room, arts and crafts, model rocketry; *Miscellaneous* ropes course, recreation room, go-cart track

Boarding: 26 cabins (electricity), 3 showers/cabin, 1 dorm; dining room (cafeteria style), special diets accommodated, kosher style, salad bar; laundry done weekly by camp

Counselors: 1 to every 3 campers, 120 counselors total; average age, 19; 30% are foreign

Camp Rules: 3 prearranged telephone calls a summer; 3 letters a week; no food in sleeping accommodations

Medical: Physician and 3 registered nurses in camp, 16–20 beds in infirmary, parent notified if child spends more than 1 night in infirmary or goes to hospital, and at discretion of director or medical director; 12 miles from Horton Hospital and Arden Hospital

Directors: Mel and Judy Stern
Summer: RD 1, Box 379A, Wurtsboro, NY 12790
914-888-5000
Winter: 67 Joyce Road, Plainview, NY 11803
516-433-5237

Judy Stern has a B.A. and has taught elementary school. She has been in camping for thirty years, first as a head counselor and for the past thirteen years as director and owner of Camp Summit. Mel Stern has a B.S. and an M.S. and has taught for thirty-three years. He is now retired from teaching. Mel has thirty-five years of camping experience and was a head counselor before becoming a director and owner of Camp Summit.

Philosophy: Camp Summit is a traditional coed camp emphasizing warmth and friendliness. There is ample opportunity for growth, enjoyment, adventure, and friendship. The staff strives to give individual attention to each camper. While the program is structured, there is opportunity for campers to receive extra instruction in the area of their choice. Directors Judy and Mel Stern pride themselves on the camp's "top facilities," which they feel provide the best opportunity for children to truly experience camp at its best.

Camper Comment: "Last summer was a great experience for me. I learned a great deal about not only others but myself. The summer was full of joy, laughter, and tears at the end of the season. Camp was one of those funny experiences that you don't fully appreciate until it is all over. You look back with hindsight and think of what a great time you had."

TIMBER LAKE CAMP
Shandaken, New York ―――――――――――――――――

Coed

Ages: 8–16

Campers: 480

Religious affiliation: None

Fees: $3,995, 8 weeks

Extra fees: Shipping of luggage, optional apparel and blanket rental, extended trips for older campers

Founded: 1965

Program: A structured and elective, competitive and noncompetitive traditional program

Facilities/Activities: *Athletics*   4 baseball fields, 2 soccer fields, 8 hard-surface tennis courts (4 lit), 5 basketball courts (3 lit), street hockey court, archery range, riflery range, weight lifting (Nautilus equipment), gymnastics; *Waterfront*   indoor and outdoor swimming pools, 2 lakes, waterskiing, sailing, sailboarding, canoeing, kayaking, rowboating; *Camping*   campfire and sleep-out sites; *Creative Arts*   outdoor theater, musicals, talent shows, 12 different arts and crafts shops, model rocketry; *Miscellaneous*   horseback riding, recreation room, Ping-Pong, ropes course

Boarding: 41 cabins (electricity), 3 showers/cabin; dining room (cafeteria style), special diets accommodated, kosher style, salad bar; laundry done weekly by commercial service

Counselors: 1 to every 3 younger campers, 1 to every 4 older campers, 160 counselors total; average age, 21; 10% are foreign

Camp Rules: Every camper calls home once a week after the first week; letters written 3 times a week; no food in cabins

Medical: Physician and 4 registered nurses in camp, counselors have first aid and CPR training, 18-bed infirmary, parents notified if child is in infirmary for more than 1 night, if child needs to go on antibiotics, or is taken out of camp for X rays or other procedures; 30 miles from Benedictine Hospital

Director: Jay S. Jacobs
Summer: Broad Street Hollow, Shandaken, NY 12480
      914-688-2266
Winter: 12 Cypress Drive, Woodbury, NY 11797
      516-367-6700

Jay S. Jacobs has been the owner and director of Timber Lake Camp since 1980. He currently serves on the board of the New York State Camp Directors Association and is a member of the board of directors of the ACA. Jay first came to Timber Lake Camp as a camper and over the years has worked in many different areas, giving him a strong background in virtually all areas of camp activity.

Philosophy: Timber Lake stresses good sportsmanship over winning; no camper plays two periods until every camper has played one. The expectation is that every camper will participate in the program. Timber Lake Camp is "unique because of the diversity its program offers. Our facilities in all areas are top-notch. We run a well-supervised, structured program."

Parent Comment: "Although Barbara and Charles have only been home for a few days, it is extremely evident that their summer was wonderful. Changing camps after five years was a difficult decision for both of them, but it seems the choice of Timber Lake was a success.

"They both said there was nothing they would change at camp. Their counselors were a good influence, kind, and helpful. My son has expressed great admiration for many counselors. He was so proud of his MVP award for baseball. Activities were great. Both children loved art, which has never been a favorite at school or camp. Evening entertainment was exciting. Canteen food was great! As a result, they were not hungry this summer. But the best is that new friends keep calling. We were so pleased to observe all the friends and counselors who came up to them to say good-bye as we left.

"Thank you for giving them both a very happy and most memorable summer. They both anxiously look forward to next year. We especially look forward to our daughter working as a waitress—do you think that experience will carry over to our home?"

TIMBER LAKE WEST

Roscoe, New York ─────────────────────────

Coed

Ages: 8–16

Campers: 280

Religious affiliation: None

Fees: $2,150, 4 weeks (2 sessions)

Extra fees: Shipping baggage

Founded: 1955

Program: A traditional structured, moderately competitive program

Facilities/Activities: *Athletics*   3 baseball fields, 2 soccer fields, 6 hard-surface tennis courts, 3 basketball courts (2 lit), 2 street hockey courts, gymnastics area, weight lifting, archery range, 2 volleyball courts, indoor gym, roller rink; *Waterfront*   swimming pool, lake, canoeing, sailing, sailboarding, kayaking, Wave Walkers, pedal boats, rowboats; *Camping*   campfire and sleep-out sites; *Creative Arts*   theater, musicals, drama, talent show, radio room, silk screening, candlemaking, macramé, ceramics, woodwork, fine arts, tie-dyeing, stained-glass making, model rocketry, electronics; *Miscellaneous*   Ping-Pong, air hockey, video games

Boarding: 31 cabins (electricity), 3 indoor showers/cabin; dining room (family style), kosher style, salad bar; laundry done weekly by commercial service

Counselors: 1 to every 3 campers, 100 counselors total; average age, 21; 10% are foreign

Camp Rules: No telephone calls home the first week, then everyone calls home once a week; 3 letters home per week; no food in cabins

Medical: Physician and 2 registered nurses in camp, some staff certified in first aid and CPR, 16-bed infirmary, parents notified by phone if child spends more than 1 night in infirmary or if child needs X rays or antibiotics; 8 miles from Community General Hospital

Directors: Bob and Alice Rosenberg
Summer: Burnt Hill Road, Roscoe, NY 12776
        914-439-4440
Winter: 12 Cypress Drive, Woodbury, NY 11797
        516-367-6700

Bob and Alice Rosenberg were head counselors at Timber Lake Camp, an affiliated eight-week camp, before becoming the directors of Timber Lake West. During the rest of the year Bob teaches in the New York City school system while Alice teaches in the Pomona, New York, school district.

Philosophy: While Timber Lake West is a traditional sleep-away camp, directors Bob and Alice Rosenberg feel that it is a camp "with a unique difference: a four-week session." The camp's general program is "a good camp for the first-time camper."

Camper Comment: "Timber Lake is the best because they treat me like I am at home."

CAMP TREETOPS
Lake Placid, New York

Coed

Ages: 7–13

Campers: 160

Religious affiliation: None

Fees: $3,100, 7 weeks

Extra fees: Transportation to and from camp

Founded: 1920

Program: Elective program with the exception of swimming and horseback riding, which are required

Facilities/Activities: *Athletics* baseball field, soccer field, hard-surface tennis court, basketball court (lit), volleyball court; *Waterfront* lake, swimming, canoeing, kayaking, rowing, sailboarding; *Camping* campfire and sleep-out sites, nature area; *Creative Arts* outdoor theater, skits, major play, modern and square dancing, instrumental and chorus instruction, weaving, ceramics, batik, tie-dyeing, leatherwork, photography; *Miscellaneous* ropes course, horseback riding, farm animals (sheep, pigs, cows, chickens, goats), use of North Country School facilities (library, music rooms)

Boarding: 40 lean-tos, 33 tents, 2 showerhouses; dining room (family style), vegetarian option, salad bar; laundry done weekly by commercial service and camp

Counselors: 1 to every 3 campers, 60 counselors total; average age, 26; 10% are foreign

Camp Rules: No telephone calls between parents and campers except on birthdays; weekly letter required (on Sunday); no food in sleeping accommodations

Medical: 2 registered nurses in camp, 23 staff certified in standard or advanced first aid, 15-bed infirmary, in case of sickness parents notified by telephone and in writing; 7 miles from Lake Placid Memorial Hospital

Director: Jeff Jonathan
Summer: Cascade Road, Box 187, Lake Placid, NY 12946
518-523-9329
Winter: Same

Jeff Jonathan received a B.A. and elementary education certification from Middlebury College in Vermont. He has worked in camping for fifteen years, the last six directing Camp Treetops. Before coming to Treetops he taught sixth grade and co-directed a high-school outdoor education program. Jeff has also been an instructor in the Adirondack Mountain Club's winter mountaineering school. In addition to his work at Treetops, he is a Standards Visitor at summer camps applying for accreditation from the ACA.

Philosophy: Treetops is a noncompetitive environment. There are two camp communities—a junior division of about sixty children (ages seven to ten), and a senior division of about ninety children (ages eleven to thirteen). Treetops is on a working farm and the entire community shares in the tasks of maintaining its two-acre vegetable garden and caring for a variety of farm animals. The children take day and overnight camping trips of up to four days' duration by foot, horse, and canoe. On a daily basis, children choose most of their activities beyond the required riding and Red Cross swimming classes. Group life is made as meaningful as possible through the enrollment of staff and children from varying racial, religious, national, economic, and geographic backgrounds.

Parent Comment: "When I picked my daughter up on Sunday she ran to me and said, 'Hi, Mom, I'm going back to Treetops next year!' As a happy parent of a happy camper, I thank you for providing my daughter with a truly wonderful summer. You have given her an opportunity to learn very valuable lessons in responsibility, sharing, and community spirit—plus you made it all such fun."

CAMP WHIPPOORWILL FOR GIRLS
Keeseville, New York

Single sex, female (brother camp, Camp Lincoln for Boys)

Ages: 8–15

Campers: 80

Religious affiliation: None

Fees: $2,300, 5 weeks / $2,700, 7 weeks

Extra fees: Transportation to and from camp, canteen deposit

Founded: 1931

Program: An elective, noncompetitive program governed by individual choice

Facilities/Activities: *Athletics* large multipurpose field for baseball, soccer, softball, touch football, and low-organization games, 2 clay tennis courts, half-court basketball court, archery range, 2 tetherball courts, volleyball court; *Waterfront* lake, swimming, fishing, 22 sailboats, 12 sailboards, 38 canoes, 24 rowboats, 6 kayaks; *Camping* campfire and sleep-out sites, nature center and trails; *Creative Arts* theater, plays, concerts, talent shows, piano, arts and crafts, pottery; *Miscellaneous* high and low ropes course, animal enclosure (llamas, goats, rabbits), vegetable garden, horseback riding, stables (10 horses), Ping-Pong, book collection, recreation building

Boarding: 18 cabins (some have electricity), 2 showerhouses; dining room (family style), special diets accommodated on request, salad bar; laundry done weekly by commercial service

Counselors: 1 to every 4 campers, 22 counselors total; minimum age, 18; majority in their 20s; 5% are foreign

Camp Rules: Campers may receive calls at mealtimes and may place calls with permission of staff, families urged to use phone sparingly; weekly letter required; no food in cabins

Medical: Physician on call, registered nurse in camp, EMT on staff, all counselors certified in first aid and CPR, 4-bed infirmary, parents notified in event of medical emergency, if child spends night in infirmary, or visits doctor; 17 miles from Champlain Valley Physicians Hospital

Director: Nancy Gucker Birdsall
Summer: RR 1, Box 188, Keeseville, NY 12944
　　　518-834-5151
Winter: P.O. Box 52, Craftsbury Common, VT 05827
　　　802-586-7731

Nancy Gucker Birdsall grew up at Camp Whippoorwill and has served as director since 1984. She has a B.S. degree in outdoor education from Empire State College. During the winter she is coordinator of the Elderhostel program in Craftsbury, Vermont.

Philosophy: Whippoorwill strives to impress upon every child her importance to the success of camp life. All campers take turns waiting on tables in the dining halls, help with cabin cleaning, participate in service projects, and assist counselors with such tasks as rolling the tennis courts or grooming and feeding the horses. A major emphasis at Whippoorwill is the extensive hiking and outdoor camping program. "From such experience children can learn comradeship, the exhilaration of accomplishment, and an appreciation for the beauty and vitality of the natural world."

Parent Comment: "I am not sure what the secret of your success is but Camp Lincoln and Camp Whippoorwill are outstanding for their lack of pretentiousness, small size, infectious enthusiasm for the wilderness, and development of camping skills in a relaxed and genial atmosphere that gives campers a sense of mastery without the pressures of competition. In a world full of nonsense these camps have remained the same steady, decent, and beautiful institutions that I attended and that my children attended."

CAMP BALLIBAY
Camptown, Pennsylvania ─────────────────────────

Coed

Ages: 6–16

Campers: 150

Religious affiliation: None

Fees: $1,350, 3 weeks / $1,850, 4 weeks / $2,990, 7 weeks; $495, 1-week arts workshop; $950, 2-week theater workshop

Extra fees: Transportation to and from camp, airport pickup, canteen

Founded: 1963

Program: An elective, noncompetitive program with heavy emphasis on the fine and performing arts

Facilities/Activities: *Athletics* baseball field, soccer field, 2 hard-surface tennis courts, gymnastics, archery range, volleyball courts; *Waterfront* swimming pool, lake, boating, kayaking, fishing, canoeing; *Camping* campfire and sleep-out sites, nature area; *Creative Arts* 2 indoor theaters, 3 outdoor platform theaters, lighting, sound, video, 5 fine-arts and crafts areas, dance, music, arts; *Miscellaneous* 6 computers (Apple, Norstar, Tandy, Leading Edge, Macintosh), horseback riding, stables, recreation rooms

Boarding: 14 cabins (electricity), 1–2 showers/cabin; dining room (family style), special diets accommodated, salad bar; laundry done weekly by commercial service

Counselors: 1 to every 3 or 4 campers, 42 counselors total; average age, 22–24; 20% are foreign

Camp Rules: No campers can make telephone calls, director and staff are always available to parents; letter writing encouraged; no food in cabins

Medical: 2 registered nurses in camp, 4-bed infirmary, parents immediately notified in situation of any severity; 7 miles from Memorial Hospital, 25 miles from Guthrie Clinic

Directors: Gerard and Dorothy Jannone
Summer: Box 1, Camptown, PA 18815
        717-746-3223, fax: 717-746-3691
Winter: Same

Gerard Jannone is the founder and director of Camp Ballibay. Prior to making Ballibay his full-time profession, Gerard was a teacher and department chairman in the New Jersey public schools for fourteen years. He has a B.S. in psychology and M.S. degrees in administration and education. He was a counselor and camp director for New Jersey "Y" camps for several years before founding Ballibay. A flight instructor, Gerard flies the camp twin-engine aircraft on camp business.

Dorothy Jannone was an art teacher in Mountainside, New Jersey, for fourteen years before making Ballibay her full-time profession. She graduated from Kean College with a B.F.A. and NYU with an M.F.A. She is president of Jane Piatek Design, an advertising agency primarily devoted to Ballibay advertising and promotion. Dorothy is active in her community in the fine arts and theater.

Philosophy: The Ballibay motto is "It's the journey, not the product," meaning that the day-to-day relationship between the staff and campers is the essence of the camp experience. A coed camp specializing in fine and performing arts, Ballibay also offers traditional camping activities such as swimming, riding, and tennis.

Parent Comment: "Ballibay is like a cove for whatever you are doing—there are no distractions from your art. With the help of staff and campers, you are intensifying *here.*"

CAMP BRYN MAWR
Honesdale, Pennsylvania ―――――――――――――――

Single sex, female

Ages: 5–16

Campers: 285

Religious affiliation: None

Fees: $4,225, 8 weeks

Extra fees: Horseback riding, specialized tennis, senior trips, canteen

Founded: 1921

Program: Structured with one choice period out of six; emphasis on instruction. There is competition but no awards

Facilities/Activities: *Athletics* 2 baseball fields, 4 soccer fields, 18 hard-surface tennis courts (8 lit), 4 basketball courts (2 lit), archery range, 2 volleyball courts, 10,000-sq.-ft. gymnastics building (free exercise, 3 uneven parallel bars, 8 balance beams, 100-ft. vaulting runway, springloaded floor, carpet), track; *Waterfront* 2 swimming pools, lake, 10 canoes, 10 sailboats, 10 Playaks, 8 rowboats, 10 water bikes, water-skiing (Ebbtide boat), Red Cross testing program for distance swimming; *Camping* campfire and sleep-out sites, nature area; *Creative Arts* 15,000-sq.-ft. multipurpose building, stage, dressing room, makeup room, mirrored dance studio, arts and crafts, ceramics, woodworking, jewelry, fine arts, batik; *Miscellaneous* English horseback riding, 3,000-sq.-ft. stable, ring, long line ring, fitness room, recreation room (piano, games, Ping-Pong)

Boarding: 20 cabins (electricity), 2–3 showers/cabin, 2 dorms (electricity and showers); dining room (buffet style), special diets accommodated, kosher style, salad bar; laundry done by camp twice weekly

Counselors: 1 for every 3 campers, 85 counselors total; average age, 21; 12% are foreign

Camp Rules: No telephone calls until after visiting day, then parents will have calls returned; at least 2 letters a week; no food in sleeping accommodations

Medical: Physician and 3 registered nurses in camp, 14-bed infirmary, parent notified of smallest detail; 4 miles from Wayne County Memorial Hospital

Directors: Herb and Melanie Kutzen
Summer: RR 5, Box 410, Honesdale, PA 18431
      717-253-2488
Winter: 81 Falmouth Street, Box 612, Short Hills, NJ 07078
      201-467-3518

Herb Kutzen has a bachelor's and a master's in education from Brooklyn College. He has owned and directed Bryn Mawr since 1972, and has spent close to forty years in camping. He has been president of the Wayne County Camping Association. Melanie Kutzen also has a bachelor's and a master's in education from Brooklyn College. She has been a director and owner of Bryn Mawr since 1972.

Philosophy: "Bryn Mawr is one of the oldest traditional eight-week camps. We believe that our highly organized program, the richness of our traditions, a strong sense of individual growth, the absence of intense competition and material rewards, and pride in uniform all contribute to create the Bryn Mawr identity. Our goals are accomplished through a fine staff of adult coaches, recreators, and educators who supervise and instruct our campers."

Parent Comment: "I'm so busy writing to my daughter daily telling her how pleased we are that she loves camp. But, I decided it was time to write and thank you for giving my daughter the opportunity of a lifetime. How lucky we are as parents to know that she is very safe and happy. This is a special gift and to say a passing thank-you just doesn't seem enough. You are very special people, camp directors, owners, parents, and the list seems endless. Thank you for allowing us to feel so relaxed and confident that our daughter is 'under your wings' for eight weeks."

CAMP CANADENSIS
Canadensis, Pennsylvania

Coed

Ages: 6–15

Campers: 350

Religious affiliation: Jewish

Fees: $3,685, 7½ weeks

Extra fees: Horseback riding lessons, tennis lessons, "Competitive Edge" daily tennis program, canteen

Founded: 1941

Program: A structured and elective, competitive and noncompetitive program

Facilities/Activities: *Athletics* 8 baseball fields, 4 soccer fields, 16 hard-surface tennis courts (12 lit), 2 street hockey courts, 13 basketball courts (12 lit), track, gymnastics (balance beam, vault, uneven bars), aerobics studio, riflery range, 2 archery ranges, 6 volleyball courts, weight room (Universal), wrestling, indoor gym; *Waterfront* 2 heated swimming pools, lake, 43 rowboats, 15 sailboards, 24 Funyaks, 15 kayaks, 4 paddleboats, 4 Hobie Cats, 3 Lazers, 3 Homars, 10 canoes, 2 waterski boats, scuba diving; *Camping* campfire and sleep-out sites, nature area; *Creative Arts* theater, drama, band, shows, arts and crafts, ceramics, puppetry, wood shop, silk screening, model rocketry, photography, radio room; *Miscellaneous* computers (Apple IIe, Apple IIGS, Commodore, Tandy, Nintendo), ropes course, 2 climbing walls, mountain bikes (Hondas), river trips, recreation rooms

Boarding: 43 cabins (electricity), 2 showers/cabin; dining room (cafeteria style), special diets accommodated, kosher style, salad bar; laundry done weekly, girls' by commercial service and boys' by camp

Counselors: 1 to every 3 campers, 150 counselors total; average age, 21½; 15% are foreign

Camp Rules: 5 telephone calls per season for campers; 4 letters written a week; food allowed in cabins

Medical: Physician and 3 registered nurses in camp, 10-bed infirmary, parents notified for anything more than a cold; 16 miles from Stroudsburg Hospital

Directors: Steve Saltzman, Terri Saltzman, William Saltzman
Summer: Canadensis, PA 18325
       717-595-7461
Winter: Box 182, Wyncote, PA 19095
       215-572-8222

William Saltzman is the founder of Camp Canadensis. He was a teacher and coached football and wrestling. Steve Saltzman and his sister Terri have both been teachers. Steve coached tennis and wrestling and won many state championships.

Philosophy: Camp Canadensis is a place operated with a "warm family feeling." The Saltzmans take pride in creating a camp in which children develop socially, physically, and mentally. Camp Canadensis provides one of the finest camping curricula for children. "Our goals are to have each camper acquire skills, make friends, work within a group setting, and develop a higher sense of self-esteem and independence."

Parent Comment: "I just wanted to thank you. Your prompt attention to our son's needs is one of the reasons why I like Canadensis and recommend it to friends. It's nice to know I can pick up the phone and call you."

CAMP CAYUGA
Honesdale, Pennsylvania ———————————————————

Coed

Ages: 5–15

Campers: 300

Religious affiliation: None

Fees: $1,700, 4 weeks / $2,700, 8 weeks

Extra fees: Transportation to and from camp, shipping baggage, canteen

Founded: 1957

Program: Combination of structured and elective, noncompetitive program

Facilities/Activities: *Athletics* 2 baseball fields, 2 soccer fields, 6 hard-surface tennis courts (lit), 2 basketball courts (lit), 2 street hockey courts, 2 gymnastics areas, 6 volleyball courts, 2 riflery ranges, 2 archery ranges, track, tetherball court, flag football, judo, indoor gym (roller hockey, aerobics), weight-lifting room, badminton, field hockey; *Waterfront* swimming pool, natural stream-fed lake, sailboats, rowboats, paddle-boats, canoes, kayaks, inner tubes, fishing; *Camping* campfire and sleep-out sites, nature area; *Creative Arts* theater, plays, arts and crafts (clay, painting, macramé), model rocketry, 2 radio stations, newspaper; *Miscellaneous* 6 computers (Commodore 64), horseback riding, stable (25 horses), 2 riding rings, 7 miles of trails, Yamaha Quad riding (4-wheel, all-terrain vehicles), cheerleading, video-game room, 2 recreation centers

Boarding: 45 cabins (electricity), 1–4 showers/cabin; dining room (cafeteria style), substitutes available, kosher style, salad bar; laundry done weekly by camp

Counselors: 1 to every 4 campers, 80 counselors total; average age, 21; 15% are foreign

Camp Rules: Campers return telephone calls after dinner every night of the week; campers must write 2 letters weekly; food allowed in cabins

Medical: Physician 5 miles from camp and on 24-hour call, 3 registered nurses and assistant in camp, 10-bed infirmary, parents notified when camper is in infirmary for 24 hours or more or if camper is taken to town to visit doctor; 5 miles from Wayne County Memorial Hospital

Director: Brian B. Buynak
Summer: RD 1, Box 1180, Honesdale, PA 18431
      717-253-3133
Winter: P.O. Box 452, Dept. FB, Washington, NJ 07882
      800-4-CAYUGA

Brian Buynak is the owner and director of Camp Cayuga. He has a B.A. and Ph.D. Residential camping has been a way of life for Brian since 1956, when his family purchased their first summer camp. For the past thirty-four summers Brian has been head counselor, waterfront director, program director, and camp director. Brian is a member of the ACA and the Wayne County Camping Association.

Philosophy: At Camp Cayuga boys and girls from five to fifteen experience "traditional camping at its best." "Making friends" is what Cayuga is all about. The camp specializes in first-time campers and strives to offer the understanding and special attention first-time campers require. Cayuga feels its instructors are specialists in their field and have demonstrated the skill and temperament required to teach beginners as well as advanced-level campers.

Daily activities are noncompetitive and designed with sensitivity to the camper's age and ability. "This ensures adequate individual attention and instruction to achieve a safe, gradual progression in each activity."

Cayuga is especially proud of its horseback riding program. A private stable which houses twenty-five horses is located on the premises. Campers can ride five days a week for a fifty-five-minute period at no extra charge.

Parent Comment: "Just a note to let you know how satisfied my wife and I were with the job you all did with our son. This is all aside from all the awards he was able to win. He gained a lot of independence. Overall, I don't see how he could have enjoyed himself anymore or taken any more advantage of all you offer. It was absolutely beyond our general expectations. Again, thanks for all your concern and caring."

CAMP CHEN-A-WANDA

Thompson, Pennsylvania ────────────────────────

Coed

Ages: 6–16

Campers: 350

Religious affiliation: None

Fees: $3,450, 8 weeks

Extra fees: Trips, canteen

Founded: 1939

Program: A structured program with some flexibility; campers have regularly scheduled individual hobby periods and supervised free play

Facilities/Activities: *Athletics* 4 baseball fields, 2 soccer fields, 5 hard-surface tennis courts (lit), 6 basketball courts (3 lit, 1 indoor), 2 street hockey courts, 2 volleyball courts, track and field area, gymnastics pavilion (exercise mats, parallel bars, vault, balance beams), archery range, golf driving range, miniature golf course (9 holes), weights, outdoor fitness center; *Waterfront* swimming pool (heated, lit), Fiddle Lake, 3 waterski boats, sailing, canoeing, kayaking, pedal-boating, rowing, waterskiing, fishing; *Camping* campfire and sleep-out sites (on grounds); *Creative Arts* theater program, fully equipped stage, ceramics, woodworking, leather crafts, clothing design, model rocketry, tie-dyeing, radio station; *Miscellaneous* 5 computers (Apple IIe), go-cart track, bicycling (24 BMX dirt bikes), air-conditioned game room (pool, Ping-Pong, hockey, Foosball, jukebox, piano)

Boarding: 31 cabins (electricity), 2–3 indoor showers/cabin; dining room (family style), weight-watching and vegetarian diets accommodated, kosher style; laundry done weekly by commercial service

Counselors: 1 to every 4 campers, 90 cabin counselors plus adult staff of 15 families; average age, 20; 25% are foreign

Camp Rules: Campers permitted to call home once a week after the first week, campers permitted to receive calls during rest hour and free play; 3–4 letters home per week required; no food in cabins

Medical: Physician and 3 registered nurses in camp, 10-bed infirmary, parents notified in case of emergency or if child requires overnight stay in infirmary; 19 miles from St. Joseph's Hospital

Directors: Caryl and Morey Baldwin, Sandy and Alan Wachman
Summer: RD 1, Thompson, PA 18465
          717-756-2016
Winter: 8 Claverton Court, Dix Hills, NY 11747
          516-643-5878

Directors Caryl and Morey Baldwin and Sandy and Alan Wachman are the backbone and spirit of Camp Chen-a-Wanda. While Morey and Alan deal with the planning of activities and work directly with the children, Caryl and Sandy are busy organizing and supervising behind the scenes. All four directors bring to Chen-a-Wanda many years of camping and education experience. The Baldwins and Wachmans describe themselves as "a happy and dedicated foursome doing what they do best—camping."

Philosophy: Camp Chen-a-Wanda calls itself "the friendly camp," which strives to fully develop campers' personalities and skills. "The staff at Chen-a-Wanda is carefully selected on the basis of maturity, experience, and enthusiasm. We feel that their influence is directly responsible for our campers' happiness." The directors claim that more than 60% of their cabin staff returns each year, while nearly 100% of their large married staff, composed of teachers and school administrators, returns each year.

Parent Comment: "Fiddle Lake is postcard pretty with the full gamut of waterfront activities. The land-based activities, including the golf driving range, go-carts, hockey courts, and batting range offer campers a full range of activities. The out-of-camp trips provide children with a break from the in-camp routine. Most important, the Baldwins and the Wachmans know all there is to know about running a camp. And the feeling that Camp Chen-a-Wanda projects is one of a safe and happy summer family."

CAMP ECHO LARK
Poyntelle, Pennsylvania ────────────────────────

Coed

Ages: 6–16

Campers: 300

Religious afffiliation: None

Fees: $2,050, 4 weeks / $3,950, 8 weeks

Extra fees: Trips

Founded: 1940

Program: A structured, competitive indoor and outdoor program

Facilities/Activities: *Athletics* 4 baseball fields, 3 soccer fields, 7 hard-surface tennis courts, 5 basketball courts, 2 street hockey courts, 2 volleyball courts, archery range, golf, miniature golf course, 2 gymnastics areas (uneven bars, balance beam, parallel bars, vault), field house; *Waterfront* lake, swimming, kayaking, waterskiing, sailing, rowboating, sailboarding; *Camping* campfire and sleep-out sites, nature area; *Creative Arts* 2 stages (5 shows a summer), radio room, arts and crafts building, model rocketry, photography room; *Miscellaneous* 15 computers (Commodore, Apple), movie theater

Boarding: 34 cabins (electricity), 1 shower/cabin; dining room (cafeteria style), special diets accommodated, kosher style; laundry done weekly by camp

Counselors: 1 to every 3 campers, 100 counselors total; average age, 20; 10% are foreign

Camp Rules: Campers may telephone parents after dinner (at parents' request); letter home required 3 times a week; no food in cabins

Medical: Physician and 2 registered nurses in camp, 20-bed infirmary, parents notified if child spends night in infirmary or requires hospital visit; 25 miles from St. Joseph's Hospital

Directors: Isaac Baumfeld, Joe Podair
Summer: Poyntelle, PA 18454
717-448-2300
Winter: 40 Halley Drive, Pomona, NY 10970
800-331-KAMP, 914-354-9267

Co-director Isaac Baumfeld has held positions at Camp Westmont, French Woods, and New England Experience. In the past, Isaac was a school guidance counselor. Joe Podair was a program director, athletic director, and head counselor at Echo Lark before becoming co-director. He is a certified soccer and basketball official.

Philosophy: Situated on five hundred acres of land and a one-hundred-acre lake, Camp Echo Lark is a coed camp in the Pocono Mountains with a philosophy of structured choice. Waterskiing and tennis programs are emphasized. "The mature staff are mostly teachers and educators whose emphasis is the individual camper and his or her specific needs. Safety is a prime consideration. Competitive sports are encouraged and we enter the county tournaments in most age groups."

Camper Comment: "Camp Echo Lark is a second home to me. I have friends of all ages and I have a lot of fun. I have improved my skills because of the great instruction and because I participate in things that I can't do at home. I can pick my favorite activities."

FRENCH WOODS SPORTS AND ARTS CENTER
Starrucca, Pennsylvania

Coed

Ages: 6–17

Campers: 300

Religious affiliation: None

Fees: $1,795, first 3 weeks / $1,950, middle 3 weeks / $1,595, last 3 weeks / $3,295, first 6 weeks / $2,995, last 6 weeks / $3,950, full 9 weeks

Extra fees: None

Founded: 1984

Program: Elective and noncompetitive. Extensive English and Western horseback riding program. Science lab emphasizing hands-on approach

Facilities/Activities: *Athletics* 2 baseball fields, soccer field, 7 hard-surface tennis courts, 2 basketball courts (1 lit), street hockey court, gymnastics area, archery range, volleyball court, golf, lacrosse, indoor complex (10-station Universal machine, karate, judo, boxing, fencing, wrestling, basketball court); *Waterfront* lake, swimming, canoeing, kayaking, rowing, sailing, sailboarding; *Camping* campfire and sleep-out sites (on island), nature area; *Creative Arts* indoor theater (3 full Broadway shows per session), voice instruction, cabaret, stagecraft, art complex, painting, sculpture (wood, steel), photography, ceramics, wood shop, stained glass, model rocketry, 2 dance studios (tap, ballet, jazz, modern), music building (rock-band guitar, keyboard, drums), radio room; *Miscellaneous* 8 computers (Apple, Macintosh), horseback riding (ring, outdoor trails, indoor facility), circus (Spanish Webb, trapeze, side-by-side and swinging trapezes, unicycle, juggling), ropes course

Boarding: 35 cabins (electricity), 2 showers/cabin; dining room (cafeteria style), special diets accommodated, salad bar; laundry done weekly by camp

Counselors: 1 to every 3 campers, 125 counselors total; average age, 22; 10% are foreign

Camp Rules: No telephone calls the first week, 2 calls per session afterward; campers must write home twice a week; no food in cabins

Medical: Physician and 3 registered nurses in camp, 12-bed infirmary, parent notified if child stays overnight in infirmary or is taken for treatment out of camp; 15 miles from Barnes-Kassen Hospital

Directors: Bev and Mike Stoltz
Summer: Starrucca, PA 18462
      717-798-2550
Winter: P.O. Box D800, Pomona, NY 10970
      800-869-6083 (outside New York)
      914-354-5517 (inside New York)

Bev and Mike Stoltz each have more than twenty-five years in education and camping. Both were teachers and supervisors in the New York City school system. Twenty years in camping as head counselors, program directors, and assistant directors in both traditional and nontraditional camp environments was excellent preparation for becoming camp directors. As both parents and educators, Bev and Mike realize the importance of a supportive atmosphere for each child.

Philosophy: At French Woods Sports and Arts Center, each camper designs his or her own program to satisfy his or her personal interests and needs. Campers are encouraged to explore and discover skills in new areas of interest. French Woods offers instruction in areas unusual to camping, such as circus arts, a "hands-on" approach to science, and an intensive on-the-premises equestrian program where horse care and maintenance are taught hand in hand with riding.

At French Woods Sports and Arts Center, each child is encouraged to develop his or her skills and creative abilities and to develop self-confidence through individual achievement rather than through peer competition. "We like to think of our camp as a family where every child is important. We cater to each camper's emotional as well as physical well-being to provide the best camping experience possible."

Parent Comment: "As the parents of six children, we have had exposure to almost every type of camping experience. As different as our children are, they are able to attend the same camp for the first time. You have the variety of activities of a very traditional camp, the choices and freedom associated with a very liberal camp, and the in-depth programs that one might expect to find in a specialty camp.

"In your freedom of choice you set the limits to eliminate confusion, while giving the children a feeling of self-confidence. In the specialty aspects you allow for intense work while forcing a mild integration that will expose the children to another activity.

"All of the above, coupled with the nurturing ability and ratio of your staff, and your presence, patience, and expertise have made these past summers a very special part of the children's growth."

INDIAN HEAD CAMP
Honesdale, Pennsylvania ─────────────────────

Coed

Ages: 7–17

Campers: 260

Religious affiliation: None

Fees: $3,850, 8 weeks

Extra fees: Canteen

Founded: 1940

Program: A structured and elective, noncompetitive personalized program for campers who are 13 years of age and older that aims to develop skills in areas of interest

Facilities/Activities: *Athletics* 3 baseball fields, soccer field, training field, 8 hard-surface tennis courts (2 lit), 3 basketball courts (1 lit), street hockey court (lit), gymnastic pavilion, archery range, 5 volleyball courts, indoor gym (weights, other equipment); *Waterfront* lake, swimming, sailing (4 Sunfish), rowing, canoeing, kayaking, sailboarding, water-skiing; *Camping* campfire and sleep-out sites, nature area; *Creative Arts* theater, full performing arts program (performing, stage and set design, lighting, music, dance), arts and crafts, ceramics, model rocketry, radio room; *Miscellaneous* 8 computers (Tandy), ropes course, recreation room (indoor games)

Boarding: 26 cabins (electricity), 1–3 showers/cabin, 1 dorm for camper waiters (ages 15 and 16), 5 platform tents at wilderness site; dining room (family style), most requests accommodated, kosher style, salad bar; laundry done weekly by commercial service

Counselors: 1 to every 3 campers, 80 counselors total; average age, 21; 30% are foreign

Camp Rules: No calls for the first 10 days, 1 call before visiting day, 2 after, appointments made; letter writing required 3 times a week; no food in sleeping accommodations

Medical: Physician and registered nurse in camp (nurses' assistants available), 15-bed infirmary, parents called if child is kept overnight in infirmary or in event of accident requiring medical intervention; 15 miles from Wayne County Memorial Hospital

Directors: Shelley and David Tager
Summer: Honesdale, PA 18431
    717-224-4111
Winter: 6 Colonial Court, East Northport, NY 11731
    516-493-0083

Shelley and David Tager have spent seventeen years in camping in Maine and Pennsylvania. David has spent twenty years in education, the last five as an elementary-school principal. Shelley has been an elementary-school teacher for sixteen years.

Philosophy: Indian Head Camp strives to provide campers with a summer of instruction and participation in land sports, water sports, creative and dramatic arts, and outdoor adventures. Indian Head is proud of its counselors. "Staff members who join the Indian Head family do so with the understanding that ours is a camper's camp! The aim is to provide the best possible experience for the young people in attendance. The rewards at Indian Head come from the relationships of people, shared experiences with friends, and the realization that we have provided a positive and meaningful direction for young people."

Parent Comment: "I attended Indian Head for many years and now send my three children from Florida. Indian Head is a 'home away from home' where I know my children will be well cared for and provided with a wide range of experiences which will enrich their lives, as the experience did mine."

LAKE OWEGO CAMP
Greeley, Pennsylvania

Single sex, male (sister camp, Camp Timber Tops)

Ages: 7–15

Campers: 170

Religious affiliation: None

Fees: $1,985, 4 weeks / $3,700, 8 weeks

Extra fees: Horseback riding, trips for older campers, canteen

Founded: 1959

Program: A structured program with electives; campers from the seventh grade on design their own program

Facilities/Activities: *Athletics*   4 baseball fields, 3 soccer fields, 6 hard-surface tennis courts (2 lit), street hockey court, track, riflery range, archery range, lacrosse field, football field, volleyball court, weight room, judo, karate; *Waterfront*   swimming pool, Red Cross swimming lessons, two lakes, sailing, canoeing, sailboarding, kayaking, rowboating, fishing, waterskiing, advanced sailing (21-ft. boat); *Camping* campfire and sleep-out sites, nature trails and center; *Creative Arts*   outdoor theater, plays, talent shows, lighting, sound, arts and crafts, model rocketry, radio station, photography, newspaper; *Miscellaneous*   5 computers (Apple II), ropes course, climbing wall, recreation room, trips program (canoeing down Delaware River, hiking on Appalachian Trail, mountain climbing), horseback riding, trails, corral, jumping

Boarding: 17 cabins (electricity), 1–2 showers/cabin, 1 central showerhouse, 3 tents (electricity); dining room (family style), special diets accommodated, kosher style, salad bar; laundry done weekly by commercial service

Counselors: 1 to every 3 campers, 60 counselors total; average age, 21; 10% are foreign

Camp Rules: Telephone calls not allowed first 10 days, parents then allowed to call at designated times during the day; letter writing every other day; no food in sleeping accommodations

Medical: Physician 2 miles away makes daily clinic calls and available at all times, registered nurse in camp, some staff members have CPR training, 7-bed infirmary, parents notified if camper stays overnight in infirmary or has serious accident; 18 miles from Mercy Community Hospital

Director: Sheldon Silver
Summer: Greeley, PA 18425
717-226-3636
Winter: 407 Benson East, Jenkintown, PA 19046
215-887-9700

Sheldon Silver has been in camping since 1972 in positions ranging from group leader, athletic director, and head counselor, to director of Lake Owego since 1986.

He has a B.A. in psychology, a B.S. in health and physical education, an M.A. in education and recreation from Brooklyn College, and a degree in educational administration from City College of New York. He has taught and coached in the New York City school system for twenty-three years. Sheldon is married with two sons.

Philosophy: At Lake Owego "campers learn to grow physically and emotionally." The camp's goals are to have campers respect each other and accept an individual for who he is. "Our staff is sensitive and trained in achieving these objectives." Boys have opportunities to develop basic skills in many activities as well as choose favorite ones. As a result, campers can be active in areas they enjoy and excel at. "Whether it be an intercamp game, a climb up a mountain, a canoe trip, or performing in a play, the boys come away with a sense of achievement and feel good about themselves."

Parent Comment: "Our son came home so happy. He loved camp. We heard a lot of stories about all the activities and people. He came back a mature, independent boy. We have you and your wonderful staff to thank.

"The morning after he came home, he woke up at 6:15, got dressed, and went outside to play basketball. This 'new' young man is energetic and ready to go. He is now interested in so many new things! The activities that you got him excited about will now last for a long time."

CAMP NETIMUS FOR GIRLS
Milford, Pennsylvania

Single sex, female (brother camp, Camp Shohola for Boys)

Ages: 7–16

Campers: 125

Religious affiliation: None

Fees: $1,450, 4 weeks / $2,650, 8 weeks

Extra fees: Horseback riding, canteen

Founded: 1930

Program: A structured, noncompetitive program with camper choice of activities

Facilities/Activities: *Athletics* baseball field, soccer field, 2 hard-surface tennis courts, basketball court, riflery range, archery range, volleyball court, lacrosse field, gymnastics (balance beam, uneven parallel bars, mats); *Waterfront* lake, swimming, canoeing, kayaking, boating, Lake Wallenpaupack, waterskiing, advanced sailing; *Camping* campfire and sleep-out sites, nature area; *Creative Arts* theater, plays, silk screen, jewelry, stained glass, woodworking, calligraphy, ceramics, dance; *Miscellaneous* 3 computers (Commodore 64), horseback riding, 2 rings, recreation room

Boarding: 15 cabins (electricity), 1 shower/cabin; dining room (family style), salad bar; laundry done weekly by camp

Counselors: 1 to every 3 campers, 45 counselors total; average age, 20; 45% are foreign

Camp Rules: Telephone calls permitted on special occasions, parents can call during mealtimes after first week; letter writing required once a week; no food in cabins

Medical: 2 nurses in camp, some staff are EMTs and certified in first aid, 8-bed infirmary, parents notified if child spends night in infirmary, visits doctor or hospital; 14 miles from Mercy Community Hospital

Directors: James and Donna Kistler
Summer: RD 1, Box 117A, Milford, PA 18337
　　　717-296-6131
Winter: 4519 Dresden Street, Kensington, MD 20895
　　　717-296-6128

Jim and Donna have been active in camping for many years as campers, counselors, and administrators. Both have undergraduate majors in education, and both have earned their master's degrees. Jim earned his degree in education administration, and Donna earned hers in physical education and health.

Philosophy: Camp Netimus seeks to create the best possible camping environment so that campers may learn more about themselves and their strengths. The camp directors and counselors believe that this can best be achieved by encouraging their campers to set individual goals for themselves and to participate in any of the camp's many sporting and extracurricular activities. Camp Netimus also believes that encouraging new friendships at the camp enhances the emotional and intellectual growth of each individual camper.

Parent Comment: "What attracted us to Netimus and Shohola? They care about our children. Quality, child-oriented programs and staff create a very special experience. Children are encouraged to develop life skills in a relaxed, sharing, supervised, happy, challenging, and safe environment. Our children participate in activities that offer a refreshing break from academic studies away from home and parental involvement. They learn new skills and build independence and self-esteem. Sharing their camp experience with other children promotes special friendships and memories that our children will always call their own. We look forward to a long association with Netimus and Shohola."

CAMP ONEKA

Tafton, Pennsylvania ─────────────────────────

Single sex, female

Ages: 7–16

Campers: 120

Religious affiliation: None

Fees: $775, first 2 weeks / $750, second 2 weeks / $1,250, first 3½ weeks / $1,200, second 3½ weeks / $2,250, 7 weeks

Extra fees: Laundry, horseback riding, canteen

Founded: 1908

Program: Combination of structured and elective activities

Facilities/Activities: *Athletics* baseball field, soccer field, 3 hard-surface tennis courts, basketball court, archery range, volleyball court, playground, hockey field; *Waterfront* lake, Red Cross swimming lessons and diving, rowing, canoeing, sailing (Sunfish and Javelin), sailboarding, Funyaks; *Camping* campfire and sleep-out sites, nature area, hiking; *Creative Arts* theater, plays, skits, ceramics, copper enameling, jewelry, basket weaving, leatherwork, art; *Miscellaneous* 2 recreation rooms

Boarding: 14 cabins (electricity), showerhouses, 8–10 tents; dining room (family style), special diets accommodated, salad bar once a week; laundry done weekly by commercial service

Counselors: 1 to every 4 campers or more, 25 counselors total; average age, 20; 20% are foreign

Camp Rules: Telephone calls only on birthdays and for emergencies; letters required for admission to certain meals and other times; no food in sleeping accommodations

Medical: 2 registered nurses in camp, some staff members have first aid, 6-bed infirmary, parents notified if camper is kept in infirmary or requires doctor or hospital visit; 15 miles from Wayne County Memorial Hospital, 3 miles from Medical Center

Directors: Dale and Barbara Dohner
Summer: Tafton, PA 18464
       717-226-4049
Winter: 10 Oakford Road, Wayne, PA 19087
      215-687-6260

Dale Dohner has sixteen years of camping experience at Resica Falls Scout Reservation as program director and director, one year at Camp Dwight, one year at Hart Scout Reservation, and four years at Oneka as program director and director. Dale is a water safety instructor trainer and a member of the National Camp School and the ACA. Dale has twenty-two years of public-school teaching (biology) and coached track and field.

Barbara Dohner is a registered nurse and a Red Cross first aid and CPR instructor. She has been a nurse at Resica, Dwight, Hart, Magar, and Oneka summer camps, as well as a school nurse.

Philosophy: Camp Oneka prides itself on its small size (120 campers). The camp maintains that this allows campers to receive quality instruction and recreation time. While Oneka provides in-camp competition, its major goals are "participation, learning, and fun. We like to think of Oneka as a large family, with campers, staff, and directors participating together in all of the camp community activities." Regular events with other camps provide times for socialization. Oneka campers can spend their camp time in a "relaxed atmosphere where trying is what counts and every camper is an appreciated camper."

Parent Comment: "My daughter had a wonderful time at Camp Oneka this year and is looking forward to returning next summer as well. She was thrilled to receive the drama award. We are proud of all her accomplishments at camp and we thank you for providing her with a very positive camping experience her first time away from home."

PINE FOREST CAMP
Greeley, Pennsylvania

Coed

Ages: 7–16

Campers: 350

Religious affiliation: None

Fees: $3,700, 8 weeks ($2,100 for 4 weeks by special arrangement)

Extra fees: Horseback riding, canteen

Founded: 1931

Program: A structured and elective, noncompetitive program with emphasis on tennis and intramural athletics

Facilities/Activities: *Athletics* 6 baseball fields, 4 soccer fields, 12 hard-surface tennis courts (3 lit), 5 basketball courts, 2 street hockey courts, track, gymnastics pavilion, riflery range, 2 archery ranges, 5 volleyball courts, indoor basketball court, wrestling, martial arts pavilion; *Waterfront* 2 swimming pools, Red Cross swimming lessons, Lake Greeley, sailboarding, sailing, canoeing, kayaking, rowing, fishing, Lake Wallenpaupack, waterskiing; *Camping* campfire and sleep-out sites, indoor and outdoor nature areas, hiking; *Creative Arts* indoor and outdoor theaters, drama lessons, plays, band, singing, instruments, model rocketry, arts and crafts, photography (darkroom), jewelry, ceramics, wood shop, drawing, painting, radio room; *Miscellaneous* 6 computers (Apple IIe), ropes course, horseback riding, trails, corral, jumping

Boarding: 40 cabins (electricity), 1 shower/cabin, showerhouses; dining room (family style), kosher style, vegetarian option, salad bar; laundry done weekly by commercial service

Counselors: 1 to every 2 campers, 150 counselors total; average age, 21; 10% are foreign

Camp Rules: No telephone calls first week, then limited to 1 or 2 for the summer; letters written 3 times a week; no food in cabins

Medical: Physician and registered nurses in camp, 12-bed infirmary, parents notified of overnight stay in infirmary or of any illness or symptoms of concern; 18 miles from Mercy Community Hospital

Directors: Marvin Black, Mickey Black, Ted Halpern
Summer: Box 242, Greeley, PA 18425
             717-685-7141
Winter: 407 Benson East, Jenkintown, PA 19046
             215-887-9700

Pine Forest Camp has been owned and operated by the Black and Halpern families since its founding in 1931. Marvin Black and Ted Halpern have held national and local leadership positions in the ACA, including serving as members on the national ACA board of directors. Marvin established the Pioneers in Camping Club, which now has over two hundred members. Both men are recipients of ACA awards for their contribution to camping. Their wives, Annette Black and Libby Halpern, have also played an active role at camp.

Mickey Black represents the third generation. Mickey is an attorney, but devotes full time to camping. He is currently serving as president of the eastern Pennsylvania section of the ACA. His wife, Barbara, is a teacher, and is in charge of the food service at camp. Mickey and Barbara have two children at camp.

Philosophy: Pine Forest Camp, founded in 1931, is one of the oldest camps still owned and operated by its founding family. Three generations and sixty years later, it remains "a fun, innovative, and exciting place for children to spend the summer. The day at Pine Forest is a busy one, structured and purposeful but relaxed and informal." Instruction emphasis is on "Did I try?" rather than "Did I succeed?" Pine Forest campers are encouraged to aim for inward satisfaction rather than outward reward.

Parent Comment: "I have sent three boys to Pine Forest over the course of about fifteen years. Each of my sons is different and has unique interests. Pine Forest made each feel good about himself in his own way. Each individual child is made to feel special. The friends my children met at camp have become lifetime companions. They had more fun at Pine Forest than at any other place or at any other time in their lives."

CAMP POCONO RIDGE
South Sterling, Pennsylvania

Coed

Ages: 7–15

Campers: 225

Religious affiliation: None

Fees: $1,925, 4 weeks / $3,450, 8 weeks

Extra fees: None

Founded: 1955

Program: An elective and structured, noncompetitive and competitive program

Facilities/Activities: *Athletics* 2 baseball fields, 2 soccer fields, 2 hard-surface tennis courts (3 more under construction), 3 basketball courts, street hockey court, track, riflery range, archery range, volleyball courts, softball fields, gymnastics area, weight room (Nautilus); *Waterfront* swimming pool, lake, canoes, kayaks, Sunfish, Funyak, rafting; *Camping* campfire and sleep-out sites, nature area; *Creative Arts* outdoor theater, radio room, multifaceted crafts room, model rocketry; *Miscellaneous* 12 computers (Apple IIe), ropes course, horseback riding (10,000-sq.-ft. indoor riding area), recreation room

Boarding: 20 cabins (electricity), 2 showers/cabin; dining room (family style), kosher style, salad bar; laundry done weekly by camp

Counselors: 1 to every 3 campers, 57 counselors total; average age, 20; 60% are foreign

Camp Rules: Telephone calls are allowed after second week; 2 mandatory letters a week; no food in cabins

Medical: 2 registered nurses living in camp, 20-bed infirmary, parents receive call if camper visits doctor; 20 miles away from Scranton Community Medical Center

Directors: Mel and Jane Wolynez
Summer: South Sterling, PA 18460
　　　717-676-3478
Winter: 826 Shari Lane, East Meadow, NY 11554
　　　516-489-4152

Mel Wolynez was head counselor and director at French Woods. He and his wife, Jane (co-director), are school administrators in New York City. Mel is an assistant principal in an elementary school for the gifted. Jane is an assistant principal in a high school and has a background in teaching children with learning disabilities.

Philosophy: Camp Pocono Ridge offers a semi-elective, coed program for boys and girls. Campers are able to choose four out of seven periods on a daily basis.

The camp is situated high in Pennsylvania's Pocono Mountains. Brooks and streams run through the camp, and it claims to have some of the tallest pine trees in the Poconos.

The program includes scuba diving in a heated pool. "A new 10,000-square-foot riding area is an exciting facility. We are in the process of building a new lodge with dining room, kitchen, infirmary, game room, and staff lounge and sleeping quarters."

Parent Comment: "After seeing many camps, Pocono Ridge is our first and only choice. Thank you so much for taking the time to show us your beautiful camp and to explain the program. It's just what we were looking for and our son is already excited about next summer."

CAMP ROBIN HOOD
Chambersburg, Pennsylvania ——————————————————

Single sex, female

Ages: 6–17

Campers: 100

Religious affiliation: None

Fees: $750, 2 weeks / $1,050, 3 weeks / $1,350, 4 weeks / $1,650, 5 weeks / $2,250, 7 weeks

Extra fees: Laundry, canteen

Founded: 1926

Program: A structured, competitive, and noncompetitive program with individualized as well as team activities

Facilities/Activities: *Athletics*   softball field, soccer field, 4 hard-surface tennis courts (2 lit), 2 basketball courts (lit), archery range, riflery range, indoor and outdoor volleyball courts, tetherball, field hockey, fencing, indoor gym, field for net sports; *Waterfront*   swimming pool, creek for canoeing, nearby lake for sailing; *Camping*   campfire and sleep-out sites, campcraft, nature trails; *Creative Arts*   indoor theater, musical productions, voice, dance, instrumental as requested, 2 pianos, 2 guitars, arts and crafts, fine arts, potter's wheel; *Miscellaneous*   2 computers (Apple), 2 English riding rings, riding hunt course, riding trails, 18-stall stable, recreation room, main lodge, learning center, cheerleading

Boarding: 4 dorms (electricity), 5 showerhouses separate from dorms (26 individual showers); dining room (family style), special diets accommodated; laundry done weekly by commercial service

Counselors: 1 to every 4 campers, 25 counselors total; age range, 18–36; 30% are foreign

Camp Rules: Parents may telephone the director anytime, telephone calls between camper and family are allowed after first week (twice a week); letter writing encouraged; nutritious food such as nuts, dried fruits allowed in dorms

Medical: Physician on call within 4 miles of camp, 2 registered nurses live in camp, all staff CPR-certified, 30%–50% of staff first aid–certified, 6-bed infirmary, parents notified when injuries require medical attention or admission to infirmary overnight; 4 miles from Chambersburg Hospital

Director: Valerie Gryniuk
Summer: 3377 Camp Robin Hood Road, Chambersburg, PA 17201
717-267-0547
Winter: 12 Downing Court, Chambersburg, PA 17201
717-267-0547

Valerie Gryniuk is a professional nurse with a B.S. degree in nursing and an M.S. in counseling. Her experience includes fifteen years of hospital, public health, and school nursing, eight years in business, and eight years in environmental health. Her camping background includes seven years as a camper, five years as a counselor, two years as a program director, and three years as a camp director. In addition to owning and operating the camp, Valerie is currently working as a health care provider at a private high school during the school year.

Philosophy: At Camp Robin Hood the staff aims to treat each camper as a unique girl. Building camper confidence and self-esteem are top goals. Girls develop both individual and team skills in the fine arts and sports. The daily schedule is designed to provide both structured and free time, "emphasizing fun, self-development, safety, and health."

Parent Comment: "In the years that our daughter has attended Camp Robin Hood, I have watched her grow in self-confidence and ability, as well as develop a sense of who she is. Camp Robin Hood is the best investment I've made in her future. It's a wonderful experience that I would highly recommend to anyone."

CAMP SHOHOLA FOR BOYS
Greeley, Pennsylvania ───────────────────────

Single sex, male (sister camp, Camp Netimus for Girls)

Ages: 7–16

Campers: 165

Religious affiliation: None

Fees: $1,450, 4 weeks / $2,650, 8 weeks

Extra fees: Horseback riding, canteen

Founded: 1943

Program: A structured, noncompetitive program with camper choice of activities

Facilities/Activities: *Athletics*   2 baseball fields, 2 soccer fields, 5 hard-surface tennis courts, 2 basketball courts, street hockey court, riflery range, archery range, volleyball court, lacrosse field; *Waterfront*   lake, swimming, canoeing, kayaking, boating, sailboarding, fishing, sailing, Lake Wallenpaupack, waterskiing, advanced sailing; *Camping*   campfire and sleep-out sites, nature area; *Creative Arts*   radio room, arts and crafts, jewelry, woodworking, model rocketry, electronics, video; *Miscellaneous*   8 computers (Tandy), horseback riding, 2 rings, trails, ropes course, recreation room

Boarding: 18 cabins (electricity), 2 shower cabins; dining room (family style), salad bar; laundry done weekly by camp

Counselors: 1 to every 4 campers, 50 counselors total; average age, 21; 40% are foreign

Camp Rules: Telephone calls permitted on special occasions, parents can call during mealtimes after first week; letter writing required once a week; no food in cabins

Medical: 2 nurses and EMTs in camp, some staff certified in first aid, 12-bed infirmary, parents notified if child spends night in infirmary, visits doctor or hospital; 18 miles from Honesdale Hospital

Directors: Frank Barger
Summer: Greeley, PA 18425
        717-685-7186
Winter: 5111 Hampden Lane, Bethesda, MD 20814
        301-652-1242

Camp Shohola has been owned and directed by the Barger family since 1943. Frank was a teacher and principal at the Sidwell Friends School in Washington, D.C.

Philosophy: Camp Shohola for Boys tries to create an environment where campers may learn more about themselves and their strengths. The camp directors and counselors believe that this can best be achieved by encouraging their campers to set individual goals for themselves and to participate in any of the camp's many sporting and extracurricular activities. Camp Shohola also believes that encouraging new friendships at the camp enhances the emotional and intellectual growth of each individual camper.

Parent Comment: "Our son had a great time at Shohola and came home happy and contented. His emotional growth in the last eight weeks is wonderful to see. Despite our pleas not to grow taller, he did so, and also grew emotionally."

CAMP STARLIGHT
Starlight, Pennsylvania

Brother/sister

Ages: 7½–15½

Campers: 430

Religious affiliation: None

Fees: $3,800, 55 days

Extra fees: Canteen

Founded: 1947

Program: Combination of structured and elective, competitive and non-competitive activities

Facilities/Activities: *Athletics*   6 softball fields, 4 soccer fields, 14 hard-surface tennis courts (5 lit), 7 basketball courts, 2 street hockey courts, gymnastics pavilion, archery range, 6 volleyball courts, indoor gym (basketball), fitness room; *Waterfront*   2 separate lakes connected by channel, swimming, sailing, waterskiing, canoeing, rowboats, Playaks, kayaks; *Camping*   campfire and sleep-out sites, nature area, nature house (small animals, library); *Creative Arts*   theater (8 Broadway-type shows and musical productions), arts and crafts, woodworking, painting, silk screening, jewelry, leatherwork, soft sculpture, ceramics (potter's wheel, hand building, slip), radio room, photography (darkroom); *Miscellaneous*   2 lounge rooms (VCRs), recreation room (fireplace, Ping-Pong, other games)

Boarding: 47 cabins (electricity), 1–2 showers/cabin; dining room (family style), special diets individually handled, kosher; laundry done 10 times by commercial service

Counselors: 1 to every 4 campers (1 to 5 for older campers), 102 cabin counselors, 20 professional staff (department heads, group leaders, etc.); average age, 21; 25% are foreign

Camp Rules: Open policy for parents to call camp, campers call home approximately 3 times or as needed; campers write home 4 times a week; no food in cabins

Medical: 1 doctor and 4 registered nurses in camp, 16-bed infirmary, parent informed by phone after child is admitted to infirmary; 26 miles from Wayne County Memorial Hospital and Barnes-Kasson County Hospital

Director: Hy Schmierer
Summer: Starlight, PA 18461
      717-798-2525
Winter: 18 Clinton Street, Malverne, NY 11565
      516-699-5239

Hy Schmierer has served as director at Starlight for over forty years. A psychologist, he was on the faculty of two universities for over twenty years. He was a director of counseling, and is now a consultant to camping and recreational organizations throughout the United States. He has served as president of the Association of Independent Camps for two terms.

Philosophy: Camp Starlight's 385 secluded acres surrounding two private lakes "were designed to provide safety for group living and all activities." Campers participate in a balanced program of athletics, waterfront activities, creative and performing arts. They are encouraged to participate in all activities but also have the opportunity to choose four electives.

The staff is guided by a large contingent of teaching and medical professionals who have been on the staff an average of twelve years. The rate of return of the campers has been 75% to 80%.

Parent Comment: "Camp Starlight has been a part of my life since I was seven years old. As a child, my summers were filled with activity, fun, and friends. My fondest childhood memories are those of my summers spent at Starlight. As a parent, I see now the true quality of the Starlight experience. It is there that strengths are enhanced, self-esteem is developed, and new tasks encouraged. Each child's personal needs, both athletic and social, are attended to by a staff that is meticulously handpicked by Hy Schmierer; they are skilled, caring, and full of spirit. Starlight is home to us and this is where we plan to stay for many years."

CAMP SUSQUEHANNOCK FOR BOYS
Brackney, Pennsylvania

Single sex, male (sister camp, Camp Susquehannock for Girls)

Ages: 7–16

Campers: 175

Religious affiliation: None

Fees: $850, 2 weeks / $1,500, 4 weeks / $2,650, 8 weeks

Extra fees: Transportation to and from camp, tutoring, horseback riding, spending money

Founded: 1905

Program: A structured and elective, competitive program; campers placed in athletic groups according to ability

Facilities/Activities: *Athletics*   3 baseball fields, 3 soccer fields, 9 tennis courts (5 clay, 4 hard surface), 4 basketball courts, 2 street hockey courts, 3 tennis backboards, 2 soccer/lacrosse backboards, 3-hole golf course, 3 volleyball courts, small building for basketball, archery range, long-jump pit, weight-lifting room, wrestling, pit for quoits; *Waterfront* lake, swimming, fishing, canoes, rowboats, sailboats, sailboards; *Camping*   campfire and sleep-out sites, nature crafts; *Creative Arts*   indoor recreation room (shows), leather, ceramics; *Miscellaneous*   horseback riding, ring, low ropes course (at girls camp), recreation room (Ping-Pong)

Boarding: 20 cabins (electricity), 1 showerhouse; dining room (family style), special diets available on a limited basis, salad bar; laundry done weekly by commercial service

Counselors: 1 to every 4 campers, 50 counselors total; average age, 21; 15% are foreign

Camp Rules: First-year campers not allowed to call, for others, phone calls made on special occasions; letters encouraged weekly; only healthy snacks allowed in cabins and under the control of the counselors

Medical: Physician and registered nurse in camp, 7-bed infirmary, camp notifies parents immediately after accident or serious illness or when camper is in infirmary for 3 days; 15 miles from United Hospital Service, Lourdes Hospital, Associates in Medicine, and Binghamton General Hospital

Director: Edwin H. Shafer
Summer: RD 1, Box 71, Brackney, PA 18812
      717-967-2323, 717-663-2188
Winter: Same

Susquehannock was founded in 1905 by G. Carlton Shafer. Edwin Shafer grew up as a camper, and then became a counselor-in-training and a cabin counselor. For twelve years he was assistant to the director, and for the past twenty-five years he has been co-director with his brother, who now directs the girls camp. Edwin has a B.A. from Princeton University and an M.A. from Columbia University. He has taught elementary and secondary school, and is an active member of the ACA. For five years he has been a Standards Visitor for ACA. Edwin is also a member of the Camp Director's Round Table.

Philosophy: Parents are asked to indicate areas in which they wish to enhance their son's personal development. Sports are an essential ingredient at Susquehannock, but many activities are noncompetitive. Campers participate according to their overall athletic proficiency, and the camp stresses the fun of play and the value of good sportsmanship. Susquehannock also encourages an appreciation for the natural environment.

"Essential for the success of these objectives is the quality of the staff. Senior staff members are experienced teachers and coaches who bring their families to camp—many have done so for more than twenty years—thereby offering an extra dimension to the supportive, friendly atmosphere. The majority of cabin counselors have been Susquehannock campers themselves, who were trained in our counselor training program."

Parent Comment: "Susquehannock is the ideal for what a boys camp should be. The days and evenings are filled with planned and chosen activities, team and individual sports. The supervised freedom of the older boys' camp life quickly gives them the feeling that the camp is their own. Their daily exposure to an exceptional senior staff strengthens good values. The younger counselors provide the highest level of sports coaching and instruction.

"My son says that he returns each summer feeling that he returns to a second home and family. There is no more a parent could desire."

CAMP SUSQUEHANNOCK FOR GIRLS
Friendsville, Pennsylvania

Single sex, female (brother camp, Camp Susquehannock for Boys)

Ages: 7–17

Campers: 90

Religious affiliation: None

Fees: $1,500, 4 weeks / $2,650, 8 weeks

Extra fees: Tutoring, horseback riding, spending money

Founded: 1985

Program: Combination of structured (juniors) and elective, noncompetitive atmosphere with some low-key competition

Facilities/Activities: *Athletics* baseball field, soccer field, basketball court, 4 clay tennis courts, gymnastics area (balance beam, horizontal bar, mats, crash mats, vault), volleyball court, archery range; *Waterfront* lake, swimming, fishing, rowboats, canoes, sailboats, sailboards, Funyaks; *Camping* campfire and sleep-out sites, nature area and museum; *Creative Arts* small indoor theater, musical shows, skits, talent night, singing, personal instruments, arts and crafts (ceramics, potter's wheel, kiln, woodworking, other crafts); *Miscellaneous* low ropes course, horseback riding, 2 rings, trails, animal care area (sheep and other animals)

Boarding: 9 cabins (electricity), 2 showerhouses; dining room (family style), special diets accommodated, salad bar; laundry done weekly by commercial service

Counselors: 1 to every 4.5 campers, 21 counselors in cabins; average age, 20; 28% are foreign

Camp Rules: No telephone calls between campers and parents except by special permission; letters written weekly; no food in cabins

Medical: Physician on call at boys camp, registered nurse at camp, some staff certified in first aid and CPR, 8-bed infirmary, 2 isolation beds, camp notifies parent whenever child goes to hospital or spends night in infirmary; 17 miles from Binghamton General, Lourdes, and Wilson Memorial hospitals

Directors: George and Dede Shafer
Summer: Lake Choconut, Friendsville, PA 18818
717-553-2343
Winter: 860 Briarwood Road, Newtown Square, PA 19073
215-353-0844

George Shafer graduated from Princeton in 1951 and received an M.A. in history from Columbia University. He teaches at Episcopal Academy. He began as a general counselor at Susquehannock for Boys forty-two years ago. Dede Shafer is co-director and has been active in the eastern Pennsylvania section of the ACA as secretary and treasurer. The Shafers have three daughters.

Philosophy: Susquehannock believes in "the moral, social, and physical development" of campers. Of equal importance is the nurturing of such qualities as self-reliance, self-confidence, and leadership ability. "In athletic competition and in cabin life campers are taught tolerance and respect for others, poise, courage, and a sense of fair play. They should learn to adapt to group living, make new friends, and cooperate with peers and counselors."

At Susquehannock an awareness of and appreciation for the natural environment is taught. Parents are asked to indicate areas in which they wish to enhance their daughter's personal development.

"The fun of play, the value of good sportsmanship" are stressed. There are competitive and noncompetitive activities.

Parent Comment: "We sent our daughter to Camp Susquehannock for Girls because we were already familiar with the camp directors. Our son had been at the boys camp for years and we had been pleased with his experience there. You can find fine facilities at many camps but beyond that we appreciate the supervision from the directors and staff at Susquehannock. They are directly involved in the camper's daily activities and serve as outstanding role models.

"Camp has provided our daughter with unique friendships and activities. The camp experience at Susquehannock has fostered independence and growth in our children. We feel Susquehannock offers campers a very special opportunity to grow and develop within a very caring environment."

CAMP TIMBER TOPS
Greeley, Pennsylvania ─────────────────────────────

Single sex, female (brother camp, Lake Owego)

Ages: 7–16

Campers: 200

Religious affiliation: Jewish

Fees: $1,985, 4 weeks / $3,700, 8 weeks

Extra fees: Horseback riding, canteen

Founded: 1961

Program: Combination of structured and elective activities

Facilities/Activities: *Athletics*   2 softball fields, soccer field, 6 hard-surface tennis courts (1 lit), field hockey, track, gymnastics pavilion (balance beam, uneven bars, mats, vault), volleyball courts, riflery range, archery range; *Waterfront*   swimming pool, lake, swimming, sailing, sailboarding, canoeing, rowboats, kayaks, Playaks; *Camping* campfire and sleep-out sites, nature area; *Creative Arts*   indoor and outdoor theaters, drama classes, shows, arts and crafts, batik, jewelry, leatherwork, ceramics, radio room; *Miscellaneous*   6 computers (Apple IIe), horseback riding, trails, corral, jumping, 20-station ropes course, extensive trips program (canoeing on the Delaware River, hiking on the Appalachian Trail, mountain climbing), recreation room

Boarding: 18 cabins (electricity), 1 shower/cabin, 2 showerhouses; dining room (family style), kosher style, low-cholesterol and vegetarian meals available, salad bar; laundry done weekly by commercial service

Counselors: 1 to every 3 campers, 75 counselors total; college age; 5% are foreign

Camp Rules: No telephone call for the first 10 days, parents must call in; letter writing 3 times a week; no food in cabins

Medical: Physician 2 miles away, registered nurse in camp, 6-bed infirmary, parent called if child stays overnight in infirmary; 18 miles from Mercy Community Hospital

Directors: Ted and Sue Weinstein
Summer: Box 236, Greeley, PA 18425
          717-226-1955
Winter: 407 Benson East, Jenkintown, PA 19046
          215-887-9700

Ted and Sue Weinstein have been the directors of Camp Timber Tops for twenty years. Ted is a high-school administrator and has served as head football coach, varsity tennis coach, and athletic director. Sue was an elementary-school teacher and has an extensive day-camp and overnight-camp background. Ted and Sue have two children.

Philosophy: At Camp Timber Tops the program is aimed at enlarging each girl's horizons. All campers have an opportunity to choose activities, with older campers afforded more freedom of choice. "The staff is the most important aspect of our organization. A year-round effort is made to recruit the best, brightest, and most caring individuals available."

Camper Comment: "Timber Tops is my second home and every summer I look forward to the type of camaraderie that can only be found at camp."

TRAIL'S END CAMP
Beach Lake, Pennsylvania ─────────────────────

Coed

Ages: 7–17

Campers: 375

Religious affiliation: Jewish

Fees: $4,075, 8 weeks

Extra fees: Counselor gratuity, canteen

Founded: 1947

Program: Combination of structured and elective activities

Facilities/Activities: *Athletics*   4 baseball fields, 2 soccer fields, 11 hard-surface tennis courts (9 lit), 4 basketball courts (lit), street hockey court (lit), track, gymnastics area, riflery range, archery range, 2 volleyball courts, physical fitness course, European handball, 9-hole golf course (par 3); *Waterfront*   lake, Red Cross swimming lessons, recreational swimming, rowing, canoeing, kayaking, catamaran, paddleboats, sailboats; *Camping*   campfire and sleep-out sites; *Creative Arts*   outdoor theater (5 shows each summer), arts and crafts, woodworking, ceramics, model rocketry, sewing center, electronics, fine arts, photography lab, filmmaking, newspaper, ham radio; *Miscellaneous*   6 computers (Apple IIe), horseback riding, library, French and Spanish labs, social hall

Boarding: 14 cabins for girls, 14 cabins for boys (all with electricity), 2 showers/cabin, 1 dorm for teenage girls, 1 dorm for teenage boys; dining room (family style), kosher; laundry done weekly on premises

Counselors: 1 to every 4.5 campers, 120 counselors total; average age, 21; 20% are foreign

Camp Rules: Campers call home once a week; letters written 3 times a week; no food in sleeping accommodations

Medical: Physician and 4 registered nurses in camp, 24-bed infirmary, parent called if child will spend more than 1 night in health center; 10 miles from Wayne County Memorial Hospital

Directors: Starr and Stan Goldberg
Summer: Beach Lake, PA 18405
717-729-7111
Winter: 1714 Wantagh Avenue, Wantagh, NY 11793
516-781-5200

Starr and Stan Goldberg were newlyweds when they started to work at Trail's End in 1964. Stan was teaching at the time and later became an assistant principal in the New York City school system. In 1965 Stan became waterfront director and Starr worked in the office. In 1967 Stan became boys' head counselor. Starr and Stan finally realized their dream by purchasing Trail's End Camp in 1987.

Philosophy: Trail's End Camp is a "diversified camp meeting the physical, educational, and cultural needs of all the campers."

Trail's End's facilities include an athletic complex, which is supervised by two athletic directors and a full athletic staff under their jurisdiction, and the health center, which is a modern building equipped with air-conditioned rooms for patients, solarium, and kitchen facility.

The staff has a five-day pre-camp orientation. When campers arrive they are welcomed by counselors who are "well trained and eagerly awaiting the campers' arrival."

The Goldbergs are proudest of the camp's "family feeling steeped in tradition." The Goldbergs claim to know every child and maintain that all campers know that Starr and Stan Goldberg are always accessible and "love being out there with the children."

Parent Comment: "Trail's End is a magnificently run camp with beautiful property. The staff is extremely friendly and caring. My daughter went to camp not knowing anyone and did so well because of the concern and care of the staff. She said that she always felt that if she didn't do well in an activity it was okay because someone was there to back her up.

"A real surprise was the condition of the clothing when the trunk was shipped back home. Just like everything else at Trail's End, the care and neatness of the clothing was impressive."

CAMP WATONKA
Hawley, Pennsylvania ─────────────────────────────

Single sex, male

Ages: 7–15

Campers: 110

Religious affiliation: None

Fees: $1,850, 4 weeks / $3,550, 8 weeks

Extra fees: Transportation to and from camp

Founded: 1963

Program: Elective, noncompetitive; emphasis on science

Facilities/Activities: *Athletics* baseball field, soccer field, 2 hard-surface tennis courts (lit), 2 basketball courts (lit), street hockey court, volleyball court, riflery range, archery range, trapshooting range; *Waterfront* lake, Red Cross swimming lessons, sailing, sailboarding, canoeing, rowing, fishing; *Camping* campfire and sleep-out sites, nature areas; *Creative Arts* radio room, drawing, leatherwork, painting, basketry, model rocketry, ham radio and robotics building, electronics, woodworking, photography (darkroom); *Miscellaneous* 20 computers (Apple IIe) with printers in air-conditioned building, recreation building (Ping-Pong, checkers, other games), minibike riding trails, chemistry, biology, and physics labs, astronomy (telescopes)

Boarding: 18 cabins (electricity), 1 shower/cabin, 1 showerhouse; dining room (family style), occasional salad bar; laundry done weekly by camp

Counselors: 1 to every 3 campers, 35 counselors total; average age, 21–23; 30%–40% are foreign

Camp Rules: Telephone calls for emergency or special events, parents can speak to counselors at any time, campers can call home when out on any of numerous trips; 2 letters home per week; no food in cabins

Medical: Registered nurse in camp, several staff have CPR and advanced lifesaving training, 5-bed infirmary, parents notified by telephone of any sickness or accident; 8 miles from Wayne County Memorial Hospital

Director: Donald Wacker
Summer: P.O. Box 127, Hawley, PA 18428
    717-226-4779
Winter: P.O. Box 356, Paupack, PA 18451
    717-857-1401

Donald Wacker has a B.S. and an M.S. from Rutgers University. He has been a science teacher and chairman of the science department in the Verona public schools in Verona, New Jersey. Donald has worked at various camps as a counselor, craft director, nature director, and assistant director before becoming the owner and director of Camp Watonka in 1963. A member of the ACA, he has been a scoutmaster for the past twenty-five years.

Philosophy: Camp Watonka prides itself on its small size of 110 boys. In addition to the traditional camp activities, Camp Watonka offers daily laboratory experiences. "Certified teachers working in well-equipped laboratory buildings make this a worthwhile experience for all boys who are interested in science." Camp Watonka does not consider itself a summer school; its "hands-on" science program is both educational and fun.

"The program at Camp Watonka is highly individualized and the campers select all of the activities in which they wish to participate." A camper may select two sciences, with the three other periods devoted to activities that the boy chooses.

Parent Comment: "Watonka was wonderful for Kim. However, I must admit I had some apprehensions going in. My son had never been away from home for so long. Because of a family tragedy, he was on shaky ground psychologically. He is also learning-disabled. Would his inability to understand some of the educational content overwhelm him as it sometimes does? None of my fears materialized. After a month at Watonka, he came back a much stronger person. He was much more independent, didn't even think of crying as he had done most of the spring, and was proud of all the things he had made at camp. Counselors, aware of his learning problems, steered him away from activities that he could expect to have trouble with, and there were obviously many left to choose from that reinforced his self-esteem and desire to learn. He often mentions some of the friends he made and looks forward to seeing them again next summer."

SOUTH

CAMP SKYLINE RANCH
Mentone, Alabama ─────────────────────────

Single sex, female

Ages: 6–16

Campers: 250

Religious affiliation: None (Christian orientation)

Fees: $735, 2 weeks / $1,395, 4 weeks

Extra fees: T-shirt shop, canteen

Founded: 1942

Program: An educational and recreational program with an extensive horseback riding program

Facilities/Activities: *Athletics* 2 basketball courts, archery range, 4 hard-surface tennis courts (2 lit), 2 backboards, open-air gymnastics area, archery range, riflery range, volleyball court; *Waterfront* swimming pool, lake, canoeing (certified Red Cross instructors), sailing; *Camping* campfire and sleep-out sites, nature area; *Creative Arts* chorus and drama classes, performance, arts and crafts, fine arts; *Miscellaneous* 4 computers (Apple IIe, IIc), strong horseback riding program (20 horses), recreation room, ropes course

Boarding: 17 cabins (electricity), 3 showerhouses; dining room (family style), special diets accommodated; laundry done every 2 weeks by commercial service

Counselors: 1 to every 5 campers (1 to every 3 for younger campers), 50–75 counselors total; average age, 20; no foreign counselors

Camp Rules: Phones available for emergencies or homesickness at director's discretion; letter writing encouraged; no food in cabins

Medical: 2 nurses in camp, entire staff certified in first aid and CPR, 7-bed infirmary, parent notified if physician is consulted; 12 miles from Baptist Medical Center

Director: Susan C. Hooks
Summer: P.O. Box 287, Highway 117, Mentone, AL 35984
205-634-3201
Winter: Same

Susan Hooks has been associated with Camp Skyline for sixteen years, seven of them as director. She is active in the ACA and Christian Camping International. She and her husband, Larry, live year-round with their two children at Camp Skyline.

Philosophy: Camp Skyline, a girls camp founded and operated on the principles of Christianity, is "dedicated to providing an exciting, successful camping experience for today's youth." Skyline is located on the banks of Little River, on top of Lookout Mountain. With over fifteen activity choices, Camp Skyline is "a summer-fun paradise for six- to sixteen-year-old campers who desire a real American camping experience." With four two-week sessions, campers may choose to stay more than one session. Campers are encouraged to select six activities, which they will participate in each day for the entire session. Teen campers live across the river in "Riverside," a pre-Depression-era hotel. Younger campers live in a group of cabins called "Hut Row," which has a big campfire circle in the center. Camp Skyline feels that "camping is truly an investment in living a lifetime of memories."

Parent Comment: "The area which I have been most impressed with has been the extremely qualified staff at Skyline. They encourage the campers to be independent and try new experiences. They help the campers interact with each other in a family-type environment."

SEACAMP ASSOCIATION, INC.
Big Pine Key, Florida

Coed

Ages: 12–17

Campers: 135

Religious affiliation: None

Fees: $1,695, 18 days

Extra fees: Transportation to and from camp, scuba program, canteen

Founded: 1966

Program: A combination of structured and elective activities that focus on marine science and scuba diving

Facilities/Activities: *Athletics* volleyball court; *Waterfront* oceanfront camp, marine science, swimming, scuba diving, sailing (Hobie Holders, Hobie Cats, Pelicans, Sidewinders), sailboarding; *Camping* campfire sites; *Creative Arts* outdoor theater, arts and crafts; *Miscellaneous* lab complex with dry and wet labs, library, running saltwater system for aquariums, trips to Looe Key National Marine Sanctuary

Boarding: 20 cabins (electricity), indoor showers and showerhouses, dorms; dining room (family style), salad bar; no laundry available

Counselors: 1 to every 5–10 campers, 20 counselors total, 25 instructors; average age, 21; 10% are foreign

Camp Rules: Telephone messages taken, campers return calls on 2 pay phones; no letter-writing policy; food discouraged in sleeping accommodations

Medical: Registered nurse in camp, all counselors certified in first aid, CPR, and National Association of Underwater Instructors diver rescue, 4-bed infirmary, parents notified if child taken to doctor; 20 miles from Fishermen's Hospital

Director: Grace Upshaw
Summer: Route 3, Box 170, Big Pine Key, FL 33043
 305-872-2331, 305-872-2205
Winter: Same

Grace Upshaw, who has a degree in education, attended Seacamp as a camper and then worked as a counselor, unit leader, and assistant director. She has been director since 1977. She is an active member of the ACA.

Philosophy: At Seacamp, campers learn marine science, use of scuba gear, and underwater exploration. Seacamp offers children the opportunity to explore blue water and coral canyons teeming with invertebrates, fish, and mammals. Seacamp's location on Newfound Harbor also makes it "an ideal place to learn and enjoy sailing and board sailing. It's an excellent way for future marine scientists to become familiar with the winds, tides, and currents that are of primary concern in oceanography. Seacamp shows the way to a sense of wonder within you that will last a lifetime."

Parent Comment: "Seacamp is probably the best thing that has happened to both my son and daughter. It has been a wonderful experience for them. Seacamp has had a very direct effect on my daughter's education and direction."

BLUE STAR CAMPS
Hendersonville, North Carolina ——————————————

Coed

Ages: 6–17

Campers: 730

Religious affiliation: Jewish

Fees: $400, 1 week pre-camp skill session / $1,800, 4 weeks / $3,250, 8 weeks

Extra fees: Elementary-school tutoring, Hebrew tutoring, horseback riding, private tennis lessons, golf, canteen

Founded: 1948

Program: A noncompetitive program with 6 independent subprograms organized by grade and gender; each subcamp is structured as an entity with its own camp leader and schedule

Facilities/Activities: *Athletics*   2 baseball fields, 2 soccer fields, 12 hard-surface tennis courts (7 lit), 3 basketball courts (lit), riflery range, archery range, weight room, indoor gym (basketball), 3 volleyball courts; *Waterfront*   swimming pool, 2 lakes, swimming, fishing, paddleboats, canoes, Playaks, kayaks, river trips by canoe and kayaks, water slide; *Camping*   campfire and sleep-out sites, nature area; *Creative Arts*   outdoor and indoor theaters, drama instruction, play production, set building, special evening program, arts and crafts, pottery studio, dance areas, video and photography studios; *Miscellaneous*   horseback riding, stable, barn, ropes course, petting zoo, library, recreation building

Boarding: 100 cabins (electricity), indoor showers (75 cabins), 5 showerhouses; 3 dining rooms (family style: grades 1–3; cafeteria style: grade 4 and up), special diets accommodated, kosher, salad bar; laundry done weekly by commercial service

Counselors: 1 to every 4 campers, 140 counselors total; average age, 20; 20% are foreign

Camp Rules: Parents may call staff, routine telephone use between parents and campers discouraged; campers required to write parents weekly; 1 care package per month permitted but must include enough for entire cabin, food not stored in cabins

Medical: Physician, 7 registered nurses, and health center administrator in camp, 45-bed infirmary, parents notified if child spends night in infirmary or in case of medical emergency; 7 miles from Margaret Pardee Hospital

Directors: Rodger and Candy Popkin
Summer: P.O. Box 1029, Kanuga Road, Hendersonville, NC 28793
  704-692-3591
Winter: 3595 Sheridan Street, Suite 107, Hollywood, FL 33021
  305-963-4494, 305-624-2267

Rodger Popkin is a second-generation camp owner and director. He and his wife, Candy, have run Blue Star Camps for twenty years. They are active in the ACA and Rodger is a trustee for the Fund for the Advancement of Camping.

Philosophy: Blue Star aims to combine the atmosphere of a traditional camp with the attributes and programming of a specialty one. Through a combination of free-choice and mandatory activities, the activity structure is tailored to the needs and aspirations of each age group. The daily program of athletic camp leagues and evening programs is enhanced by the tradition of "theme days." Each week campers go on out-of-camp trips. "We offer an environment where children are challenged and supported, and, as a result, succeed."

Parent Comment: "This will be my daughter's second year at Blue Star, and I think Rodger is extremely nurturing and good with children. It makes a big difference. There are also a lot of special activities and the other kids seem friendly."

GWYNN VALLEY CAMP
Brevard, North Carolina ————————————————————

Coed

Ages: 5–12

Campers: 200

Religious affiliation: None

Fees: $750, 2 weeks / $1,075, 3 weeks

Extra fees: Transportation to and from camp

Founded: 1935

Program: A noncompetitive program for younger children. Educational focus is on expanding horizons through an international and multicultural population

Facilities/Activities: *Athletics* soccer field, basketball court, gymnastics area, archery range; *Waterfront* swimming pool, lake, canoeing, French Broad River, Playaks, rafting, tubing; *Camping* campfire and sleep-out sites, nature trails; *Creative Arts* indoor stage, dramatics, costume room, pottery shop, general crafts, operational gristmill, weaving room, 2 pianos; *Miscellaneous* stable (12 horses), lodge, barn, minor farm buildings, fireplaces in several buildings, ropes course, recreation room

Boarding: 26 cabins (electricity), indoor bathrooms (ages 5–9), 4 showerhouses for older campers; dining room (family style), special diets accommodated; laundry done twice a week by camp

Counselors: 1 to every 3 campers, 70 counselors total; average age, 30; 15% are foreign

Camp Rules: Parents may call director or counselors, routine telephone use by campers discouraged; counselors write parents weekly and campers encouraged to write; no food in cabins

Medical: Physician and 2 registered nurses in camp, assistant director is an EMT, 11-bed infirmary, parents notified if child spends night in infirmary or in case of medical emergency; 6 miles from Transylvania County Hospital

Director: Howard Boyd
Summer: Route 4, Box 292, Brevard, NC 28712
        704-885-2900
Winter: Same

Howard and Betty Boyd have owned and directed Gwynn Valley Camp since 1967. Howard has an M.Sc. and a Ph.D. in botany from Ohio State. He was a naval aviator for six years and is a past president of the southeastern section of the ACA. Betty has an elementary-education certificate from Kent State University. The Boyds have three children.

Philosophy: Gwynn Valley Camp has been in continuous operation with the same family since 1935. At Gwynn Valley, competition is minimized and activities are varied to give every child a chance to succeed. A working farm and an operating gristmill offer opportunities for children to feel needed and involved in the lives of their companions. "An international staff is carefully selected for professionalism and a genuine caring attitude toward children." The crafts program is creative, utilizing no kits or molds but preferring free-form and native materials. Individual sports and fine arts are emphasized.

Parent Comment: "My daughter's first stay at Gwynn Valley this year was indeed a wonderful experience. Because I am a single parent and must work in the summer, I was concerned about her. Her camp experience was full of stimulating, artistic, and life-enriching activities. I have nothing but praise for the counselors and camp. Thank you for letting her share your lives at what sounds like a little piece of paradise."

CAMP ROCKMONT
Black Mountain, North Carolina

Single sex, male

Ages: 7–16

Campers: 386

Religious affiliation: None (Christian orientation)

Fees: $795, 2 weeks / $1,395, 4 weeks

Extra fees: Skiing, rafting, riding, trapshooting, trips

Founded: 1956

Program: A structured and elective, noncompetitive and competitive program for building Christian values

Facilities/Activities: *Athletics*   2 baseball fields, 3 soccer fields, 5 hard-surface tennis courts, 2 basketball courts, track, riflery range, archery range, volleyball courts, indoor gym, golf driving range; *Waterfront* lake, swimming, sailing, canoeing, waterskiing, zip line, Blob; *Camping* campfire and sleep-out sites, nature area; *Creative Arts*   stage, audio-visual equipment, arts and crafts, model rocketry; *Miscellaneous*   24 computers (Apple IIe), ropes course (50-ft. rappel tower), 3 radio-controlled tracks for model cars and trains, recreation room, BMX bike track

Boarding: 39 cabins (electricity), showers in cabins; dining room (family style), special diets accommodated; laundry done weekly by camp

Counselors: 1 to every 3.5 campers, 110 counselors total; average age, 20; 3% are foreign

Camp Rules: Recommended that there be no phone contact between camper and parent; at least 1 letter written a week; no food in cabins

Medical: 4 registered nurses in camp, some EMTs in camp, 20-bed infirmary, written notice to parents of any overnight stay in infirmary or visit to doctor's office, telephone call made if child has to go to hospital; 3 miles from a medical facility, 15 miles from Memorial Mission Hospital

Director: R. David Bruce
Summer: Lake Eden Road, Black Mountain, NC 28711
704-686-3885
Winter: Same

R. David Bruce has a B.A. from Emory University and eighteen years of camp staff experience. He has been director of Camp Rockmont for four years and is a member of the ACA.

Philosophy: Camp Rockmont is a privately owned Christian camp for boys. They believe that camp can be a parent's best tool for developing Christian values, moral character, and high self-esteem. They also believe summer camp plays a large role in a child's development through competitive and noncompetitive activities. Campers from all around the world benefit from these activities because the staff of Christian young men and women "are fully committed" to the ideals and "high destiny of their service."

Parent Comment: "Wanted to drop a note to you folks for giving my son a wonderful camp experience. He bubbled with enthusiasm, excitement, and laughter as he told us about his two weeks at Rockmont. I have noticed a self-reliance, contentment, and air of confidence in him that I have not seen before. My husband and I are both most grateful to you and your outstanding staff for all that was done to make his first time at camp such a success. We will see you next year."

CAMP HORIZONS
Harrisonburg, Virginia ————————————————————

Coed

Ages: 7–16

Campers: 120

Religious affiliation: None

Fees: $595–$685, 2 weeks

Extra fees: Horseback riding

Founded: 1982

Program: A structured and elective, noncompetitive program; emphasis on an international program

Facilities/Activities: *Athletics* large all-purpose field, basketball court, volleyball court; *Waterfront* swimming pool, lake, canoeing, swimming, zip line; *Camping* campfire and sleep-out sites, nature area; *Creative Arts* theater, arts and crafts; *Miscellaneous* horseback riding, trails, ring, high and low ropes course, recreation room

Boarding: 10 cabins (electricity), 8 tents, 2 showerhouses; dining room (family style), salad bar; laundry done weekly by camp

Counselors: 1 to every 5 campers, 25 counselors total; average age, 22; 50% are foreign

Camp Rules: Only in case of emergency can camper call home or receive call; letters written home once a week; no food in sleeping accommodations

Medical: Registered nurse in camp, 6-bed infirmary, parents notified if child must go to doctor; 16 miles from Rockingham Memorial Hospital

Director: William John Hall
Summer: Route 3, Box 374, Harrisonburg, VA 22801
703-896-7600
Winter: Same

John Hall is the founder, owner, and director of Camp Horizons. He has been a counselor, program director, and assistant resident manager at other camps. John is a graduate of Colorado Outward Bound and was an Eagle Scout. He is currently working toward a degree in camp directing at James Madison University. In addition to his camping experience, John traveled worldwide with "Up with People," an international singing group.

Philosophy: Camp Horizons is a group-oriented summer experience for children ages seven to sixteen. "Each individual camper receives all the attention he or she needs, becomes a contributing group member, and learns that the goal is not to reach the top of the mountain first but to help the *whole* group reach the top."

Camper Comment: "I have made friends here that I could have never made at home. These two weeks challenged me and I did things I never thought I could do. It was a terrific summer."

CAMP MONT SHENANDOAH

Millboro Springs, Virginia

Single sex, female

Ages: 7–16

Campers: 110

Religious affiliation: None

Fees: $1,050, 3 weeks / $1,725, 6 weeks

Extra fees: Horseback riding, canteen

Founded: 1927

Program: Structured and elective activities with competition

Facilities/Activities: *Athletics* baseball field, soccer field, 2 clay tennis courts, basketball court, archery range, volleyball court; *Waterfront* river, canoeing, swimming; *Camping* campfire and sleep-out sites, nature area; *Creative Arts* theater, junior and senior musicals, arts and crafts; *Miscellaneous* recreation room

Boarding: 12 cabins (electricity), 2 showerhouses; dining room (family style); laundry done by commercial service

Counselors: 1 to every 4.5 campers, 21 counselors total; average age, 22; 5% are foreign

Camp Rules: Telephone calls only on birthdays; weekly letter home required; no food in cabins

Medical: Registered nurse in camp, several counselors with first aid training, 8-bed infirmary, parent notified if camper is seriously hurt, injured, or ill; 20 miles from Allegheny Regional Hospital

Director: William T. Carrington
Summer: Route B, Box 19, Millboro Springs, VA 24460
      703-997-5994
Winter: P.O. Box 505, Orange, VA 22960
      703-672-2807

William T. Carrington has a B.A. in history from Hampton City College, Hampton City, Virginia, a master's degree in education from the University of Richmond, and a master's degree in history from Columbia University. He is a headmaster of a school and has been in education for over twenty years. He has been director and owner of Camp Mont Shenandoah since 1967.

Philosophy: Camp Mont Shenandoah is a small residential summer camp for girls. Founded in 1927, it enjoys a long history of traditions. Girls are placed in cabins by age, but have many opportunities to mix with campers of all ages. The camp consistently averages a 70% return of old campers; the Five-Year Club contains about 25% of the camp. Mont Shenandoah attracts counselors who are excellent role models, and many of the counselors are former campers.

A wide variety of activities allows girls to pursue many interests: horseback riding, swimming, canoeing, arts and crafts, land sports. The two teams, Buffs and Greens, engage in spirited but friendly competition.

The camp plans a six-week program, which attracts approximately 80% of the campers. The rest of the campers come for three-week periods, but do not get the full benefit of the Mont Shenandoah camping experience.

Parent Comment: "Camp Mont Shenandoah takes over where home leaves off, reinforcing the values and ideals that all parents seek for their children.

"Campers are encouraged to be themselves, respecting each other for their similarities as well as for their differences. Summers at CMS are filled with opportunities for leadership and personal growth. Positive self-esteem is developed and nurtured in an atmosphere that abounds with love and concern for every camper.

"My daughter's seven summers at Camp Mont Shenandoah will undoubtedly be remembered as seven of the best of her life. Words really don't do Camp Mont Shenandoah justice!"

CAMP GREEN BRIAR (Timber Ridge Camps, Inc.)
High View, West Virginia —————————————————————

Coed

Ages: 6–12

Campers: 250

Religious affiliation: None

Fees: $2,050, 4 weeks (2 sessions)

Extra fees: Spending fund

Founded: 1956

Program: Structured and elective

Facilities/Activities: *Athletics* 2 baseball fields, 2 soccer fields, 6 hard-surface tennis courts (lit), 2 basketball courts (lit), street hockey court, track, gymnastics with trampoline, riflery range, archery range, volleyball court, 18-hole golf course, lacrosse; *Waterfront* 2 swimming pools, lake, waterskiing, sailboarding, sailing, canoeing, kayaking, hydrosliding; *Camping* campfire and sleep-out sites, nature area; *Creative Arts* outdoor theater, plays, dance, arts and crafts (ceramics and wood shop), model rocketry; *Miscellaneous* 7 computers (IBM), ropes course, cycling, circus skills (flying trapeze, tight wire, juggling, Spanish Webb, clowning), petting farm, Indian lore, horseback riding (15 horses)

Boarding: 26 cabins (electricity), at least 2 showers in each cabin, 2 showerhouses; dining room (family style), kosher style, salad bar; laundry done weekly by camp

Counselors: 1 for every 3 campers, 85 counselors total; average age, 19; 3% are foreign

Camp Rules: No telephone calls unless camper calls when he or she is on trip out of camp, parents communicate through staff; letter writing 3 times a week; no food in cabins

Medical: Physician and 3 registered nurses in camp, medical driver (EMT) on duty 24 hours a day, 12-bed infirmary, parent notified by letter if child is in infirmary for 1 night and called if for 2 nights; 20 miles from Winchester Medical Center

Director: Frederick I. Greenberg
Summer: High View, WV 26808
304-856-2630
Winter: 10 Old Court Road, Baltimore, MD 21208
301-484-2233

Fred ("Uncle Fred") Greenberg is president and owner of Timber Ridge Camps, Inc. and Camp Green Briar. He is a speech pathologist practicing in Baltimore and has a lifelong interest in dealing with the needs of children in daily life. He is active on the boards of civic organizations.

Philosophy: Green Briar is a four-week camp for youngsters from kindergarten through the sixth grade. "We don't compete with an eight-week camp. Instead we concentrate on providing the best four-week program one will find. Our goal is to provide your child with an enjoyable experience while he or she discovers every aspect of camp life and learns to live and share as part of a total community away from home."

Parent Comment: "I want to thank you and everyone involved for making my son's summer such an enjoyable and unique experience. In reading his letters, I'm sure that these last four weeks will always be remembered as one of the busiest and happiest times of his life. This summer has boosted his level of confidence and his skills have been greatly developed."

CAMP GREENBRIER FOR BOYS
Alderson, West Virginia —————————————————

Single sex, male

Ages: 7–15

Campers: 150

Religious affiliation: None

Fees: $1,190, 3½ weeks / $2,190, 7 weeks

Extra fees: Academic tutoring, personal allowance

Founded: 1898

Program: Combination of structured and elective, mostly noncompetitive program; boys select their schedules for the mornings, and the afternoons are used for playing team games

Facilities/Activities: *Athletics* 3 baseball fields, soccer field, 7 hardsurface tennis courts, 2 basketball courts (lit), riflery range, archery range, volleyball court, 5-hole golf course, fitness and play area, indoor gym, wrestling mat, track; *Waterfront* river, Red Cross swimming lessons, snorkeling, fishing, 30 canoes, 8 kayaks, 70-ft. water slides, nationally rated white-water canoe run; *Camping* campfire and sleepout sites, woodcraft cabin, nature area; *Creative Arts* 2 grass amphitheaters, stage, crafts lodge, power tools, pottery wheel; *Miscellaneous* recreation room (fireplace), Ping-Pong, library, rock climbing, rappelling

Boarding: 50 tents, 2 showerhouses, 8 cabins used by staff and guests (electricity), 1 shower/cabin; dining room (family style), special diets accommodated; laundry done weekly by camp

Counselors: 1 to every 3 campers, 50 counselors total; average age, 21; 15% are foreign

Camp Rules: No telephone calls made by camper; letters written once a week and campers encouraged to write more; no food allowed in tents

Medical: Part-time physician available, 2 registered nurses in camp, 10-bed infirmary, parents notified of illness or injury by telephone or letter except in minor cases (upset stomach, sore muscles, etc.); 12 miles from Humana Hospital

Director: Robert W. Hood
Summer: Route 2, Box 5A, Alderson, WV 24910
        304-445-7168
Winter: Box 585, Exmore, VA 23350
        804-442-7972

Robert W. Hood has been in camping since 1962 when he first became a counselor. He has been head of woodcrafts, crafts, and waterfront at another camp. In 1973 he became camp director at Greenbrier. In the winter, he is the technology coordinator for Northhampton County schools. He has taught math and computing from kindergarten to college and has also been a guidance counselor. Robert holds a B.S., M.S., and a post-professional teaching certificate.

Philosophy: Although there are 150 campers, Greenbrier strives to achieve a "family feeling." Greenbrier's aim is to strengthen a boy's self-confidence and self-esteem by teaching him new skills in a non-pressured environment. "Our continuous operation for nearly a century attests to our ability to change with the times without abandoning our traditional values." Athletically talented campers will find appropriate instruction and team competition, as will those who are not competitive. Boys select their own program of activities which are taught by counselors who are chosen primarily because they are "nice people and good role models as well as skilled instructors. We are known for our superior staff, beautiful facilities, and delicious food. But above all, we are best known for our campers, who are great kids."

Parent Comment: "A traditional girls or boys camp that offers a variety of activities and an atmosphere that leads to carefree, good memories is rare. However, such camps do exist; Greenbrier is one."

CAMP RIM ROCK
Yellow Spring, West Virginia —————————————————

Single sex, female

Ages: 7–17

Campers: 147

Religious affiliation: None

Fees: $800, 2 weeks / $1,090, 3 weeks / $1,500, 4 weeks / $1,800, 5 weeks / $2,160, 6 weeks / $2,800, 8 weeks

Extra fees: Canteen

Founded: 1952

Program: A structured, noncompetitive camp with extensive horseback riding activities

Facilities/Activities: *Athletics*　softball field, 2 volleyball courts, archery range, soccer field, 2 hard-surface tennis courts; *Waterfront*　swimming pool, frontage on Cacapon River for canoeing; *Camping*　campfire and sleep-out sites; *Creative Arts*　drama and dance pavilion, arts and crafts; *Miscellaneous*　English horseback riding (41 horses), 5 rings, cross-country riding course, trails, pavilion

Boarding: 29 cabins (electricity), indoor showers; dining room (family style), vegetarian option, salad bar; laundry done weekly by commercial service

Counselors: 1 to every 4 campers, 38 counselors total; average age, 23; 25% are foreign

Camp Rules: Campers may make and receive family calls; letters required twice a week; food from home kept in metal container in counselor's cabin

Medical: Doctors nearby, 2 nurses in camp, 5-bed infirmary, parents telephoned in event of medical emergency; 26 miles from Winchester Medical Center

Director: James L. Matheson
Summer: Box 69, Yellow Spring, WV 26865
   800-662-4650
Winter: Box 88, Winchester, VA 22601
   800-662-4650

James L. Matheson is a clergyman in the United Methodist Church with B.A. and M.A. degrees from Duke University. Matheson has run his own nonsectarian camp for twenty-five years. He has been pastor of three churches in the Washington, D.C., area.

Philosophy: Camp Rim Rock emphasizes each camper's individuality and her specific readiness for the various levels of camp life. Activities are organized, physically challenging, and oriented toward personal development in a friendly cohesive environment. "This provides a framework within which each child can more readily build self-confidence." Safety and nutritious meals are also key components at Rim Rock.

Parent Comment: "The staff, program, and natural setting, as well as the careful attention given to each camper, surpass any publicity we have seen about Camp Rim Rock. Its unique excellence should be seen to be appreciated."

CAMP TEEN TOWN (Timber Ridge Camps, Inc.)
High View, West Virginia

Coed

Ages: 13–16

Campers: 150

Religious affiliation: None

Fees: $2,050, 4 weeks (2 sessions)

Extra fees: Spending money

Founded: 1966

Program: Combination of structured and elective activities

Facilities/Activities: *Athletics* baseball field, soccer field, 4 hard-surface tennis courts (lit), 2 basketball courts (lit), street hockey court, track, lacrosse, indoor gym (gymnastics, trampoline), riflery range, archery range, volleyball court, 18-hole golf course; *Waterfront* swimming pool, lake, waterskiing, kayaking, canoeing, sailing, hydrosliding, sailboarding; *Camping* campfire and sleep-out sites, nature trails; *Creative Arts* outdoor theater, theater arts, dance, musical performances, arts and crafts (ceramics), model rocketry, radio room; *Miscellaneous* 7 computers (IBM PC), horseback riding, cycling, ropes course, circus arts (trapeze rig, Spanish Webb, others), petting farm, recreation room, Indian lore

Boarding: 2 dorms (electricity) with showers, 40 tents (electricity), 4 showerhouses; dining room (cafeteria style), kosher style, salad bar; laundry done weekly by camp

Counselors: 1 to every 3 campers, 50 counselors total; average age, 20; 3% are foreign

Camp Rules: No direct calls unless camper is out of camp on trip, parents can communicate through camp staff; letter writing 3 times a week; no food in sleeping accommodations

Medical: Physician and 2 registered nurses in camp, medical driver (EMT) on duty 24 hours a day, 7-bed infirmary, parents notified by letter if child stays in infirmary 1 night and by phone if 2 nights; 20 miles from Winchester Medical Center

Director: Jerry Smith
Summer: High View, WV 26808
     304-856-2630
Winter: 10 Old Court Road, Baltimore, MD 21208
     301-484-2233

Jerry Smith is co-owner and director of Camp Teen Town. Jerry is a former teacher, coach, and athletic director. He is a graduate of the University of Maryland. He and his wife, May, have three children, all former campers, who still lend a hand during the summer. Jerry has been with Camp Teen Town since 1960.

Philosophy: Camp Teen Town is a traditional camp with two four-week sessions. Low-key competition is encouraged. Children are recognized as individuals, the program reflecting that boys and girls of the same age have different interests and desires. "There is a spirit that is achieved only in a community of teenagers living, working, and playing together. Songs and cheers fill the air as our Teen Town campers compete in all activities throughout the camp."

Parent Comment: "Many thanks to you and the staff, especially our son's counselors, who took the time to communicate with me as well as with him. Please thank them for encouraging my son in a positive way, being sensitive to his needs, recognizing his concerns and even his fears, responding to his likes and dislikes, and for maximizing his strengths while minimizing his weaknesses. I also commend you on your high standards of excellence in selecting these fine counselors (often emulated by our youngsters)."

CAMP WHITE MOUNTAIN (Timber Ridge Camps, Inc.) *High View, West Virginia* ─────

Coed

Ages: 6–16

Campers: 325

Religious affiliation: None

Fees: $3,636, 8 weeks

Extra fees: Spending money

Founded: 1955

Program: Combination of structured and elective activities

Facilities/Activities: *Athletics* 3 baseball fields, 2 soccer fields, 9 hard-surface tennis courts (lit), 2 basketball courts (lit), street hockey court, track, indoor gym (gymnastics, trampoline), riflery range, archery range, volleyball courts, 18-hole golf course, lacrosse; *Waterfront* swimming pool, lake, waterskiing, sailboarding, sailing, hydro-sliding, kayaking, canoeing; *Camping* campfire and sleep-out sites, nature area; *Creative Arts* outdoor theater, dance, musicals, arts and crafts (ceramics, wood shop), model rocketry, radio room; *Miscellaneous* 7 computers (IBM PC), horseback riding (15 horses), ropes course, cycling, petting farm, recreation room, Indian lore, circus arts (trapeze rig, Spanish Webb, others)

Boarding: 34 cabins (electricity), at least 2 showers/cabin, 2 showerhouses; dining room (family style), kosher style, salad bar; laundry done weekly by camp

Counselors: 1 to every 3 campers, 110 counselors total; average age, 20; 3% are foreign

Camp Rules: No direct telephone calls unless camper is out of camp on trip, parents communicate through staff; letter writing 3 times a week; no food in cabins

Medical: Physician and 3 registered nurses in camp, medical driver (EMT) on duty 24 hours a day, 12-bed infirmary, parents notified by letter if camper stays 1 night in infirmary and by phone if camper stays 2 nights; 20 miles from Winchester Medical Center

Director: Frederick I. Greenberg
Summer: High View, WV 26808
     304-856-2630
Winter: 10 Old Court Road, Baltimore, MD 21208
     301-484-2233

Fred ("Uncle Fred") Greenberg is president and owner of Timber Ridge Camps, Inc. and Camp White Mountain. Uncle Fred is a speech pathologist practicing in Baltimore, and he has a lifelong interest in dealing with the needs of children in daily life. He is active on the boards of civic organizations.

Philosophy: Camp White Mountain is located in the Shenandoah Valley, next to the Capon River. White Mountain considers itself one of the last strongholds of traditional camping, set in an atmosphere of low-keyed competition. Children are recognized as individuals. "Owned by one family for the past thirty years, Timber Ridge and White Mountain have provided, and will continue to provide, excellent summer opportunities for children of all ages."

Parent Comment: "I am pleased to tell you that I intend to recommend Camp White Mountain to parents who are interested in providing an enriching and rewarding (first) 'summer away from home' for their children. I do hope that my son will be among the many who will return to Camp White Mountain in the future. Again, thanks for everything."

MIDWEST

CULVER SUMMER CAMPS
Culver, Indiana —————————————————————

Coed

Ages: 9–17

Campers: 1,400

Religious affiliation: None

Fees: $800, 2 weeks / $2,450, 6 weeks

Extra fees: Transportation to and from camp, uniform

Founded: 1901

Program: A structured, competitive program with camper choice of activities

Facilities/Athletics: *Athletics* 10 baseball fields, 6 soccer fields, 17 tennis courts (15 hard surface, 2 indoor), 3 basketball courts, 6 indoor basketball courts, gymnastics area, riflery range, archery range, golf, volleyball courts, ice arena, track, indoor racquetball and handball, weight room, fencing, wrestling; *Waterfront* indoor swimming pool and diving tank, lake, sailing, canoeing, waterskiing, scuba diving, fishing; *Camping* campfire and sleep-out sites, nature center and museum; *Creative Arts* indoor and outdoor theaters, stagecraft, dance, acting, vocal instruction, bands, private music instruction, choirs, arts and crafts, model rocketry; *Miscellaneous* over 100 computers (all types), recreation room, aviation program (own airport and aircraft), indoor and outdoor horseback riding, libraries and classrooms

Boarding: 60 cabins (electricity), showerhouses; 2 dining rooms (cafeteria style), salad bar; laundry done weekly by camp

Counselors: 1 to every 5 campers, 250 counselors total; average age, 35; 5% are foreign

Camp Rules: Telephone calls permitted by campers in emergencies; weekly letter writing required; no food in cabins

Medical: 2 physicians and 12 registered nurses in camp, many staff members certified in first aid and CPR, 60-bed infirmary, parents notified by phone if child spends night in infirmary; 10 miles from Holy Cross Parkview Hospital

Director: Frederick D. Lane
Summer: Box 138 CEF, Culver, IN 46511
                800-221-2020 (outside Indiana), 219-842-8207 (in Indiana)
Winter: Same

Frederick Lane has more than twenty-five years of experience in various programs at Culver. He is a licensed guidance counselor and principal in Indiana. He is also a member of the board of directors of the ACA.

Philosophy: Culver Summer Camps has as its primary aim the development of each camper's leadership potential. Culver believes that by encouraging its campers to become leaders, they will evolve into more confident, determined, and responsible citizens. Culver believes that this aim can best be accomplished by encouraging each of its campers to assume various leadership positions in any of the camp's wide variety of activities.

Parent Comment: "The one thing that stands out from Culver Summer is its leadership philosophy. My son went to Culver Summer Camps one summer as a shy, quiet boy. He came back after six weeks more talkative and responsive to other people. He is confident and more aware of the possibilities before him."

CRYSTALAIRE CAMP

Frankfort, Michigan ———————————————————

Coed

Ages: 8–17

Campers: 88

Religious affiliation: None

Fees: $500, 2 weeks / $740, 3 weeks

Extra fees: Horseback riding, canteen

Founded: 1921

Program: An elective, noncompetitive program stressing camper responsibility

Facilities/Activities: *Athletics* large multipurpose playing field, 2 hard-surface tennis courts, basketball court, touch football, cricket, volleyball court; *Waterfront* Crystal Lake, swimming, sailing, sailboarding, kayaking, canoeing, water polo, water ballet; *Camping* campfire and sleep-out sites, nature area; *Creative Arts* theater, dramatics, pottery, jewelrymaking, leather tooling, drawing, newspaper, sewing, baking, silk screening; *Miscellaneous* gazebo, horseback riding, bicycling and bicycle repair, animal care, backpacking

Boarding: 12 cabins (no electricity), 1 tent showerhouse; dining room (family style), special diets accommodated; laundry done once per session by campers

Counselors: 1 to every 7 campers, 13 counselors total; average age, 21; 15% are foreign

Camp Rules: Outgoing calls not permitted, parents may call staff; letter required once a week; no food in sleeping accommodations

Medical: Registered nurse in camp, 5-bed infirmary, parents notified by phone if child spends night in infirmary or requires outside medical attention; 3 miles from Paul Oliver Hospital

Director: David Reid
Summer: 1327 South Shore Road, Frankfort, MI 49635
616-352-7589
Winter: Same

David Reid has over twenty-five years of camp experience and has owned and directed Crystalaire since 1980. Before buying Crystalaire he was a teacher in Washington, D.C., for fifteen years. David is past president of the Michigan section of the ACA. Katherine Houston, David's wife, is active in camp operations. She is a special education teacher and job study coordinator for a local school district.

Philosophy: Crystalaire stresses its noncompetitive, loosely structured program. Campers and staff plan daily activities together and share responsibility for establishing many camp policies and rules. Campers choose their activities and share in camp chores such as meal preparation and dishwashing. At Crystalaire, games and activities are for camper satisfaction, not for winning awards. "We offer activities that require an active involvement as opposed to a passive involvement."

Camper Comment: "One of the reasons I like Crystalaire Camp so much is that there isn't a social caste system. People do end up in bunches but that isn't the same as cliques because bunches are based on you and what you do. Not 'who you are'—i.e., homecoming queen or varsity football player or pretty or your family makes more than $60,000. Also at Crystalaire people aren't as likely to prejudge, or, if they do, they learn to change pretty fast."

INTERLOCHEN NATIONAL MUSIC CAMP

Interlochen, Michigan ———————————————

Coed

Ages: 8–17

Campers: 1,400

Religious affiliation: None

Fees: $2,780, 8 weeks

Extra fees: Transportation to and from camp, private lessons

Founded: 1928

Program: For serious music and art students as well as those just trying art areas; competitive and structured or noncompetitive and elective

Facilities/Activities: *Athletics* soccer field, hard-surface tennis courts, basketball court, gymnastics area, archery range, volleyball courts, badminton, indoor gym (Nautilus); *Waterfront* 2 lakes, swimming, advanced lifesaving, canoeing, sailing, rowing; *Camping* campfire and sleep-out sites, nature area; *Creative Arts* junior string orchestra, intermediate orchestra, concert orchestra, world youth symphony, junior wind and percussion ensemble, intermediate band, high-school symphonic band, high-school concert band, junior chorus, intermediate chorus, intermediate festival chorus, intermediate operetta workshop, high-school choir, girls chorus, high-school operetta workshop, chamber music, classical guitar, composer's forum, Shakespeare's music, high-school jazz band, jazz ensemble, stage band, instrumental lessons (wind, harp, percussion, organ, piano), dance (improvisational, jazz, ballet, modern), theater arts (musical productions, Shakespeare productions), radio room, arts and crafts, ceramics, painting, metalsmithing, sculpture, printmaking, photography, video production; *Miscellaneous* computers, recreation room, Ping-Pong, galleries

Boarding: 420 cabins (electricity), indoor showers; dining room (cafeteria style), salad bar; laundry done weekly by camp (younger campers) or by campers (older campers) at coin-operated machines

Counselors: 1 to every 2 campers, 140 counselors and instructors total (special instructors who spend shorter amounts of time at the camp are an important part of the staff); average age, 20; no foreign counselors

Camp Rules: Pay phones available; letter writing encouraged; no food in cabins

Medical: 2 physicians and several registered nurses in residence, 27 beds in 3 infirmaries, parent notified if child stays in infirmary overnight; 16 miles from Munson Medical Center

Director: Edward J. Downing
Summer: P.O. Box 199, Interlochen, MI 49643
      616-276-9221
Winter: Same

Edward J. Downing has been director of the National Music Camp at Interlochen since 1979. His association with Interlochen began in 1972, when he became administrator for the University of Michigan state programs, a position he held for three years. In addition to being director of the National Music Camp, Downing is artistic director of the Interlochen Arts Festival, which runs concurrent with the National Music Camp. He has been a band conductor in several Michigan schools and has toured the U.S. and Europe as a conductor of youth groups. Downing has a B.A. and an M.A. in music from the University of Michigan.

Philosophy: National Music Camp is recognized as the premier fine arts camp in the country. The faculty come from professional arts organizations or teach at prestigious colleges, universities, and public schools around the country. "Interlochen is committed to developing the leaders of tomorrow as well as artists and those who appreciate the arts." The approach is thus a holistic one. Everyone—campers, faculty, and staff—wears blue corduroy trousers and light blue shirts during the 8-week session. "Self-discovery through self-discipline and challenge is an exciting adventure for young people."

Camper Comment: "I spent two summers at the National Music Camp. I wasn't by a long stretch one of the many great musicians and artists that attended camp. I didn't have a very successful year as far as obvious progress. But I learned how to accept the challenges before me and I learned how to accept the values and ideas that other people very unlike me had. I learned responsibility for my own self as well as for others."

CAMP MAPLEHURST
Kewadin, Michigan ──────────────────

Coed

Ages: 7–17

Campers: 200

Religious affiliation: None

Fees: $900, 2 weeks / $1,600, 4 weeks / $2,950, 8 weeks

Extra fees: Transportation to and from camp, horseback riding, canteen

Founded: 1955

Program: An elective, noncompetitive program with optional participation in organized team competition

Facilities/Activities: *Athletics*   2 baseball fields, soccer field, 3 hard-surface tennis courts (2 lit), basketball court, track, gymnastics area (rings, parallel and uneven bars, balance beams, mats), riflery range, archery range, 2 volleyball courts, fencing, tetherball courts, golf driving range and 5-hole course; *Waterfront*   2 lakes, swimming, waterskiing, scuba diving, snorkeling, fishing, sailing (Lazers), water games, pontoon boats, 8 rowboats, 8 canoes, 14 Funyaks, Flying Scot, paddleboats, 4 sailboards; *Camping*   campfire and sleep-out sites, nature area; *Creative Arts*   auditorium, musicals, arts and crafts (ceramics, painting, drawing, textiles, woodworking, model rocketry), photography lab (black and white), dance room (ballet, modern, jazz, aerobic); *Miscellaneous*   9 computers (Apple IIe, Apple IIe+, Franklin, Macintosh, IBM), English and Western horseback riding, stable, 20 miles of trails, telescope, microscopes, aquariums, library, recreation room (Ping-Pong, table soccer, bumper pool)

Boarding: 19 cabins (electricity), at least 1 indoor shower/cabin; dining room (cafeteria style), kosher style and vegetarian meals available, salad bar; laundry done weekly by camp

Counselors: 1 to every 4 campers, 36 counselors total; average age, 20; 10%–15% are foreign

Camp Rules: Parents can call director to arrange camper call; letter home required once or twice a week; food discouraged in cabins

Medical: Physician and health director in camp, 8-bed infirmary, parents notified by physician if child requires medical treatment; 20 miles from Munson Medical Center

Director: Laurence Cohn
Summer: Box 315, Winters Road, Kewadin, MI 49648
        616-264-9675
Winter: 1455 Quarton Road, Birmingham, MI 48009
        313-647-2646

Laurence Cohn, who has a B.A. in biophysics and a Ph.D. in psychology and education, taught educational psychology at the University of Michigan. He is currently teaching psychology at the University of Michigan, Dearborn. He has been associated with Camp Maplehurst for thirty-four years, first as a camper and then as a staff member. A licensed pilot, Laurence is also a scuba diver and water safety instructor.

Philosophy: Maplehurst was founded as a summer camp that offered "an alternative to the autocratic, hierarchically organized school and social systems that campers experience during the regular school year." The camp encourages the participation of the campers in decisionmaking. At Maplehurst, the spirit of play is fundamental.

Parent Comment: "Our children attended Maplehurst Camp for many years, always returning happy, rested, and full of life, eager to impart their experiences to us. Apart from all the wonderful activities, what was always apparent was the loving, warm, family-type atmosphere that pervaded the whole camp. The various guest experts who participated throughout the summer sessions—computer whizzes to psychologists, authors, musicians, and sports experts—also impressed us."

PINE RIVER CAMP
Barbeau, Michigan ———————————————————————

Coed

Ages: 9–17

Campers: 50

Religious affiliation: None

Fees: $520, 2 weeks / $1,080, 4 weeks

Extra fees: Transportation to and from camp, spending money

Founded: 1966

Program: An elective, noncompetitive program with an emphasis on outdoor skills and multiple-day and week trips

Facilities/Activities: *Athletics* volleyball court, archery range, riflery range, tetherball court; *Waterfront* Munuscong Bay (camp is on an island), swimming, sailing, fishing, canoeing, Playaks; *Camping* campfire and sleep-out sites, nature areas, ecology, survival skills workshop; *Creative Arts* arts and crafts; *Miscellaneous* zip line, backpacking, bike trips, gardening, carnivals, saunas, canoe trips

Boarding: 7 cabins, shower; dining room (family style and cafeteria dining), occasional salad bar; laundry done as needed by campers and staff

Counselors: 1 to every 4 campers, 15 counselors total; average age, 21; 5% are foreign

Camp Rules: Telephone calls permitted after first week; letter writing encouraged; no food in cabins

Medical: EMT in residence, counselors trained in first aid and water safety, 2-bed infirmary, parents notified in medical emergencies; 20 miles from War Memorial Hospital

Director: Clifford P. Borbas
Summer: Neebish Island, Barbeau, MI 49710
    906-632-9076
Winter: 918 Lantern Hill Drive, East Lansing, MI 48823
    517-332-3991

Clifford Borbas founded Pine River Camp with his brother in 1966 and is now its owner and director. He has a Ph.D. in secondary education from Michigan State University and works from September to June as an emergency services mental health therapist for a community agency. He is also a registered social worker in the state of Michigan. Clifford has taught at the secondary and college levels and is on the board of directors of the Michigan section of the ACA. His wife, Barbara, an artist, assists in the running of Pine River.

Philosophy: Pine River Camp is a small, unstructured camp that emphasizes camper decisionmaking and activity choice. Multiple-day and week outings are offered and older campers may enroll in challenging backpacking and canoeing trips. Campers help determine trip itineraries, supervise their own free time, plan and pack for trips, help prepare meals, and do cleanup chores. Pine River feels "self-confidence and maturity come from meeting successfully the fun, safe challenges of an outdoor environment that is initially unfamiliar to most campers. The staff's job is to assist in this growth."

Parent Comment: "I want to thank you for the obviously marvelous time our son had at Pine River Camp. He's in the middle of writing a journal so he can remember it all in the years to come. I've always dreaded those first few weeks after he's come home from camp. He's always had 'reentry' problems but this year was so different. He's really mellow. Much more sure of himself but not in a cocky way—so much readier to accept responsibility and initiate things without being told to. Great!"

CAMP SEQUOIA
Adrian, Michigan

Coed

Ages: 6–15

Campers: 50

Religious affiliation: None

Fees: $260 per week (based on 2 or more weeks; camp season lasts 7 weeks)

Extra fees: Weekly horsemanship

Founded: 1955

Program: A noncompetitive program

Facilities/Activities: *Athletics* baseball field, soccer field, basketball court, volleyball court, tetherball court, riflery range; *Waterfront* swimming pool, lake, 2 rowboats, fishing; *Camping* campfire and sleep-out sites, nature area; *Creative Arts* arts and crafts; *Miscellaneous* 4 computers, English and Western horseback riding (corral), dart arena, obstacle course, conservation area

Boarding: 8 cabins (electricity), 10 indoor showers; dining room (cafeteria style); laundry done weekly by commercial service

Counselors: 1 to every 3 campers, 16 counselors total; average age, 21; no foreign counselors

Camp Rules: Campers not allowed to use phone except in case of emergency; minimum of 1 letter home per week; no food in cabins

Medical: Physician 5 miles away, 2-bed infirmary, parents notified if child becomes ill; 5 miles from Bixby Hospital

Director: Robert J. Welke
Summer: 2675 Gady Road, Adrian, MI 49221
517-263-2039
Winter: 620 Company Street, Adrian, MI 49221
517-263-2039

Bob Welke is the owner and director of Camp Sequoia and has over thirty years of camping experience and youth work. He has an M.A. in camping and counseling from the University of Michigan and has worked in the classroom and as a swimming coach. He has served on the Michigan Camping Association's board of directors.

Philosophy: Sequoia strives to meet the individual needs of each camper. It offers a noncompetitive experience where a camper may try many of the camp activities and then choose those that he or she really enjoys. "Our first and last concern is always the children and their well-being."

Parent Comment: "Our daughter loved the family atmosphere at Camp Sequoia. Everyone played together, ate together, brushed their teeth together, did their exercises together. And she loved the riding. The camp is horse crazy. They teach English and Western which is great for horse nuts."

CAMP WALDEN
Cheboygan, Michigan ————————————————————

Coed

Ages: 7–16

Campers: 275

Religious affiliation: None

Fees: $1,675, 4 weeks / $3,100, 8 weeks

Extra fees: Transportation to and from camp, insurance, bedding, laundry, riding, yearbook

Founded: 1959

Program: Elective, noncompetitive camping, canoeing, tripping, and backpacking programs

Facilities/Activities: *Athletics* 3 baseball fields, 3 soccer fields, 8 hard-surface tennis courts (6 lit), basketball court, smaller practice basketball court, street hockey court, track, gymnastics area (high and low balance beams, even and uneven parallel bars, side horse, vault, rings, mats), riflery range, archery range, volleyball courts, golf driving range, lacrosse field, fencing, floor hockey pavilion; *Waterfront* Long Lake, swimming, fishing, waterskiing, sailing (23-ft. sloop, 7 15-ft. sloops, 8 Sunfish), 12 kayaks, 30 canoes, 5 motorboats, 12 sailboards, 4 paddle wheelers, pontoon boat, 8 Playaks, 2 Force 5 racing boats; *Camping* campfire and sleep-out sites, nature area; *Creative Arts* indoor and outdoor theaters, musicals, drama, dance, ceramics (10 wheels), jewelry, lapidary, batik, painting, drawing, photography (darkroom), radio station; *Miscellaneous* 10 computers (Apple IIe), English and Western horseback riding (25 horses), 6 rings, barn, recreation building

Boarding: 33 cabins (electricity), 2 indoor showers/cabin, 1 large showerhouse; dining room (family style), salad bar; laundry done weekly by commercial service

Counselors: 1 to every 3 campers, 90 counselors total; most counselors, 18–22; 10% are foreign

Camp Rules: Telephones available for special occasions; 2 letter-writing days per week; parents requested not to send food, snacks provided as part of regular camp menu, no food in cabins

Medical: Physician and registered nurse in camp, 10-bed infirmary, parents notified if child requires overnight stay in infirmary or in case of emergency; 8 miles from Community Memorial Hospital

Directors: Lawrence Stevens, Neal Schechter
Summer: 5606 South River Road, Cheboygan, MI 49721
      616-625-2050
Winter: 31070 Applewood Lane, Farmington Hills, MI 48331
      313-661-1890

Directors Lawrence Stevens and Neal Schechter have B.A.s and M.A.s in education with extensive teaching experience. They have been active members of the ACA since founding Camp Walden in 1959. Each one has over thirty-five years of professional camping and child development experience.

Philosophy: Walden is a distinctive summer camp for youngsters. The camp is dedicated to furthering the mental and physical well-being of each young camper. The following five objectives guide the directors and staff at Walden: 1) to give each child ample opportunity to enjoy every kind of fun activity, 2) to encourage physical fitness, because physically fit children develop confidence and self-assurance at an accelerated pace, 3) to help each child develop socially by providing experiences in group living, 4) to provide children with an educational experience they will carry with them into adult life, 5) to allow each child the opportunity to decide which of the wide range of activities he or she wants to engage in. This freedom of choice is important in helping youngsters achieve greater self-reliance.

Parent Comment: "Another wonderful summer was had by all three of my daughters. They loved the freedom and responsibility that came with it. Their true love is Camp Walden. It can do no wrong in their eyes. Thanks for a great time from our girls."

CAMP CHIPPEWA FOR BOYS
Cass Lake, Minnesota ─────────────────────

Single sex, male

Ages: 7–17

Campers: 60

Religious affiliation: None

Fees: $1,450, 4 weeks / $2,800, 8 weeks

Extra fees: Canadian wilderness trip, Canadian fishing expedition, canteen

Founded: 1935

Program: A varied land and water program; structured for the first week, then elective. Campers' programs tailored to age and ability; extensive individual instruction

Facilities/Activities: *Athletics*　baseball field, soccer field, 3 hard-surface tennis courts, basketball court, riflery range, 2 archery ranges (target, field), volleyball court; *Waterfront*　2 lakes, swimming, waterskiing, 17 canoes, 5 fishing boats, 9 sailboats; *Camping*　campfire and sleep-out sites, nature area; *Creative Arts*　arts and crafts, arrowmaking; *Miscellaneous*　recreation room

Boarding: 9 cabins (electricity), 2 showerhouses; dining room (family style); laundry done weekly by commercial service

Counselors: 1 to every 3 campers, 20 counselors total; average age, 23; 5% are foreign

Camp Rules: Telephone calls permitted for special occasions; letter home required once a week; no food in cabins

Medical: Physician in camp, 4-bed infirmary, parents notified if child requires medical treatment beyond routine first aid; 24 miles from Northwest Hospital

Director: John P. Endres
Summer: RR 2, Cass Lake, MN 56633
       218-335-8807
Winter: 11427 North Pinehurst Circle, Mequon, WI 53092
       414-241-5791

The son of the founders of Chippewa, John P. Endres has a B.S. and an M.S. from the University of Wisconsin. A camper and then a counselor, he has been director since 1960. John has also been a teacher and administrator in the Fox Point, Wisconsin, school system for thirty-five years.

Philosophy: It is Camp Chippewa's goal to "provide each boy with the opportunity to grow physically and to develop an awareness of self-worth and discipline while living and working within the group." Chippewa maintains limited enrollment (sixty boys) and a "mature staff," and location of the camp in the Chippewa National Forest "ensures freedom from resorts and vacationers."

Parent Comment: "My son attended Chippewa for five years. I can think of no single influence greater than those years under the guidance and counseling of the Endres family in making him an adult. His love for the wilderness is very much a part of his daily life. His development of self-confidence can be traced back to his days at Cass Lake."

CAMP FOLEY
Pine River, Minnesota ————————————————————

Coed

Ages: 6–16

Campers: 140

Religious affiliation: None

Fees: $370 per week (1- to 3-week stays)

Extra fees: Transportation to and from camp, art supplies, ammunition for rifle range, canteen

Founded: 1925

Program: A structured, noncompetitive program with an emphasis on sailing

Facilities/Activities: *Athletics* baseball field, soccer field, 2 hard-surface tennis courts, basketball court, riflery range, trapshooting area, archery range, volleyball courts (regular, sand); *Waterfront* 4,000-acre lake (connects to 22-lake chain), swimming, sailing (C-scows, X-Boats, M-16s, E-scow, Tanzer 22, Sunfish, Vanguard 470), canoeing, water-skiing, sailboarding, rowing, fishing; *Camping* campfire and sleep-out sites, nature area; *Creative Arts* arts and crafts, textile crafts, model rocketry, robotics lab, woodworking shop; *Miscellaneous* all-terrain biking, recreation room, Ping-Pong, tepees

Boarding: 20 cabins (electricity), 3 showerhouses; dining room (family style), special diets accommodated, salad bar; laundry done weekly by commercial service

Counselors: 1 to every 5 campers, 30 counselors total; average age, 20–21; 10%–15% are foreign

Camp Rules: Campers may receive emergency telephone calls but are not permitted to phone home; minimum of 1–2 letters home required, depending on length of session; no food in cabins

Medical: Registered nurse in camp, 4-bed infirmary, parents notified in medical emergencies; 35 miles from St. Joseph's Medical Center

Director: Marie Schmid

Summer: County Road 77, Box 172, Pine River, MN 56474
218-543-6161

Winter: 160 Windsor Court, New Brighton, MN 55112
612-633-4881

Marie Schmid is a second-generation camp director and has grown up with Camp Foley. Before becoming director in 1985 she was a cabin counselor, waterfront director, program director, and swimming, canoeing, and waterskiing instructor. She has a B.A. in elementary education from the College of St. Catherine in St. Paul, Minnesota.

Philosophy: Camp Foley's purpose is to provide children with the opportunity to develop new friendships and skills in a natural, informal setting, free from the tensions and pressures of today's society. Foley prides itself on its specialized sailing program, which it claims is one of the finest inland sailing programs in the country.

Parent Comment: "When we brought our kids up the first day the staff and counselors were so nice and by talking to them you could tell they were there because they really loved kids and wanted them to have a great time. I could go on and on about Camp Foley but the most important feeling I got from Foley is that our kids were in good hands."

CAMP LAKE HUBERT FOR GIRLS/CAMP LINCOLN FOR BOYS Lake Hubert, Minnesota ———

Brother/sister

Ages: 8–17

Campers: 200

Religious affiliation: None (Christian orientation)

Fees: $850, 2 weeks / $1,635, 4 weeks / $3,210, 8 weeks

Extra fees: Transportation to and from camps, laundry, special trips, yearbook

Founded: 1927 (girls), 1909 (boys)

Program: An elective, noncompetitive program

Facilities/Activities: *Athletics*   3 baseball fields, 3 soccer fields, 10 hard-surface tennis courts, 2 basketball courts, 3 riflery ranges, 2 trapshooting ranges, 2 archery ranges, field target archery range, 6 volleyball courts, track, gymnastics area, karate, fencing, aerobics; *Waterfront*   spring-fed lake, swimming, 50 sailboats, 35 sailboards, 70 canoes, 10 Playaks, 8 Fun Bugs, 8 rowboats, 2 pontoons, houseboat; *Camping*   campfire and sleep-out sites, 2 nature areas; *Creative Arts*   outdoor theater, minor plays, mime, 5 different arts and crafts areas, model rocketry; *Miscellaneous*   high and low ropes courses, horseback riding (65 horses), 5 rings, 2 barns, extensive canoe trips, ecology center, recreation room

Boarding: 14 cabins (electricity), indoor showers; 6 dining rooms (family style), salad and fresh fruit bar; laundry done every 10 days by commercial service

Counselors: 1 to every 4 campers, 40 counselors total; average age, 22; 8% are foreign

Camp Rules: Phone use by campers discouraged except for emergencies; staff writes 3 times per month; no food in cabins

Medical: Physician and 2 registered nurses in camp, 20 beds in 2 infirmaries, parents notified if child spends night in infirmary or visits local hospital; 12 miles from St. Joseph's Medical Center

Directors: Sam Cote, Bill Jones
Summer: Lake Hubert, MN 56459
      218-963-2339, 218-963-2281
Winter: 5201 Eden Circle, Minneapolis, MN 55436
     612-922-2545

Co-director Sam Cote grew up at camp and follows his father's leadership in the camping industry. He is currently president of the Northland section of the ACA.

Bill Jones was a camper and counselor before becoming co-director of Camp Lincoln and Camp Lake Hubert. He is currently treasurer of the Northland section of the ACA and national board member of the ACA.

Philosophy: Camp Lincoln and Camp Lake Hubert have over 150 years of camping tradition between them. A special diversity of backgrounds exists, with campers coming from forty-one states and twelve foreign countries. Separated by a mile of water, these brother/sister camps offer a "special, safe, and richly rewarding place for today's camper."

Parent Comment: "Camp Lincoln and Camp Lake Hubert are special because of the bonding between the kids and staff. There is a sharing of ideas and an affection and sensitivity that are always present. Activities are enjoyable because everyone has so much energy. The best part of camp is the opportunity to be yourself and be accepted by others. That is what Lincoln and Lake Hubert are like."

CAMP MISHAWAKA
Grand Rapids, Minnesota ―――――――――――――――――

Brother/sister

Ages: 7–16

Campers: 80 boys, 80 girls

Religious affiliation: None

Fees: $775, 2 weeks / $1,495, 4 weeks / $2,840, 8 weeks

Extra fees: Chartered bus transportation to and from camp, laundry, trips, canteen

Founded: 1910 (boys), 1963 (girls)

Program: An elective, competitive program combining recreational activities with hands-on educational activities

Facilities/Activities: *Athletics* 2 baseball fields, soccer field, 4 hard-surface tennis courts, basketball court, street hockey court, track, badminton, archery range, gymnastics area, horseshoe pits, 2 volleyball courts, riflery range, 4 square courts; *Waterfront* Lake Pokegama, swimming, waterskiing (2 70-hp waterski boats, 1 35-hp boat), sailing (X-Boats, Dolphins, Sunfish), 2 fishing boats (motor), 7 rowboats, 4 sailboards, 40 canoes, houseboat, pontoon boat; *Camping* campfire and sleep-out sites, nature cabin and trail; *Creative Arts* theater, 2 operettas (girls), Saturday night shows (boys), arts and crafts, radio room, model rocketry, newspaper, ham radio; *Miscellaneous* horseback riding, stables, jump course, rings, library, 2 recreation rooms (pool, table games), astronomy room, Ping-Pong, ropes course

Boarding: 36 cabins (some with electricity), 2 tents, indoor showers and 1 showerhouse; dining room (family style), emphasis on low-sugar, low-fat meals, salad bar; laundry done weekly by commercial service

Counselors: 1 to every 5 campers, 18 boys counselors, 14 girls counselors; average age, 32 (boys), 25 (girls); 12% are foreign

Camp Rules: Phone use discouraged except for emergencies; 2 letters home required per week; care packages discouraged, some food allowed in sleeping accommodations

Medical: Registered nurse, backup LPN, and EMT in camp, 6-bed infirmary, parents notified by phone and letter in medical emergencies; 4 miles from Itasca Medical Center

Directors: Jon Erickson (boys), Holly Wilson (girls)
Summer: P.O. Box 368, Grand Rapids, MN 55744
          218-326-5011
Winter: Same

Jon Erickson started out as a camper at Mishawaka, then became a trip outfitter, campcraft leader, and cabin counselor. A 1976 graduate of the University of Montana, Jon has been co-director since 1984.

Holly Wilson and her husband, Dan, have served on the Mishawaka staff since 1980. She has been head of arts and crafts, head counselor, and program director. Holly earned a degree in education and sociology from Cornell College and has taught second grade and junior high for ten years.

Philosophy: Mishawaka believes the keys to successful camping are "safety, health, and happiness." They strive to help young people grow in health, self-worth, outdoor skills, and responsibility. "Evidence of our success comes from the hundreds of second- and third-generation campers. The staff is mature and dedicated (they average nine years at Mishawaka)." Mishawaka has been profiled in *Outside* magazine and the "Today" show.

Parent Comment: "I have been acquainted with Mishawaka for thirty-five years as a camper, counselor, and parent of two children who have spent several summers there. The opportunity to experience the outdoors and learn and grow under the close supervision of a qualified staff is an invaluable experience. One of the most satisfying experiences of my life has been watching my son and daughter learn to live and work with their peers, to develop self-confidence and leadership skills, and to appreciate the beauty of the outdoors through the Mishawaka experience."

SHERWOOD FOREST CAMP

Deer River, Minnesota

Single sex, female

Ages: 7–17

Campers: 75

Religious affiliation: None

Fees: $1,485, 4 weeks / $2,870, 8 weeks

Extra fees: Transportation to and from camp, laundry, canteen

Founded: 1932

Program: A noncompetitive program

Facilities/Activities: *Athletics* baseball field, 2 hard-surface tennis courts, riflery range, archery range, volleyball courts; *Waterfront* lake, swimming, sailing, canoeing, sailboarding, aquaplaning, rowboating, waterskiing, paddleboating, fishing, Playaks; *Camping* campfire and sleep-out sites, campcraft area, nature area; *Creative Arts* dramatics, arts and crafts, dance; *Miscellaneous* vespers area, pet-raising area, recreation rooms

Boarding: 9 cabins (electricity), indoor showers; dining room (family style), special diets accommodated, salad bar; laundry done weekly by commercial service

Counselors: 1 to every 3 campers, 25–28 counselors total; average age, 22; 20% are foreign

Camp Rules: Campers must have parent's request or director's approval to call home, parents requested not to call; weekly letter home required; no food in cabins

Medical: Registered nurse in camp, some staff trained in first aid and CPR, 5-bed infirmary, parents notified by letter if nurse feels it necessary, by phone in more serious cases; 15 miles from Itasca Medical Center

Director: Maxine Gunsolly
Summer: RR 1, Box 200, Deer Lake, Deer River, MN 56636
        218-246-8670
Winter: 805 Second Avenue, NW, Grand Rapids, MN 55744
        218-326-3823

Maxine Gunsolly has been the owner and director of Sherwood Forest Camp for thirty-eight years. A college graduate with a degree in physical education, she was a camp counselor before operating Sherwood Forest Camp. Maxine continues to teach horseback riding and waterskiing.

Philosophy: Sherwood Forest Camp strives "to develop in each girl those skills and traits that will make her a better citizen and better able to live in and contribute to the community to which she returns." Safety is their first concern. "We try to achieve our goals in an atmosphere of informality and fun, with the addition of plenty of good food, good medical care, and a highly qualified staff."

Parent Comment: "Sherwood has been an important part of my life for over thirty years, first as a riding counselor and now as a parent of a six-year camper (presently a senior counselor). Natural beauty, individual attention, and a noncompetitive atmosphere make Sherwood special. Long-lasting friendships among girls from many states are a plus. As a pediatrician, I appreciate the emphasis on safety, health, and age-appropriate activities. Sherwood represents the best camping has to offer."

CAMP TAUM SAUK
Lesterville, Missouri ————————————————————————

Coed

Ages: 8–15

Campers: 120

Religious affiliation: None

Fees: $550, 2 weeks / $825, 3 weeks / $1,350, 5 weeks / $1,590, 6 weeks

Extra fee: Canteen

Founded: 1946

Program: A noncompetitive program that encourages teamwork, comradeship, and responsibility. Campers are involved in planning of programs

Facilities/Activities: *Athletics* baseball field, soccer field, 2 hard-surface tennis courts (lit), 2 basketball courts, gymnastics area, track, 2 volleyball courts, archery range, riflery range, track, skeet range, free weights, aerobics, tetherball, indoor gym (tumbling mats); *Waterfront* swimming pool, lake, canoeing, sailing, kayaking, fishing, pontoons, splash boats; *Camping* campfire and sleep-out sites, campcraft, nature area; *Creative Arts* theater, creative dance, drama, skits, arts and crafts, model rocketry, video room, camera room, radio room; *Miscellaneous* 2 computers (XT and AT clones), horseback riding, stables, rings, zip wire, ropes course with rappelling, recreation room

Boarding: 13 cabins (electricity), 7 indoor showers, 3 showerhouses; dining room (family style); laundry done weekly by commercial service

Counselors: 1 to every 4 campers, 35 counselors total; average age, 20; 5% are foreign

Camp Rules: Campers not allowed to use phone except for special occasions and in case of emergency; 3 letters home per week; no food in cabins

Medical: Physician on call, 3 registered nurses in camp, entire staff certified in first aid and CPR, 3-bed infirmary, parents notified if child becomes ill or runs temperature for over 2 days; 25 miles from Arcaia Valley Hospital

Director: George D. Smith
Summer: Route 1, Box 26, Lesterville, MO 63654
          314-637-2489
Winter: 13 Litzsinger Lane, St. Louis, MO 63124
          314-961-5538

George D. Smith has been the owner and director of Taum Sauk for thirty-two years. He has a B.S. and an M.A. in education from the University of Missouri and he taught elementary physical education for fifteen years. He also spent two years in the U.S. Army Medical Corps.

Philosophy: Camp Taum Sauk's philosophy is one of "living and planning together for a real summer's camping experience." The camp shows its interest in the "total growth of the camper by helping to develop a well-integrated individual. The program is not bound by tradition or requirements but is adaptable to satisfy the needs and interests of the camper.

Parent Comment: "Taum Sauk gave our son the 'best time ever.' I had hoped that this camp would give him rewards and many memories of summer and I was right on target! He had a great time and he will always have fond memories of his two weeks with all of you wonderful and caring people."

CAMP ALGONQUIN
Rhinelander, Wisconsin

Coed

Ages: 7–17

Campers: 150

Religious affiliation: None

Fees: $1,095, 3 weeks / $1,470, 4 weeks / $2,490, 7 weeks

Extra fees: Rafting trip, canteen

Founded: 1975

Program: A structured, noncompetitive program with electives; emphasis on learning program

Facilities/Activities: *Athletics* baseball field, 2 soccer fields, 2 hard-surface tennis courts, basketball court, riflery range, archery range, badminton, 2 volleyball courts; *Waterfront* lake, swimming, sailing, canoeing, waterskiing, inner tubing, kayaking; *Camping* campfire and sleep-out sites, nature center and trails; *Creative Arts* informal theater, skits, plays, creative arts (painting, sculpture), art shop, newspaper; *Miscellaneous* 4 computers (3 Apple, 1 Compaq), low ropes course, natural wetland area, recreation room, outdoor recreation court, state forest learning program areas

Boarding: 30 cabins (no electricity), large indoor shower facility; dining room (family style), special diets accommodated; laundry done weekly by commercial service

Counselors: 1 to every 8 campers, 18 counselors total; average age, 21–22; 5% are foreign

Camp Rules: Telephone calls only in case of emergency but parents may speak to child if parents desire; letter writing strongly encouraged; no food in cabins

Medical: Registered nurse living in camp, some staff have first aid certification, 5-bed infirmary, parents immediately notified by phone of sick camper; 8 miles from St. Mary's Hospital

Director: Donald W. McKinnon
Summer: 4151 Camp Bryn Afon Road, Rhinelander, WI 54501
715-369-1277
Winter: Same

Don McKinnon is the owner and acting director of Camp Algonquin. He has been involved in the camping and recreation industry for the past seventeen years, ten of which he has spent at Camp Algonquin. Don has worked at four other camps as program director, consultant, and camp director. He holds a master's degree in recreational services.

Philosophy: Camp Algonquin utilizes a combination of individualized learning and outdoor recreation to improve a child's skills in reading, writing, and self-expression, while strengthening a concept of self and independent thinking. "Camp Algonquin is founded on the belief that each child is a unique individual deserving of love, understanding, and the opportunity to realize his or her true potential. We strive to unlock each child's unique talents. This is accomplished through a nationally recognized learning program and a well-structured but flexible outdoor recreation program."

The learning center uses brain-compatible learning techniques to develop skills in reading, writing, and self-expression, and strives to permit each child to experience success at every level of learning. Included are a variety of outdoor sports, games, and activities "in the belief that having fun and enjoying the outdoors is more important than just winning games. We want every child to have a memorable summer of fun."

Parent Comment: "Our son's first experience at Camp Algonquin was so terrific for him that we wondered if a second summer could measure up. But measure up it did. His 'camp tales' are peppered with many names of campers, new ones and alumni, several of whom are referred to as 'my good friends . . .' The stories range from campfires, canoe trips, and cabin antics, to how beautiful and peaceful the woods are in early morning. John's second summer at camp was a successful one for him and he wants to return again to have fun and see friends and because 'at camp, they let you be just yourself and you're accepted.' Enough said."

CAMP BIRCH KNOLL FOR GIRLS
Phelps, Wisconsin

Single sex, female

Ages: 7–16

Campers: 150

Religious affiliation: None

Fees: $1,650, 4 weeks / $2,950, 8 weeks

Extra fees: Transportation to and from camp, laundry, sheets and pillowcases, extra horseback riding, yearbook, canteen

Founded: 1944

Program: A structured, noncompetitive program with the opportunity to choose electives

Facilities/Activities: *Athletics* baseball field, 2 soccer fields, 5 hard-surface tennis courts, 2 basketball courts, 2 street hockey courts, 2 volleyball courts, gymnastics area (carpeted/padded indoor center) with all events, rhythmic gymnastics, archery range (all bows compound), 3 racquetball courts; *Waterfront* 630-acre lake, swimming, lap swimming, skin diving, synchronized swimming, waterskiing, springboard diving, inner tubing, canoeing, sailing (12 Sunfish, X-Boat, Rebel), pontoon boat; *Camping* campfire and sleep-out sites, nature area; *Creative Arts* indoor and outdoor theaters, plays, mime, skits, singing classes, art workshop, jewelry, pottery, graphics, sketching, painting, dance (ballet, jazz, tap), newspaper; *Miscellaneous* 4 computers (3 Compaq, 1 Apple), English horseback riding, Hunter Jumper facility, trails, children's petting farm, hiking, cheerleading, recreation room (fireplace), cooking classes

Boarding: 18 cabins (electricity), central showerhouse; dining room (family style), special diets accommodated, salad bar; laundry done weekly by commercial service

Counselors: 1 to every 4 campers, 30 counselors total; average age, 21; no foreign counselors

Camp Rules: Campers may receive telephone calls from parents after 2 weeks; 2 letters required per week; no food packages from home, food from canteen allowed in cabins

Medical: Pediatrician available daily, 2 registered nurses in camp, assistant director is certified in first aid, CPR, and lifesaving, 6-bed infirmary, parents notified immediately in medical emergencies; 8 miles from Eagle River Memorial Hospital

Director: Gary Baier
Summer: 3500 Dam Lane, P.O. Box 67, Phelps, WI 54554
       715-545-2556
Winter: 5589 Treehaven Circle, Fort Myers, FL 33907
      800-843-2904, 813-275-7919

Before becoming director, Gary Baier was Birch Knoll's program director for thirteen years. During the rest of the year he is a high-school tennis coach and tennis professional. He is assisted in camp by six other members of the Baier family, including Ed Baier and Neva Baier, owners of Birch Knoll.

Philosophy: At Birch Knoll, participation and improvement in activities are stressed. Campers elect activities and are encouraged "to go for it" in these areas. All instructed activities have red, white, and gold achievement levels which serve as a curriculum guide for the counselors and a motivational tool for the girls. A big-sister and secret-sister program eases the entrance of first-time campers to Birch Knoll, helping everyone feel a part of "one giant family."

Parent Comment: "The facilities at Camp Birch Knoll are first rate in every way and the competence of the counselors in their given fields is top-notch. What impressed us from the very beginning was that the most important thing to everyone connected with Birch Knoll was that the girls had a good time. While there are many learning activities, there are also many activities designed for the girls to simply have a good time—it all adds up to a fun summer."

CAMP BIRCH TRAIL FOR GIRLS
Minong, Wisconsin

Single sex, female (brother camp, North Star Camp for Boys)

Ages: 8–16

Campers: 180

Religious affiliation: None

Fees: $1,600, 28 days / $2,950, 56 days

Extra fees: Transportation to and from camp, medical insurance, horseback riding, photo album, canteen

Founded: 1959

Program: A structured, noncompetitive program with camper choice of activities

Facilities/Activities: *Athletics* 2 baseball fields, soccer field, 4 hard-surface tennis courts (1 lit), basketball court, archery range, gymnastics area, 2 volleyball courts; *Waterfront* lake, swimming, diving, sailing (5 Sunfish, 4 mini-scows, 1 X-Boat), aerobics, water ballet, 7 sailboards, 38 canoes, 2 kayaks, 12 Funyaks, 5 rowboats, 3 waterski boats, 2 pontoon boats; *Camping* campfire and sleep-out sites, nature and ecology center; *Creative Arts* outdoor theater, plays, musicals, crafts, pottery, ceramics, nature crafts, stained glass, jewelry, tie-dyeing, weaving, macramé, dance; *Miscellaneous* high and low ropes courses, roller skating, recreational building

Boarding: 24 cabins (electricity), 3 showerhouses; dining room (family style), special diets accommodated, salad bar; laundry done 4 days a week by commercial service

Counselors: 1 to every 3 campers, 60 counselors total; average age, 22; 12% are foreign

Camp Rules: Telephone calls not permitted except in emergencies; letter required once a week; no food in cabins

Medical: Physician and 2 registered nurses in camp, 12-bed infirmary, parents notified by phone if child spends night in infirmary or requires prescription medication or requires outside medical attention; 16 miles from Community Memorial Hospital

Directors: Richard and Barbara Chernov
Summer: P.O. Box 527, Minong, WI 54859
        715-466-2216
Winter: 5146 North Woodburn Street, Whitefish Bay, WI 53217
        414-962-2548

Richard was a high-school teacher and attorney before becoming co-director of Birch Trail. His association with Birch Trail began as a camper and counselor at North Star Camp for Boys, Birch Trail's brother camp. Barbara served as North Star's secretary, crafts instructor, and dramatic-show supervisor before becoming co-director at Birch Trail. Currently, Richard sits on the board of the Wisconsin section of the ACA and both Chernovs are active members of the ACA.

Philosophy: Birch Trail believes that it is the willingness to risk failure in expanding one's horizon that best signals personal growth. Birch Trail aims to provide campers with a nurturing setting in which they can learn new skills according to their own goals, abilities, and interests. "This supportive atmosphere also encourages girls to express their feelings and think about themselves and the world around them." The aim is to give "each camper a happy and meaningful experience that will contribute to each camper's physical, emotional, social, mental, and spiritual growth."

Parent Comment: "Our daughter has attended Birch Trail for five years. In that time we know she has thoroughly enjoyed herself, gained skills in activities, and made lifelong friendships with campers from all over the world. Beyond those benefits, she has become a more self-confident, independent, and self-assured person because of the nurturing environment and outstanding staff at Camp Birch Trail. Each staff member takes a special interest in every camper and helps her reach her potential."

CAMP MENOMINEE
Eagle River, Wisconsin —————————————————————

Single sex, male

Ages: 6–17

Campers: 150

Religious affiliation: None

Fees: $800, 2 weeks / $2,300, 6 weeks; $275 / 1-week basketball seminar

Extra fees: Transportation to and from camp, laundry, canteen

Founded: 1928

Program: A structured, competitive program with the opportunity for noncompetitive activities and electives; emphasis on sports

Facilities/Activities: *Athletics*   7 baseball fields, 2 soccer fields, 5 hard-surface tennis courts, 2 basketball courts (1 lit), street hockey court, track, riflery range, archery range, 2 volleyball courts, beach volleyball court, 5-hole golf course; *Waterfront*   lake, Red Cross swimming lessons, fishing, waterskiing, sailboarding, kayaking, canoeing, sailing, pontoon boat; *Camping*   campfire and sleep-out sites, nature area; *Creative Arts*   theater, skits, plays, game shows, woodworking, ceramics, model rocketry, photography (darkroom), newspaper, radio room; *Miscellaneous*   recreation room, pool table, Ping-Pong, air hockey, board games, library

Boarding: 17 cabins (electricity), showerhouses; dining room (family style), special diets accommodated, salad bar; laundry done weekly by commercial service

Counselors: 1 to every 4 campers, 38 counselors total; average age, 20; 15% are foreign

Camp Rules: Telephone calls not permitted except on birthdays, emergencies, or unless prearranged with directors; 2 letters home required weekly; no food in cabins

Medical: Physician and 2 registered nurses in camp, waterfront director certified in Red Cross first aid, CPR, and advanced lifesaving, 11-bed infirmary, parents notified by telephone in case of medical emergency; 15 miles from Eagle River Memorial Hospital

Directors: Glenn and Dawn Klein
Summer: 4985 Highway D, Eagle River, WI 54521
715-479-2267
Winter: South 2756 Villa Ruhe, Marshfield, WI 54449
715-387-2267

Glenn and Dawn met at the University of Wisconsin–Madison, where they both received their undergraduate degrees. In 1983 they got married at Menominee and purchased the camp. Both are ACA-certified camp directors, and they are the parents of three sons. Glenn first came to Menominee in 1969 as a camper, while Dawn began in 1981 as a member of the medical staff.

Philosophy: Menominee emphasizes "making your best effort, learning from your mistakes, and forming close relationships." Each camper's program is tailored to his needs with input from both the camper and his parents. "We have a tremendously diverse and caring staff of camping professionals, educators, former campers, and college students who honestly love the work and realize the impact camp has on the development of young men."

Parent Comment: "The time that I enjoy my sons the very best is the time right after they return home from Camp Menominee. There seems to be a metamorphosis that takes place while they are in the north woods, breathing that air, and living in a community of fellowship, brotherhood, and teamwork that abounds there. They are both more self-sufficient and they help out much more around the house. For a period of time, they are truly 'team players' and a pleasure to have around the house."

CAMP NEBAGAMON FOR BOYS
Lake Nebagamon, Wisconsin ―――――――――――――

Single sex, male

Ages: 9–15

Campers: 220

Religious affiliation: None

Fees: $1,800, 27 days / $2,950, 55 days

Extra fees: Transportation to and from camp, canteen

Founded: 1929

Program: A structured program with electives; emphasis on basic swimming, canoeing, campcraft, and tennis skills

Facilities/Activities: *Athletics* 2 baseball fields, 2 soccer fields, 7 hard-surface tennis courts (2 lit), 2 basketball courts (1 lit), track, 2 riflery ranges, archery range, 2 volleyball courts; *Waterfront* 934-acre lake, swimming, fishing, 14 rowboats, 48 canoes, sailboats (Phantoms, X-class sloops), pontoon boat, 4 sailboards, 14 kayaks, 4 motorboats; *Camping* campfire and sleep-out sites, nature trails, campcraft, orienteering; *Creative Arts* theater (skits, talent shows, choir), arts and crafts, photography (darkroom); *Miscellaneous* logging museum, bicycling, recreation room

Boarding: 24 cabins (electricity), showerhouses; dining room (family style), special diets accommodated; laundry done weekly by commercial service

Counselors: 1 to every 3 campers, 90 counselors total; average age, 20; 10% are foreign

Camp Rules: Telephone calls permitted on camper's birthday and in emergencies; 2 letters home required weekly; no food in cabins

Medical: Physician, registered nurse, and 2 nurse's aides in camp, 8-bed infirmary, parents notified by telephone in medical emergencies or in case of illness; 38 miles from St. Mary's Hospital

Directors: Roger and Judy Wallenstein
Summer: Lake Nebagamon, WI 54849
      715-374-2275
Winter: 5237 North Lakewood Avenue, Chicago, IL 60640-2220
      312-271-9500

Roger Wallenstein started at Nebagamon in 1955 as a camper, later becoming a counselor and administrator. He has an M.Ed. in educational psychology and has taught in Chicago for fifteen years. Roger has two sons. Judy began in camping as an administrator in the wilderness outdoor camping and hiking program. She has a B.S. in elementary education and has experience in business management and social work.

Philosophy: Nebagamon emphasizes achievement of individual goals. Individual and team competition is available but never forced. "We see the program as a means to an end—our goal being that each camper feel a sense of personal worth." A nucleus of mature supervisors (average age, 31) provides guidance for all camp participants. Extensive backpacking, bicycling, canoeing, and fishing trips are offered in addition to regular in-camp activities.

Parent Comment: "This is our son's third summer at Nebagamon and each year he comes home happy, self-confident, and full of camp stories and memories. Again, this summer was a positive growing experience because of the planning and oversight of a fine professional staff. Twelve-year-old boys are easily influenced by older kids, and we are pleased that you provided such fine role models. Also, I had the opportunity to hit a tennis ball with him and it was a toss-up to determine who was more pleased with his progress, me or him. We are additionally proud that he tends to be a leader in the cabin."

NORTH STAR CAMP FOR BOYS
Hayward, Wisconsin ─────────────────────────────

Single sex, male (sister camp, Birch Trail for Girls)

Ages: 8–16

Campers: 150

Religious affiliation: None

Fees: $1,600, 4 weeks / $2,900, 8 weeks

Extra fees: Transportation to and from camp, horseback riding, canteen

Founded: 1945

Program: A structured program, some competition, with individual choice of activities

Facilities/Activities: *Athletics*   2 baseball fields, soccer field, 5 hard-surface tennis courts (1 lit), basketball court (lit), archery range, riflery range, volleyball court; *Waterfront*   lake, swimming, sailing (5 Sunfish, 5 mini-scows, X-Boat), waterskiing, canoeing, 5 sailboards, catamaran, Funyaks, pontoon boat for fishing; *Camping*   campfire and sleep-out sites, nature trails; *Creative Arts*   outdoor theater, musical production, silk screening, leatherwork, ceramics, photography, model rocketry, arts and crafts; *Miscellaneous*   horseback riding, recycling program, recreation room, Ping-Pong, garden, mountain biking

Boarding: 19 cabins (electricity), showerhouses; dining room (family style), special diets accommodated, emphasis on low-fat, low-sugar diet, salad bar; laundry done weekly by commercial service

Counselors: 1 to every 4 campers, 54 counselors total; average age, 22; 2% are foreign

Camp Rules: Telephone calls not permitted except on birthdays or in case of illness; 2 letters required per week, directors write weekly; no food in cabins

Medical: Physician and 2 registered nurses in camp, some staff trained in first aid and CPR, 8-bed infirmary, parents notified by phone in medical emergencies and by letter in case of minor problems; 14 miles from Hayward Area Memorial Hospital

Directors: Robert and Sue Lebby
Summer: Route 1, Hayward, WI 54843
715-462-3254
Winter: 7540 North Beach Drive, Milwaukee, WI 53217
414-352-5301

Robert Lebby received a bachelor's degree in business from Duke University and a teaching certificate in physical education from Cleveland State. He has studied camping administration at George Williams College and is an ACA-certified camp director. Sue received a bachelor's degree in nursing from the University of Wisconsin–Madison and has over fifteen years of experience as an emergency and pediatric intensive care nurse.

Philosophy: North Star tries to impart to campers the value of individual differences, self-reliance, and good sportsmanship. Campers are encouraged to practice decisionmaking by choosing their activities. North Star considers its staff its most important asset: "Through their enthusiasm and caring they help campers feel comfortable enough to just be themselves."

Parent Comment: "We are so pleased that we have become a North Star family and applaud North Star on the excellent way they run camp. Not only is it organized and fun, but the boys learn so much about values, feelings, and themselves. Our son returned home a much more sensitive boy and learned to be aware of others' feelings before his own. He really benefited from the caring attitude that prevails at North Star. Anyone can run an organized program but it's really a special person who can run one from the heart. The summer was everything you promised it would be and more. Our son can't wait to return."

RED ARROW CAMP FOR BOYS

Woodruff, Wisconsin

Single sex, male

Ages: 8–15

Campers: 100

Religious affiliation: None

Fees: $2,350, 7 weeks

Extra fees: Transportation to and from camp, horseback riding, special trips, canteen

Founded: 1921

Program: A structured program with the opportunity for electives; emphasis on improving skills. Extensive trip program

Facilities/Activities: *Athletics* 2 softball fields, soccer field, 3 hard-surface tennis courts, basketball court, street hockey court, track, riflery range, archery range, volleyball court, lacrosse field, wrestling mat, weight and fitness area, trapshooting; *Waterfront* 4,000-acre Trout Lake, swimming, skin and scuba diving, fishing, sailing (MC scows, Lazer II, Butterfly, Skipjack, Sailfish), 7 sailboards, 37 canoes, 2 war canoes, 6 rowboats, 3 waterski boats, pontoon boat; *Camping* campfire and sleep-out sites, nature areas; *Creative Arts* theater, musical production, choir, woodworking, photography (darkroom); *Miscellaneous* horseback riding, rings, trails, library, recreation room, high and low ropes courses

Boarding: 12 cabins (electricity), showerhouse; dining room (family style), special diets accommodated; laundry done weekly by commercial service

Counselors: 1 to every 4 campers, 26 counselors total; average age, 22; 1% are foreign

Camp Rules: Campers permitted to receive calls during mealtimes, outgoing calls permitted in emergencies only; letter required for 2 meal tickets a week; no food in cabins

Medical: Registered nurse in camp, 2-bed infirmary, nurse notifies parents if child is sick; 10 miles from Howard Young Medical Center

Directors: Sue and Bob Krohn
Summer: 3980 Day Lake Road, Woodruff, WI 54568
      715-385-2769
Winter: 590 Sherry Lane, Deerfield, IL 60015
      708-945-3058

Bob and Sue Krohn have B.S. and M.S. degrees in psychology, education, physical education, and recreation. They have taught at the elementary, secondary, and university level for twenty years. Bob and Sue were both directors of different camps before marrying. They have operated Red Arrow Camp since 1967.

Philosophy: Red Arrow Camp's motto is "Don't wait to be a great man, be a great boy." The goals of Red Arrow Camp are friendship, achievement through short-term goal setting, and the development of self-confidence and self-esteem through a program of challenge and adventure. Because of its relatively small size, Red Arrow tries to offer a family setting where all campers and staff come to know and respect one another. "Red Arrow aims to inspire every camper to live unselfishly, thoughtfully, confidently—and have fun while he is doing it!"

Parent Comment: "When we visited our sons at Red Arrow this summer both were so enthused about camp. Our younger son was talkative and 'up'—a real improvement over the withdrawn, depressed son we sent off in June. Our eldest's weight loss is fabulous. He did not like the weight loss camp he attended last summer. We are thrilled he has lost weight while having such a wonderful time! Both boys have learned to waterski. Thank you and your staff again for a terrific job!"

RED PINE CAMP FOR GIRLS
Minocqua, Wisconsin

Single sex, female

Ages: 6–16

Campers: 125

Religious affiliation: None

Fees: $1,400, 27 days / $2,800, 55 days

Extra fees: Horseback riding

Founded: 1938

Program: An elective and structured, noncompetitive program

Facilities/Activities: *Athletics* 4 hard-surface tennis courts, basketball court, gymnastics area (balance beams, mats), archery range, volleyball courts; *Waterfront* 1,200-acre lake, swimming, canoeing, sailing, sailboarding, waterskiing, rowboating, paddleboating; *Camping* campfire and sleep-out sites, nature area; *Creative Arts* drama, arts and crafts; *Miscellaneous* natural amphitheater, recreation room, horseback riding, ring

Boarding: 16 cabins (electricity), 2 showers/cabin, 2 showerhouses; dining room (family style), special diets accommodated, salad bar; laundry done weekly by private laundress out of camp

Counselors: 1 to every 3 campers, 35 counselors total; most college age; percentage of foreign counselors varies

Camp Rules: Director notifies parents if anything is wrong, foreign campers may phone home; letters written once a week; no food in cabins

Medical: 2 registered nurses in camp, 8-bed infirmary, parents immediately notified when child is sick; 4 miles from Howard Young Medical Center

Directors: Sarah Wittenkamp Rolley, Irene Boudreaux
Summer: Box 69, Minocqua, WI 54548
       715-356-6231
Winter: Same

Sarah Wittenkamp Rolley is a graduate of Monticello Junior College and the University of Kansas. A former camper, she has been on staff since 1953. Irene Boudreaux has a B.S. in health and physical education from the University of Southwestern Louisiana. She has twenty-three years of teaching experience in elementary and secondary schools and has been affiliated with Red Pine since 1954.

Philosophy: Red Pine emphasizes harmonious and responsible group living as well as an appreciation and utilization of nature. "Red Pine is an opportunity to meet girls from a wide geographic representation. We strive to provide not only a safe, fun experience, but one with guidance and values useful and influential in later life. It is our firm belief that a happy, positive camping experience is a true treasure of youth."

Parent Comment: "Congratulations on a superbly run camp. It is beautifully manicured and your maintenance is in A-No. 1 condition. You can both be proud of your work and of your beautiful and inviting camp. We were very impressed with the excellent condition of the camp's physical facilities and the well-balanced, safety-conscious program which effectively achieves the camp's objectives. While professionalism is manifested by the camp staff, who possess all the certified and technical skills, there exists a special quality of warmth, a caring concern, and a desire to develop each child's potential to the fullest. It was evident that the staff had received superior leadership training. Also, a real sense of values is highly visible."

TOWERING PINES CAMP FOR BOYS/
WOODLAND FOR GIRLS *Eagle River, Wisconsin* ——

Brother/sister

Ages: 7–16

Campers: 160

Religious affiliation: None

Fees: $2,775, 7 weeks

Extra fees: Transportation to and from camp, special tutoring, canteen

Founded: 1945

Program: An elective program with emphasis on horsemanship, tennis, sailing, aquatics, marksmanship, and creative arts

Facilities/Activities: *Athletics* baseball field, soccer field, 9 hard-surface tennis courts, basketball court, gymnastics area, 2 riflery ranges, 2 archery ranges, 4 volleyball courts, track; *Waterfront* lake, swimming, sailing, boating, waterskiing, racing shell; *Camping* campfire and sleep-out sites, nature area, ecology center; *Creative Arts* outdoor theater, radio room, arts and crafts; *Miscellaneous* 8 computers (Apple), ropes course, recreation building

Boarding: 18 cabins (electricity), 1 shower/cabin, 1 showerhouse (located at waterfront); dining room (cafeteria and family style), salad bar; laundry done weekly by commercial service

Counselors: 1 to every 3.5 or 4 campers, 45 counselors total; average age, 19; 2% are foreign

Camp Rules: Telephone calls restricted; letters written weekly; no food in cabins

Medical: 2 registered nurses in camp, 12 beds in 2 infirmaries, parents notified when child is sick; 9 miles from Eagle River Memorial Hospital

Director: John M. Jordan
Summer: Eagle River, WI 54521
  715-479-4540
Winter: 242 Bristol Street, Northfield, IL 60093
  708-446-7311

John M. Jordan has a master's degree from Northwestern University. He began his camping career in 1946 and has thirty years of teaching experience. He is a member of the Midwest Association of Private Camps and the ACA.

Philosophy: Towering Pines and Woodland emphasize strong leadership. The goal is to develop skills for new interests and greater confidence. "A caring and sensitive staff assures safety and structure."

Parent Comment: "My husband and I would like to express our appreciation to you and your staff. Our son seems to have had a wonderful summer. He has lots of very nice memories which he recounts daily and, in our opinion, he has changed enormously. He seems so much more confident of himself. He seems to have a greater sense of who he is and is happy with what he sees. He has always had very low self-esteem. We thank you."

CAMP WE-HA-KEE
Winter, Wisconsin ——————————————————————————

Single sex, female

Ages: 7–17

Campers: 100

Religious affiliation: Catholic

Fees: $800, 2 weeks (2 sessions) / $1,200, 3 weeks (2 sessions) / $1,500, 4 weeks (2 sessions) / $2,100, 6 weeks / $2,400, 7 weeks / $2,700, 8 weeks

Extra fees: Transportation to and from camp, weekly horseback riding, canteen

Founded: 1923

Program: A noncompetitive program in which campers choose their activities and create individualized schedules. Social development, problem solving, values reinforcement, and physical skills emphasized

Facilities/Activities: *Athletics* soccer field, 4 hard-surface tennis courts, 2 basketball courts, indoor and outdoor gymnastics areas, archery range; *Waterfront* lake, swimming, waterskiing, sailing (Zuma, mini-fish), canoeing, rowboating, paddleboats, kayaks, pontoon; *Camping* campfire and sleep-out sites, nature areas; *Creative Arts* theater, dance, 2 arts and crafts buildings (pottery); *Miscellaneous* 2 computers (Apple IIe), horseback riding, trails, tepee, play equipment, recreation room

Boarding: 12 cabins (electricity), 3 showerhouses; dining room (cafeteria style), special diets accommodated, salad bar; laundry done weekly by commercial service

Counselors: 1 to every 4 campers, 21 counselors total; average age, 19–20; 20% are foreign

Camp Rules: Campers not allowed to use phone; letters home encouraged; food in cabin allowed if shared with other campers

Medical: Physician and registered nurse in camp, entire staff certified in basic first aid and CPR, waterfront staff have advanced lifesaving, 4-bed infirmary, parents notified if child becomes ill; 35 miles from Puck County Hospital

Director: Sister Arturo Cranston, O.P.
Summer: Route 1, Box 251, Winter, WI 54896
715-266-3263
Winter: Same

Sister Arturo Cranston, O.P., is a Dominican sister who was a music teacher in elementary and high schools for twenty-eight years before she began her work for the Tennessee Valley Authority in recreation and natural resources management. She has directed Camp We-Ha-Kee since 1984 and has served on the Wisconsin board of the ACA.

Philosophy: Camp We-Ha-Kee stresses social skills necessary for life with both peers and adults in an environment away from the normal supports of family. "It is an opportunity for a girl to test her own values against those of girls from completely different backgrounds and cultures. We stress acceptance, understanding, and bonding within the camp community."

Camper Comment: "I came from a suburb of Chicago and I loved the outdoors of We-Ha-Kee, the sunshine, the rain, the woods. I was a camper here for four years and it was a great place to be—with so much fun and laughter. Now I am a counselor here—this is my second year—and I realize also how emotionally healthy an environment it is. There are wonderful, supportive women here with a lot of love and guidance to give the campers."

CAMP WOODBROOKE

Richland Center, Wisconsin —————————————————

Coed

Ages: 7–12

Campers: 34

Religious affiliation: Quaker (diversity welcomed)

Fees: $600, 13 days / $880, 20 days

Extra fees: None

Founded: 1979

Program: A structured, cooperative program with electives. Emphasis placed on group decisionmaking and raising camper environmental awareness

Facilities/Activities: *Athletics* activity fields, archery range, volleyball court; *Waterfront* 200-acre pond, swimming, canoeing; *Camping* campfire and sleep-out sites, nature areas; *Creative Arts* informal outdoor theater, dramatics, nature and pioneer crafts, woodworking, carpentry, baking; *Miscellaneous* garden, recreation room, nature pavilion

Boarding: 6 cabins, showerhouses; dining room (family style), vegetarian diet available; laundry done weekly by camp staff

Counselors: 1 to every 3 campers, 10 counselors total (4 additional counselors in training); average age, 22; 20% are foreign

Camp Rules: Parents may telephone director at any time; letter writing strongly encouraged; no food in cabins

Medical: Counselors certified in first aid, 2-bed infirmary, parents notified by director in case of medical emergency; 7 miles from Richland Center Hospital

Director: Jenny Lang
Summer: Route 4, Box 202, Richland Center, WI 53581
          608-647-8703
Winter: 795 Beverly Place, Lake Forest, IL 60045
          708-295-5705

Jenny Lang has an M.A. in child development and is also the mother of four children. She has worked as a counselor and program director in summer camps and has served as a volunteer with the Girl Scouts and church groups. She is an ACA-certified camp director and the newsletter editor for the Illinois section of the ACA.

Philosophy: Camp Woodbrooke is a small, diverse, ecologically oriented camp in which all campers and staff are involved in making program decisions and assigning living tasks. "Campers develop lasting friendships while camping at an outpost site, digging for clay, singing, baking, watching butterflies, or creating a puppet show." The Woodbrooke staff emphasizes the Quaker principles of caring, simplicity, and cooperative responsibility.

Parent Comment: "Both our children returned from Camp Woodbrooke healthy, relaxed, and with increased self-confidence. We heard many stories of friendships, adventures, and a new awareness of the natural world. Woodbrooke is unique for many reasons. However, three stand out. Life is simple there (no TV, radios, video games, junk food, etc.). The natural setting is beautiful and children spend their days entirely outdoors. And the staff is exceptional. Camp Woodbrooke has been a valuable part of our children's lives."

WEST

ORME SUMMER CAMP
Mayer, Arizona

Coed

Ages: 7–16

Campers: 250

Religious affiliation: None

Fees: $1,000, 2 weeks / $1,800, 4 weeks / $2,500, 6 weeks, $3,000, 8 weeks

Extra fees: Transportation to Phoenix, laundry, craft supplies, Prescott Rodeo, private horse stall, Green River trip

Founded: 1929

Program: A structured Western riding camp

Facilities/Activities: *Athletics* baseball field, 3 soccer fields, 4 hard-surface tennis courts (1 lit), basketball court (lit), gymnastics area, track, riflery range, archery range, volleyball court, weight room, wrestling mats; *Waterfront* swimming pool, fishing pond; *Camping* campfire and sleep-out sites, nature area; *Creative Arts* 2 outdoor theaters, leatherwork, ceramics, woodworking, photography, stained glass, handicrafts, model rocketry; *Miscellaneous* 20 computers (Apple, Hewlett-Packard), recreation room, 24,000-volume library, 40,000-acre working cattle ranch, rodeo arena, riding rings, survival training, classrooms

Boarding: 8 cabins (electricity), 2 showerhouses; dining room (cafeteria and family style), special diets accommodated, salad bar; laundry done weekly by camp

Counselors: 1 to every 6 campers, 35 counselors total; average age, 21; 5% are foreign

Camp Rules: Pay phones available, messages taken for campers; 1 letter per week required; no food in cabins

Medical: 2 registered nurses in camp, 12-bed infirmary, parent notified of camper illness at nurse's discretion; 40 miles from Marcus Laurence Hospital

Director: William S. Hart, Jr.
Summer: H.C. 63, Box 3040, Mayer, AZ 86333
602-632-7601
Winter: Same

William S. Hart, Jr., has been with the Orme Summer Camp for thirty-four years, first as director of the Orme horsemanship program, and for the past twenty-one years as director of the camp. Mr. Hart is past president of the Western Association of Independent Camps and is a member of the board of the Coronado section of the ACA. Mr. Hart has participated in numerous rodeos and roundups in his thirty-four years at Orme.

Philosophy: The Orme Summer Camp is primarily a Western riding camp, and is located on the 40,000-acre Quarter Circle V Bar Ranch. Each camper can expect to ride at least one hour a day whether he or she is an expert or novice. Pack trips, rodeos, and gymkhanas are offered throughout the session. The last two weeks of camp are devoted either to a motor caravan throughout the Southwest (camping out every night) or an intensified horsemanship option. The Orme Summer Camp uses the facilities of the Orme School, a college-preparatory boarding school. Optional academics are taught by Orme faculty. "Democracy and liberty stand firmly in the background of the Orme Summer Camp. Our purpose for over sixty years has been that the camper leave camp at the end of the season with something more than the feeling of having been well entertained."

Parent Comment: "A long overdue 'thank you' for encouraging our daughter to come to Orme camp last summer. She had a wonderful time . . . Her counselor did everything she could to ensure that our daughter had a successful summer. We all appreciated her loving concern."

CATALINA SEA CAMP/JR. SEA CAMP
Avalon, California

Coed

Ages: Sea Camp, 12–17, Jr. Sea Camp, 8–12

Campers: 220

Religious affiliation: None

Fees: $400, 1 week (Jr. Sea Camp) / $1,400, 3 weeks (Sea Camp)

Extra fees: Camp store

Founded: 1979

Program: A moderately structured, noncompetitive program emphasizing marine science, island ecology, snorkeling, scuba diving, and underwater photography

Facilities/Activities: *Athletics* baseball field, 2 hard-surface tennis courts, 2 basketball courts, 2 volleyball courts, soccer field; *Waterfront* Pacific Ocean, swimming, sailing (basic, intermediate, advanced, racing techniques, catamaran), crewing aboard larger boats, basic seamanship, sailboarding (basic and intermediate), ocean kayaking, snorkeling, scuba diving; *Camping* campfire and sleep-out sites; *Creative Arts* arts and crafts, talent show; *Miscellaneous* recreation room (Ping-Pong, air hockey), marine biology labs, terrestrial labs, invertebrate lab, algae lab, fish lab, plankton lab, marine mammal center, shark petting tank

Boarding: Dorms (electricity), 8–12 showers/facility; dining room (family style), special diets accommodated, salad bar; laundry done by counselors twice per Sea Camp session, not done for Jr. Sea Camp

Counselors: 1 to every 5 campers, 23 counselors, 25 instructors; average age of counselors, 19, instructors, 23; 2% are foreign

Camp Rules: Emergency calls only; letter writing encouraged; no food in dorms

Medical: Registered nurse in camp, instructors trained in first aid, CPR, and water safety, 4-bed infirmary, parent notified when camper unable to participate in activities; Bay Watch paramedics 15 minutes by helicopter, Avalon Municipal Hospital 2 miles by sea, 7 by land

Directors: Ross and Kristi Turner
Summer: P.O. Box 796, Toyon Bay, Avalon, CA 90704
213-510-1622
Winter: P.O. Box 1360, Claremont, CA 91711
714-949-0687

Ross Turner has a degree from Brigham Young University in biology and physical education. Kristi Turner has a degree from San Diego State in elementary education. After seven years of teaching at Anaheim High School they decided to start an outdoor educational program on Catalina Island. From 1976 to 1978, they developed and operated the Marine Science Program of Cherry Cove. In 1979 this grew into the nonprofit Catalina Island Marine Institute (CIMI). In 1979 CIMI ran the first Catalina Sea Camp.

Philosophy: Catalina Sea Camp and Jr. Sea Camp are the only marine science camps on the West Coast. Campers explore the wonders of Santa Catalina Island at Toyon Bay in the southern California Channel Islands with qualified instructors. All levels of scuba certification are offered. "All of our instructional and counseling staff are handpicked to provide campers with courteous instructional and counseling staff as well as safe and exciting programs. A variety of social activities is also offered."

Parent Comment: "The camp did our son so much good. We basically brought a very scared and apprehensive kid to San Pedro and were surprised and delighted to see a much matured, more self-assured, and happy young man at the end of the session. He talked nonstop about everything he had done. It was obvious that he had won many battles during the previous two weeks. These positive feelings appear to have carried over into the seventh grade. He has a much more positive attitude toward school, and he is striving for 'A's' this year. And he is much more confident socially and therefore has more friends. We have tried many other things to try to get him motivated. This seems to be the one thing that has worked."

COPPERCREEK CAMP
Greenville, California ─────────────────

Coed

Ages: 6–17

Campers: 60

Religious affiliation: None

Fees: $895, 2 weeks / $1,295, 3 weeks / $1,995 (regular) or $2,195 (advanced) 4-week trek session (white-water rafting, backpacking)

Extra fees: Transportation to and from San Francisco

Founded: 1966

Program: A noncompetitive program emphasizing crafts, water activities, riding, and out-of-camp activities

Facilities/Activities: *Athletics*   multipurpose field, hard-surface tennis courts at nearby high school, riflery range, archery range, volleyball courts; *Waterfront*   swimming pool, Lake Almanor 10 miles from camp, waterskiing (19-ft. Ski Nautique), fishing, skin diving, 4 sailboards; *Camping*   campfire and sleep-out sites, nature area; *Creative Arts*   drama, arts and crafts, photography lab; *Miscellaneous*   mountain bikes, hiking, low-level ropes course, climbing wall, English horseback riding (10 horses), stables, ring, jumping, trails, overnight rides, backpacking

Boarding: 10 cabins (electricity), indoor showers; eat outdoors under umbrellas on a covered porch (cafeteria style: breakfast and lunch; family style: dinner), special diets accommodated; laundry done weekly by camp

Counselors: 1 to every 7 campers, 12 counselors total; average age, 24; 10% are foreign

Camp Rules: Telephone use permitted for emergencies and special occasions; letter home required once a week (Sundays); no food in cabins

Medical: Registered nurse in camp, 2 staff members are EMTs, some staff have advanced first aid training, 2-bed infirmary, parents notified if child is sick for more than 1 day or requires physician; 3 miles from Indian Valley Hospital

Directors: John S. Lindskog, Lynne Evarts
Summer: Box 749, Greenville, CA 95947
    916-284-7617
Winter: Box 512, Oakhurst, CA 93664
    209-683-7252

John Lindskog has owned and operated Coppercreek Camp with Lynne Evarts since 1966. A graduate of California Polytechnic, John has nine years of experience in city recreation. Lynne has over thirty-five years of camping experience and an M.B.A. from the University of Southern California.

Philosophy: The emphasis at Coppercreek is traditional. Campers choose from such activities as photography, drama, fishing, waterskiing, backpacking, pottery, and rock climbing. Campers also have responsibilities such as tent cleanup and setting the tables for meals. "Coppercreek is a small camp with big adventures—a magic place where campers can learn and have fun with sixty other campers from all over the world. It is a camp where everybody knows you by the end of the first day and friends are forever."

Parent Comment: "My child had a wonderful experience at Coppercreek Camp. The emotional growth in just two weeks was astounding. At age six, we were worried that two weeks would be too much. Coppercreek was so successful that he will attend for at least three weeks as a seven-year-old."

DOUGLAS RANCH CAMPS
Carmel Valley, California ——————————————

Brother/sister

Ages: 7–14

Campers: 100

Religious affiliation: None

Fees: $1,175, 2 weeks (new campers only) / $1,700, 3 weeks / $2,050, 4 weeks

Extra fees: Medical insurance, laundry, canteen

Founded: 1925

Program: A structured, competitive program with some electives

Facilities/Activities: *Athletics* baseball field, soccer field, 4 hard-surface tennis courts, 2 riflery ranges, 2 archery ranges, volleyball court; *Waterfront* swimming pool; *Camping* campfire and sleep-out sites, nature areas; *Creative Arts* outdoor theater, skits, arts and crafts; *Miscellaneous* Western-style horseback riding (25 horses), ring, barn, recreation room

Boarding: 25 cabins (electricity), showerhouses; dining room (family style); laundry done weekly by commercial service

Counselors: 1 to every 3.5 campers, 26–29 counselors total; average age, 20–21; 20% are foreign

Camp Rules: No telephone calls permitted except for emergencies, parents can speak to staff at any time; letter home required once a week; no food in cabins

Medical: Doctor 3 miles away, registered nurse in camp, 6-bed infirmary, parent notified in case of medical emergency as noted on child's medical form; 3 miles from paramedic-staffed Red Cross ambulance station, 20 miles from Monterey Community Hospital

Director: Carole Douglas Ehrhardt
Summer: 33200 East Carmel Valley Road, Carmel Valley, CA 93924
        408-659-2761
Winter: 8 Pala Avenue, Piedmont, CA 94611
        415-547-3725

Carole Douglas Ehrhardt has been the director of the Douglas Ranch Camps (brother/sister camps) for twenty-two years. Since her grandmother founded the camp in 1925, Carole has been a camper, counselor, and program director before assuming her current position as director. A graduate of the University of California at Berkeley, she has taught school for several years.

Philosophy: Douglas Ranch Camps are located in California's Carmel Valley. Building character and self-confidence and encouraging new interests and skills are the main goals of the camp. "Pride in accomplishment and individual growth for each camper is provided with the help of quality instruction in our major sport skills of Western riding, swimming, tennis, archery, and riflery. Our counselors are carefully chosen for their experience in working with children. Every precaution is observed to ensure the health and safety of our campers." Although the setting is a structured one, each camper has the opportunity to focus on the activities he or she enjoys most in unstructured hours that are built into the program.

Camper Comment: "As a young girl, Douglas Ranch Camps guided me, gave me strength, love, and education to help me through life. Douglas gave me the chance to experience childhood in the truest, purest sense, and now I rekindle those experiences as an adult. Douglas gave me confidence, and taught me responsibility and compassion."

GOLD ARROW CAMP

Lakeshore, California

Coed

Ages: 7–16

Campers: 250

Religious affiliation: None

Fees: $1,175, 2 weeks / $1,650, 3 weeks / $2,220, 4 weeks

Extra fees: Yearbook, canteen

Founded: 1933

Program: A noncompetitive program designed to increase campers' self-esteem through outdoor activities

Facilities/Activities: *Athletics* riflery range, archery range; *Waterfront* lake, swimming, motorboating, waterskiing, canoeing, kayaking, sailing (55 national class boats), jet waterskiing, hydro-sliding; *Camping* campfire and sleep-out sites, nature areas; *Creative Arts* outdoor theater, arts and crafts, 5 potter's wheels, ceramics; *Miscellaneous* rock climbing, ropes course, backpacking, horseback riding, nature games and study, day hikes

Boarding: 30 cabins (no electricity), several tents, showerhouses; dining room (cafeteria style), salad bar; laundry done weekly by camp

Counselors: 1 to every 3 campers, 100 counselors total; average age, 21; 8% are foreign

Camp Rules: No telephone calls except for emergencies; letter home required once a week; no food in sleeping accommodations

Medical: 2 registered nurses in camp, waterfront and riding personnel trained in first aid, 6-bed infirmary, nurse notifies parent in medical emergency; 45 miles from Clovis Community Hospital

Director: Ken Baker
Summer: Box 155, Lakeshore, CA 93634
209-893-6641
Winter: 2100 North Sepulveda Boulevard, #2,
Manhattan Beach, CA 90266
213-545-3233

Ken Baker, director of Gold Arrow Camp, spent eight years in day camping before coming to Gold Arrow. For ten years he worked closely with Manny Vezie, the founder of Gold Arrow, before becoming the camp's director.

Philosophy: Gold Arrow aims to develop each camper's interest in wholesome outdoor sports. The program is designed to permit each camper to participate according to his or her own skill level. "We intend to build self-confidence through accomplishment in a noncompetitive atmosphere."

Parent Comment: "What a privilege to be able to send your child to such a beautiful spot in the High Sierras with an emphasis on every water sport imaginable. Gold Arrow offers horses, arts and crafts, hiking, archery—everything that increases self-confidence and fun."

JAMESON RANCH CAMP

Glennville, California

Coed

Ages: 6–14

Campers: 75

Religious affiliation: None

Fees: $790, 2 weeks (5 2-week sessions)

Extra fees: None

Founded: 1935

Program: An elective, noncompetitive program designed to get camp-ers involved in all aspects of a working ranch

Facilities/Activities: *Athletics* gymnastics area (vault), riflery range, archery range, volleyball courts (on sand); *Waterfront* swimming pool, lake, sailing, canoeing, rowing, fishing; *Camping* campfire and sleep-out sites, nature areas; *Creative Arts* outdoor theater, outdoor arts and crafts; *Miscellaneous* Western horse program, working ranch, trails, riding arena, large garden, animal care, rock climbing, mountain bikes, overnight horseback trips, singing, barn dances

Boarding: Sleep outside on porches; dining room (cafeteria and family style); laundry done weekly by commercial service

Counselors: 1 to every 4.5 campers, 18 counselors total; average age, 20–21; 15% are foreign

Camp Rules: No telephone calls except for emergencies; letter home required once a week; no junk food

Medical: Registered nurse in camp, some staff have first aid training, 3-bed infirmary, parents notified in medical emergencies; 40 miles from Memorial Hospital

Directors: Ross and Debby Jameson
Summer: Box SPG, Glennville, CA 93226
        805-536-8888
Winter: Same

Ross Jameson is a second-generation camp director who grew up at Jameson Ranch Camp. Debby is a registered nurse and teacher. They have four children and have directed the camp since 1975. Ross served on the board of directors for the Western Association of Independent Camps for four years.

Philosophy: At Jameson Ranch Camp, a rustic wholesome life-style continues from generation to generation. "In today's high-tech society, it is rare to sleep outside, gather eggs, and pitch hay to calves." Campers choose daily from a variety of programs offered. "Our size and staff ratio promote a close family atmosphere where children can feel a sense of belonging and grow in self-esteem by making friends and learning skills."

Parent Comment: "I have only positive things to say. I sent two kids of different sexes, interests, personalities, and opinions, and they both came back enriched. They have a deeper appreciation of nature, other people, spiritual values, and each individual's contribution toward a harmonious whole."

CAMP O-ONGO
Running Springs, California ───────────────────

Coed

Ages: 8–15

Campers: 112

Religious affiliation: None (Christian orientation)

Fees: $1,250, 3 weeks / $2,395, 6 weeks

Extra fees: None

Founded: 1940

Program: A general, noncompetitive program

Facilities/Activities: *Athletics* baseball field, hard-surface tennis courts, basketball court, riflery range, archery range, volleyball court; *Waterfront* swimming pool; *Camping* campfire and sleep-out sites, nature area; *Creative Arts* arts and crafts; *Miscellaneous* recreation room, hiking, outdoor chapel, Western riding ring

Boarding: 16 cabins (electricity), indoor showers, showerhouses at pool; dining room (family style), special diets accommodated; laundry done weekly by camp

Counselors: 1 to every 7 campers, 16 counselors total; average age, 19–20; 20% are foreign

Camp Rules: Messages delivered, outgoing phone calls discouraged; mandatory weekly letter home; no food in cabins

Medical: Registered nurse in camp, counselors required to have first aid and CPR, 12-bed infirmary, parent notified when child requires care from physician; 12 miles from Mountains Community Hospital

Director: Tom Preston
Summer: P.O. Box 60, Running Springs, CA 92382
      714-867-7041
Winter: Same

Tom Preston has been involved with Camp O-Ongo since its inception in 1940 (his father started the camp when Tom was nine years old). Tom received a teaching degree from the University of California at Santa Barbara and began running Camp O-Ongo when his father passed away in 1968. He is an ACA-certified camp director and has been active in both the ACA and the Western Association of Independent Camps.

Philosophy: Camp O-Ongo's goal is to help children grow physically, emotionally, and spiritually. YMCA camp ideas have been incorporated into the programs. Each camper is encouraged to try every activity. Competition, peer pressure, and negative comments are discouraged in order to build self-confidence and emotional stability. In addition, each camper is asked to try a portion of each food at each meal. "The camp's spiritual influence is limited to taking principles to live by from the Bible and encouraging the campers to practice these ideas. We are nonevangelical and welcome campers of all faiths. We try to create a family atmosphere where friendships started will last through the years."

Parent Comment: "In a nutshell, the whole camp experience was great for our son. I couldn't begin to tell you how wonderful it was for him and how much he enjoyed it. However, you created a monster—he won't be denied a return trip. Fortunately, we have almost earned enough to ensure his next session."

SKYLAKE RANCH CAMP
Ahwahnee, California

Coed

Ages: 6–16

Campers: 90–100

Religious affiliation: None

Fees: $855, 2 weeks / $1,640, 4 weeks / $3,200, 8 weeks

Extra fees: Transportation to and from camp, canteen (includes laundry)

Founded: 1966

Program: A structured and elective program

Facilities/Activities: *Athletics* baseball field, soccer field, hard-surface tennis court, gymnastics area, riflery range, archery range, volleyball court, badminton; *Waterfront* swimming pool, pond, canoeing, swimming, fishing, Playaks, inner tubes, Bass Lake (20 miles from camp), waterskiing; *Camping* campfire and sleep-out sites, nature areas; *Creative Arts* outdoor theater, drama classes, musical productions, craft house (variety of arts and crafts), dance; *Miscellaneous* recreation room, horseback riding (riding and vaulting arena), library, leadership training, Ping-Pong

Boarding: 14 cabins (7 with electricity, 7 without), 7 cabins with indoor showers, 7 cabins use showerhouses; dining room (family style); laundry done once a week by commercial service

Counselors: 1 to every 6 campers, 20–24 counselors; average age, 21; 10%–20% are foreign

Camp Rules: Phones available for emergencies only; letter home required once a week; no food in cabins

Medical: Registered nurse in camp, 2 staff members qualified EMTs, 4-bed infirmary, parent notified if child needs to see physician or spends night in infirmary; 18 miles from Fremont Hospital, 54 miles from Saint Agnes Hospital

Director: Marian Howe Andersen
Summer: P.O. Box 298, Ahwahnee, CA 93601
       209-683-4460
Winter: 7518 North 6 Street, Fresno, CA 93710
       209-435-6993

Marian H. Andersen graduated from California State University, San Jose, and taught in public schools for fifteen years. She has done graduate work at the University of Nevada and California State University, Sacramento. For the last five years she has taught and written about special education. Marian grew up in camping and is a second-generation camp director. She has been active in the ACA and is past president of the northern California section of the Western Association of Independent Camps.

Philosophy: "The uniqueness of Skylake Ranch Camp comes with the family atmosphere and the loving and accepting attitudes found in camp." The staff strives to make sure that "every person in camp is successful at something each day." With a variety of traditional camp activities, campers choose daily the activity they want to pursue. Though the camp does not specialize, a camper can. "Campers leave camp with memories of fun and feeling good about themselves."

Parent Comment: "My daughter loves Skylake Ranch Camp. She loves the friends she has made there. She can hardly wait to return for her third summer and will be taking her little brother this year. We like the caring atmosphere we have found at camp. Our daughter learned some new skills each summer and we know that both she and her brother will return this summer with more skills."

SNOW MOUNTAIN CAMP
Nevada City, California

Coed

Ages: 7–16

Campers: 60

Religious affiliation: None

Fees: $920, 2 weeks

Extra fees: Canteen

Founded: 1970

Program: An individualized noncompetitive program

Facilities/Activities: *Athletics*   hard-surface tennis courts, archery range, volleyball court; *Waterfront*   swimming pool, reservoir, water-skiing, canoeing, sailing, kayaking, overnight canoe trips; *Camping* campfire and sleep-out sites, nature area; *Creative Arts*   outdoor theater (production every 2 weeks), arts and crafts; *Miscellaneous*   riding ring, BMX bike course

Boarding: 3 winterized cabins (electricity), 6 summer platform cabins (no electricity), indoor showers, showerhouses; dining room (family style), special diets accommodated, salad bar; laundry done once per session by commercial service

Counselors: 1 to every 5 campers, 16–17 counselors total; average age, 20–21; 6% are foreign

Camp Rules: Telephone calls limited; letter home encouraged daily; no food in cabins

Medical: Physician on 24-hour call, 3-bed infirmary, parents notified if child sick for 24 hours or if child's illness or accident requires a doctor's visit or emergency care; 7 miles from Sierra Nevada Memorial Hospital

Director: Ray Kalman
Summer: P.O. Box 476, Nevada City, CA 95959
        916-265-4439
Winter: Same

Ray Kalman, who has a B.A. in recreation, enjoyed camp so much as a child that he dreamed of re-creating that unique experience and sharing it with others. Snow Mountain Camp is the realization of that dream. Ray is a life member of the ACA and has been a member of the Western Association of Independent Camps for the past fourteen years. He has been the northern California ACA board and standards chairman for the past six years.

Philosophy: At Snow Mountain Camp, everyone contributes to what happens. The camp's small size permits flexibility and an opportunity for campers to participate in a variety of activities based on their interests and abilities. "At Snow Mountain Camp, we have a real commitment to providing a fun, challenging, and nurturing experience— one that builds self-confidence and friendships and encourages self-reliance and cooperation."

Parent Comment: "We have nothing but praise for your camp. You are organized and business-oriented, yet personal and caring. This was the first camp experience for both children. It proved to be a marvelous experience."

THUNDERBIRD RANCH SUMMER CAMP

Healdsburg, California

Coed

Ages: 6–15

Campers: 45

Religious affiliation: None

Fees: $845, 2 weeks

Extra fees: Laundry, waterskiing, camp photo, camp T-shirt, canteen

Founded: 1961

Program: Located on a working ranch, Thunderbird emphasizes riding and combines structured and elective activities

Facilities/Activities: *Athletics* baseball field, soccer field, basketball court, archery range, volleyball courts, playground; *Waterfront* swimming pool, Russian River, canoeing, inner tubing, Lake Sonoma (30 minutes away), waterskiing; *Camping* campfire and sleep-out sites, nature areas; *Creative Arts* outdoor theater, arts and crafts; *Miscellaneous* working ranch, horseback riding (riding and vaulting arena), barns, blacksmith shop

Boarding: No cabins, but 2 covered wagons, 1 caboose, 3 tepees, 1 train depot, central bathhouse (6 showers); dining room (cafeteria style); laundry done weekly by commercial service

Counselors: 1 to every 5 campers, 12 counselors total; average age, 21; 50% are foreign

Camp Rules: No telephone calls except for emergencies, parents can call director at any time; letters home encouraged; no food in sleeping accommodations

Medical: Physician across road from camp, all counselors certified in first aid and CPR, 2-bed infirmary, parents notified if child requires medical treatment; 8 miles from Healdsburg General Hospital

Director: Bruce F. Johnson
Summer: 9455 Highway 128, Healdsburg, CA 95448
        707-433-3729
Winter: Same

Bruce Johnson was a California State Champion Western Youth Rider in 1967. He studied recreational business management at the University of Nevada on a 4-H scholarship and is a past 4-H Lite horse leader. A second-generation camp director, he is an active member of the ACA.

Philosophy: Thunderbird Ranch provides young people with the opportunity to develop and improve their riding skills while experiencing life on a working ranch. It is a small camp and all campers share in the general farm chores. "Thunderbird Ranch perpetuates the Johnson family's commitment to youth from around the world and sets the stage for the positive, maturing experience young people encounter when they work with horses. We believe the old adage, 'The outside of a horse is good for the inside of a child.' "

Parent Comment: "We wanted you to know what a good time our daughters had at Thunderbird Ranch this summer. They have talked about it a lot and must have liked every single thing about camp. The riding program has helped one daughter tremendously . . . Your instructors and riding program have given her the confidence she needed to do something she has always wanted to do."

ANDERSON CAMPS
Gypsum, Colorado

Coed

Ages: 7–17

Campers: 125

Religious affiliation: None

Fees: $1,560, 4 weeks ($1,680, Wilderness Program) / $1,860, 5 weeks ($1,980, Wilderness Program) / $3,260, 9 weeks ($3,380, Wilderness Program); $440, 10 days, area children's program

Extra fees: One-way airport transportation, sheets and blankets, rafting trips, canteen

Founded: 1962

Program: A noncompetitive program with daily choice of activities; all programs outdoor-oriented with a variety of camping trips offered

Facilities/Activities: *Athletics* baseball field, soccer field, tennis court, basketball court, riflery range, archery range, football field, volleyball court, horseshoe pit, badminton, croquet; *Waterfront* swimming pool (heated), pond, fishing, Playaks, white-water rafting trips out of camp; *Camping* campfire and sleep-out sites; *Creative Arts* model rocketry; *Miscellaneous* recreation room, English and Western horseback riding, trails, barn, 3 arenas, corrals, pastures, extensive camping trips—horseback, rafting, cave exploration, mountain climbing, rappelling, backpacking, tours of Colorado sites

Boarding: 15 cabins (electricity), some showers in cabins, showerhouse, tents for camping trips; dining room (family style), salad bar; laundry done weekly by camp

Counselors: 1 to every 7 campers, 16–18 counselors total; average age, 20; no foreign counselors

Camp Rules: Telephones available only for emergencies, parents may call on camper's birthday; campers must write home every Sunday (letter serves as Sunday lunch ticket); food in cabins discouraged, no junk food allowed

Medical: Retired general practitioner lives 8 miles from camp, RN or EMT in camp, entire staff trained in first aid and certified in CPR, wilderness coordinator is an EMT, 3-bed infirmary, parents notified if child needs a physician or if child spends night in infirmary or visits nurse for more than minor injury; 25 miles from Valley View Hospital

Directors: Janet M. Martin, Sandy Jackson
Summer: 7177 Colorado River Road, Gypsum, CO 81637
          303-524-7766
Winter: Same

Janet Martin has worked at Anderson Camps since 1975 and became a director in 1981. She is a member of the ACA and has a B.S. from Colorado State University. Sandy Jackson has worked at Anderson Camps since 1977 and became a director in 1988. She has seven years of teaching experience and received a B.S. from Fort Lewis College and an M.A. from Colorado State University.

Scott Stuart has owned Anderson Camps since 1979. He has a B.S. from the University of Southern California and an M.A. from the University of Denver.

Philosophy: Anderson is an outdoor summer adventure camp in the Colorado Rockies. Located between Vail and Aspen it offers a general program for boys and girls from seven to seventeen. Anderson emphasizes outdoor, noncompetitive activities, individual attention, and weekly camping trips. Three specialty programs are offered to older campers: High Country Riding (ages twelve to seventeen), the Wilderness Pioneer Program (ages fourteen to seventeen), and the Team Leadership Program (ages fifteen to seventeen). "Staff at Anderson Camps are chosen first for their love of children. The small enrollment allows the staff to focus on each camper's individual success." The camp motto is "Teamwork dedicated to camper enrichment."

Parent Comment: "Anderson has afforded our daughter the opportunity to become reliant on herself. We have seen her flourish from a shy, quiet little girl to an outgoing, independent, young maturing woman. The experiences she has had encourage her to use herself to meet new challenges. She has also made lifetime friends at camp from the 'little guys' to the counselors and directors. It always warms my heart to visit camp and see her reach out and hug a little fellow who is six, then hear a twelve-year-old holler 'Hi, ya.' Anderson is the greatest!"

BLUE MOUNTAIN RANCH

Florissant, Colorado ———————————————————————

Coed

Ages: 7–15

Campers: 150

Religious affiliation: None (nonsectarian ecumenical services)

Fees: $850, 2 weeks / $1,425, 25 days

Extra fees: Canteen

Founded: 1946

Program: A structured, noncompetitive program

Facilities/Activities: *Athletics* 2 baseball fields, soccer field, 2 hard-surface tennis courts, basketball court, track, gymnastics area, riflery range, archery range, volleyball court; *Waterfront* swimming pool (heated), 2 small lakes, canoeing, fishing; *Camping* campfire and sleep-out sites, nature area; *Creative Arts* outdoor theater, drama, skits, special activities, new arts and crafts facility; *Miscellaneous* 6 computers (Tandy), recreation room, Ping-Pong, museum, library, ropes course

Boarding: 13 cabins (electricity), 2 showers/cabin, living room with fireplace in each cabin; dining room (family style), special diets accommodated, salad bar; laundry done weekly by commercial service

Counselors: 1 to every 5 campers, 30 counselors total; average age, 21; 2% are foreign

Camp Rules: Campers not allowed to use phone except in case of emergency; minimum of 1 letter home per week; food allowed in cabins

Medical: Registered nurse in camp, all staff CPR-certified, 5 certified in first aid, 8-bed infirmary, parent notified if child stays in infirmary or is taken to doctor; 14 miles from Langstaff/Brown Emergency Center

Directors: Coach Bill Allen, Suzie Allen Graf
Summer: P.O. Box 146, Florissant, CO 80816
719-748-3279
Winter: 3517 Rogers Avenue, Fort Worth, TX 76109
817-927-8844

Coach Bill Allen, who founded Blue Mountain Ranch in 1946, has worked in the field of education his entire life as a teacher, a coach, and as director of Blue Mountain Ranch. He has an M.A. from West Texas State University and he taught and coached in the Fort Worth, Texas, public schools for thirty-five years. Suzie Allen Graf, director of the girls section since 1972, has a B.A. degree and has taught for two years.

Philosophy: Blue Mountain Ranch is a small camp founded on the idea that summer should be a time for children to relax from the social, academic, and athletic pressures that they are under during the school year. The directors strive to know each child as an individual and to make everyone feel that he or she is a member of a greater family. Campers choose new activities weekly. "We hope to help each child according to his or her particular needs, to teach our campers love of country, family, and friends, and to give each an awareness of the needs of others."

Camper Comment: "I was a slightly scared eleven-year-old first-time camper when I first came to Blue Mountain Ranch, but I soon forgot this feeling and fell in love with Blue Mountain. I learned good values and the meaning of friendship as well as the significance of honesty and love. Camp became very important to me not just because of such things as climbing my first mountain or seeing my first falling star but because of something deeper. We became a family. This summer marks my fifth year as a counselor."

COLVIG SILVER CAMPS
Durango, Colorado

Coed

Ages: 8–18

Campers: 200

Religious affiliation: None

Fees: $1,200, 3 weeks (ages 8–10) / $1,680, 4 weeks / $1,980, 5 weeks / $3,500, 9 weeks

Extra fees: Transportation to and from camp, canteen

Founded: 1969

Program: An elective, noncompetitive outdoor wilderness adventure program with an emphasis on minimum environmental impact

Facilities/Activities: *Athletics*   2 game fields, hard-surface tennis court, basketball court, riflery range, archery range, 2 volleyball courts (1 cement, 1 dirt); *Waterfront*   3 small man-made lakes, canoeing, swimming, Playaks; *Camping*   campfire and sleep-out sites (next to 2-million-acre San Juan National Forest), nature area; *Creative Arts*   one craft shop, photography, lapidary, pottery, model rocketry; *Miscellaneous* 2 large recreation rooms, ropes course

Boarding: 35 cabins (electricity), 8 showers in cabins, 3 showerhouses; dining room (family style), special diets accommodated, salad bar; laundry done weekly by camp

Counselors: 1 to every 4 campers, 45 counselors total; average age, 24; no foreign counselors

Camp Rules: Phones available for emergencies only; campers must write home once a week; food in cabins limited

Medical: 3 registered nurses in camp, 6-bed infirmary, parent notified in case of serious medical condition, postcard if routine; 10 miles from Mercy Medical Center

Director: Jim Colvig
Summer: 9665 Florida Road, Durango, CO 81301
            303-247-2564
Winter: Same

Jim Colvig has worked with Colvig Silver Camps for twenty years. Jim helped design and build the cabins, and was in charge of maintenance and repair for eight years. For the last seven years he has been in the administration, the last three as director.

Philosophy: Colvig does not specialize in its programming. Instead, its goal is to provide a special program for each camper, "one that will build confidence, self-reliance, tolerance, friendship, enjoyment of simple pleasures, and love of nature." It is their hope that at Colvig children will "develop new interests and goals while experiencing acceptance and encouragement and positive leadership without concern for peer pressure, schedules, bells ringing, or concern for what parents or teachers expect."

Parent Comment: "Our son has told us some wonderful stories, regaled us with some interesting songs, and shared experiences that I'm sure he will never forget. His first words off the plane were 'Hi, Mom, I'm going back again next year.' "

CIMARRONCITA RANCH CAMPS
Ute Park, New Mexico

Single sex, female (brother camp, Cimarroncita Ranch)

Ages: 7–16

Campers: 125

Religious affiliation: None

Fees: $1,375, 3 weeks / $2,190, 6 weeks

Extra fees: Transportation to and from camp, laundry, canteen

Founded: 1931

Program: Combination of a structured and elective, moderately competitive program; emphasis on horseback riding

Facilities/Activities: *Athletics* 2 softball fields, soccer field, 2 hard-surface tennis courts, volleyball court, riflery range, archery range, gymnastics area (elementary); *Waterfront* swimming pool, wading and inner tubing in shallow water by river, 2 ponds for fishing; *Camping* campfire and sleep-out sites, nature areas; *Creative Arts* theater, drama, set design, costuming, other related skills, stage with sound and lighting equipment, arts and crafts, looms, lapidary, jewelry, potter's wheel, silk-screen/stenciling equipment, kiln, leather tools; *Miscellaneous* recreation room, Ping-Pong, piano, horseback riding, 2 rings, vaulting ring

Boarding: 14 cabins (electricity), all have indoor showers, 1 shower-house; dining room (family style, with evening buffet); laundry done weekly by commercial service

Counselors: 1 to every 3 campers, 40 counselors total; average age, 20½, no junior counselors; 1% are foreign

Camp Rules: Telephone use by campers restricted, phone calls from parents discouraged except on special occasions (birthdays); letter writing encouraged; food in cabins discouraged

Medical: 1 registered nurse in camp, all staff members have first aid training and are CPR-certified, 5-bed infirmary, parents notified by camp nurse in event of sickness or injury; 12 miles from nearest doctor and 42 miles from Miner's-Colfax Medical Center Hospital

Directors: Michael U. and Joyce N. Burk
Summer: P.O. Box 68, Ute Park, NM 87749-0068
          505-376-2376
Winter: Same

Mike Burk, a second-generation camp director, grew up in the camping business and has over thirty years of professional camping experience. For over twenty-five years he has been Cimarroncita's girls camp director. Joyce, his wife, has been co-director with him for over twenty years. Both are former educators.

Philosophy: Cimarroncita is kept small enough for each camper and staff member to know all other camp "family" members by name. Making new campers feel a part of this family is a first priority. Instruction in all activities and recognition of campers' skills result in improved self-image and pride of accomplishment. The youngest campers sample all of the camp's activities. Older campers select activities of their choice.

Cimarroncita offers challenge and adventure, and is structured to promote success for each individual camper. Fun and friendship are second only to campers' health and safety.

Parent Comment: "Thank you for the memories that our daughter will have the rest of her life. Memories of this wonderful place, of touching nature, of warm friendships, and of the guidance you have given to make this a very special six weeks year after year. My wife and I also will carry fond memories. We have been introduced to a most beautiful part of our country, one we may not have found were it not for Cimarroncita Camp."

CIMARRONCITA RANCH CAMPS
Ute Park, New Mexico

Single sex, male (sister camp, Cimarroncita Ranch)

Ages: 7–14

Campers: 65

Religious affiliation: None

Fees: $1,375, 3 weeks / $2,190, 6 weeks

Extra fees: Transportation to and from camp, laundry, canteen

Founded: 1944

Program: Combination of a structured and elective, moderately competitive program; emphasis on horseback riding

Facilities/Activities: *Athletics* baseball field, soccer field, 2 hard-surface tennis courts, basketball court, free weights area, mats, riflery range, trapshooting, archery range; *Waterfront* swimming pool, wading and inner tubing in shallow water by river, 2 ponds for fishing; *Camping* campfire and sleep-out sites, nature areas; *Creative Arts* basic crafts; *Miscellaneous* recreation room, Ping-Pong, piano, horseback riding, 2 rings, vaulting ring

Boarding: 8 cabins (electricity), most have showers, 1 showerhouse; dining room (family style, with evening buffet); laundry done weekly by commercial service

Counselors: 1 to every 3 campers, 22 counselors total; average age, 20½ (must have completed first year of college and no junior counselors); 1% are foreign

Camp Rules: No telephone calls from campers unless special permission from director; letter writing encouraged; food in cabins discouraged

Medical: Registered nurse living in camp, all staff members have first aid training and are CPR-certified, 5-bed infirmary, parents notified by camp nurse in the event of sickness or injury; 12 miles from nearest doctor and 42 miles from Miner's-Colfax Medical Center Hospital

Director: Marietta Scurry Johnson
Summer: P.O. Box 68, Ute Park, NM 87749-0068
        505-376-2376, 505-376-2392
Winter: Same

Marietta Scurry Johnson, the boys camp director, is the mother of four and a graduate of Stanford University and the University of Texas law school. She has been on the faculty of St. Mark School of Texas for sixteen years and is a board member of the Hockaday School and Trinity Christian Academy as well as of other civic organizations in Dallas, Texas, where she resides in the winter. A former camper at Cimarroncita, she has been the director of the boys camp for ten years.

Philosophy: Cimarroncita's first priority is making new campers feel at home. The health and safety of all campers is also important. The camp staff strives to create a family feeling by learning everyone's name. With the mountain environment and cool summer temperatures, Cimarroncita is "ideal for daily horseback riding, as well as other traditional camp activities." Healthy living is strongly promoted, and no junk food is permitted in camp. "Every boy is made to feel part of a group, yet is encouraged to develop his own God-given talents and individual strengths. It is our goal to love, challenge, and encourage each camper, and then love him some more."

Parent Comment: "This camp is a character builder. It is full of joy. The emotional and spiritual growth that my son experienced is unparalleled . . . and it's in the majestic mountains of New Mexico."

ECHO HILL RANCH
Medina, Texas ————————————————————————

Coed

Ages: 6–14

Campers: 110

Religious affiliation: None

Fees: $1,750, 4 weeks

Extra fees: Transportation to and from camp, laundry, canteen

Founded: 1953

Program: A structured, noncompetitive program emphasizing interpersonal skills

Facilities/Activities: *Athletics* 2 baseball fields, soccer field, 2 hard-surface tennis courts (lit), basketball court (lit), gymnastics area, 3 riflery ranges, archery range, fencing, volleyball court; *Waterfront* 2 swimming pools, small lake, fishing, kayaking, boating; *Camping* campfire and sleep-out sites, nature area; *Creative Arts* outdoor theater, radio room, creative dramatics, folk dancing, kiln, ceramics, arts and crafts; *Miscellaneous* 3 computers (IBM, Apple), horseback riding, trails, recreation room

Boarding: 13 cabins (electricity), indoor showers; dining room (family style), special diets accommodated, kosher style; laundry done twice weekly by commercial service

Counselors: 1 to every 4 campers, 25 counselors total; average age, 23; 5% are foreign

Camp Rules: Telephone calls discouraged; letters home encouraged; food generally not permitted in cabins

Medical: Doctor on call, infirmary counselor certified in first aid and CPR, 6-bed infirmary, parents notified in medical emergencies; 20 miles from Sid Peterson Hospital

Director: S. Thomas Friedman
Summer: Route 16, Box 70, Medina, TX 78055
　　　　512-589-7739
Winter: Same

S. Thomas Friedman did his undergraduate and early graduate work at the University of Illinois, Northwestern University, and the University of Chicago. He received his Ph.D. in psychology at the University of Texas at Austin. A professor at the University of Texas for twenty-five years doing work in social psychology and child development, he has been the director of Echo Hill Ranch since its founding.

Philosophy: Echo Hill aims to stimulate and enhance a child's development into a mature adult. The atmosphere is noncompetitive and child-centered, with an emphasis placed on individual differences and appreciation of the skills of others. Echo Hill promotes enthusiasm, discipline, and good sportsmanship. "Activities are merely mechanisms to help children grow and develop insight into who they are and what they can accomplish. Over four hundred acres surrounded by hills and crystal streams provide a natural, peaceful setting for activity, challenge, and excitement."

Parent Comment: "Thank you for creating our daughter's favorite place in Texas! She made many new friends and enjoyed the many social and recreational outlets that Echo Hill has to offer. We are delighted to hear that her experience has been such a positive one. Thank you and your talented staff for another great year."

CAMP OLYMPIA
Trinity, Texas ——————————————————

Coed

Ages: 7–16

Campers: 270

Religious affiliation: None (nonsectarian daily program, Christian Sunday vespers)

Fees: $419, 6 days / $829, 13 days / $969, 15 days / $1,309, 3 weeks

Extra fees: None

Founded: 1968

Program: A structured, competitive program with opportunity for electives and noncompetitive activities

Facilities/Activities: *Athletics* baseball field, soccer field, 3 hard-surface tennis courts, basketball court (lit), gymnastics area (balance beam, 2 sunken trampoline pits, large mat for tumbling), riflery range, archery range, 2 grass volleyball courts, football field, skeet range, indoor gym (basketball); *Waterfront* swimming pool (Junior-Olympic size), water slide, waterwheel, 3 diving boards (1 meter, 3 meters), diving platform, Lake Livingston, 8 waterski boats, 10 sailboats, 13 canoes, 22 sailboards, 6 kayaks, 2 rescue boats, fishing, Blob, tubing, other activities; *Camping* campfire and sleep-out sites, nature area; *Creative Arts* outdoor theater, drama classes, radio room, arts and crafts (silver, jewelry, painting), model rocketry; *Miscellaneous* 7 computers (Apple IIe), recreation room (Ping-Pong, games), science library, movie theater, greenhouse, model farm, chapel, log cabin, BMX bike course, horse barn (22 horses), ropes course

Boarding: 22 cabins (electricity, air-conditioned), indoor showers; dining room (family style), special diets accommodated, salad bar; laundry done weekly by camp

Counselors: 1 to every 4 campers, 120 counselors total, 12 administrators; average age, 20; no foreign counselors

Camp Rules: Telephone calls not permitted, but parents can call staff at any time; counselors write parents twice per term, camper encouraged to write; no food in cabins

Medical: Registered nurse in camp, counselors certified in first aid and CPR, 6-bed infirmary, parents notified by nurse after camper returns from doctor; 10 miles from Trinity Memorial Hospital

Director: Tommy Ferguson
Summer: Route 2, Box 25-B, Trinity, TX 75862
  409-594-2541, 713-443-1153
Winter: Same

Tommy Ferguson has been the director of Camp Olympia for fifteen years. He has served as president of the Texas chapter of the ACA and for the past four years has been an elected representative to the Southern American Camping Association for Private Independent Camps.

Philosophy: Camp Olympia is operated on the principles of the Greek tradition of strengthening the body, spirit, and mind. Activities are designed to challenge the maturity and physical capabilities of each age group. Each camper spends time in activities that he or she is most interested in, and there are thirty-five activities from which to choose.

Parent Comment: "I chose Camp Olympia because of the counselors. My sense was that my children would be safe, supervised, happy, and involved. My children needed to experience being on their own and have the opportunity to make responsible choices. I hoped this would happen in a nurturing, supportive, and caring environment. I chose people who I thought would make a contribution to my children's lives. I know I chose well."

CAMP NAVAJO TRAILS
Bicknell, Utah

Coed

Ages: 7–17

Campers: 50

Religious affiliation: None

Fees: $1,600, 3 weeks / $2,600, 5 weeks / $4,000, 8 weeks

Extra fees: Transportation to and from Salt Lake City International Airport, canteen

Founded: 1966

Program: An elective, noncompetitive program that combines a traditional weekend skill-building in-camp program with weekly out-of-camp 5-day adventure excursions

Facilities/Activities: *Athletics* baseball field, soccer field, 2 basketball courts, riflery range, archery range (target, field), volleyball courts; *Waterfront* weekly 5-day excursions to Lake Powell for boating, waterskiing, skin diving, and camping on lakeshore (other activities include sailboarding, swimming, and sailing), weekly 5-day excursions to Green River for white-water kayak training, Fish Lake excursions for fishing and canoeing; *Camping* campfire and sleep-out sites, nature areas; *Creative Arts* outdoor theater, plays, costuming, staging, acting, videotaping, musicals, dance, arts and crafts; *Miscellaneous* recreation hall, horseback riding (instruction, trips), tack barn, ropes course, mountain climbing, survival training, hiking (Grand Canyon), backpacking, bike trekking, most activities set in the wilderness

Boarding: 6 cabins (electricity), indoor showers, tepees; dining room (family style); laundry done weekly by campers

Counselors: 1 to every 3 campers, 17 counselors total; average age, 24; 5%–8% are foreign

Camp Rules: Telephone use discouraged; letter home required once a week; no food in sleeping accommodations

Medical: 4-bed infirmary, parents notified if child requires medical treatment beyond routine first aid; 3 miles from Wayne County Medical Clinic, 55 miles from Sevier Valley Hospital

Director: Don "J" Sampson
Summer: Box 88, Department P, Bicknell, UT 84715
  801-425-3469
Winter: Box 886, Department P, Los Altos, CA 94022
  408-245-6789

Don Sampson, owner and director of Navajo Trails, is assisted in running the camp by his wife, Nancy. Don has a B.A. in economics and an M.B.A. from the University of Utah. Don teaches at Foothill Community College in Los Altos Hills, California. He has directed Navajo Trails since its founding in 1966. His wife, Nancy, has taught, raised their five children, and serves as office manager.

Philosophy: Camp Navajo Trails gathers campers from all parts of the U.S. and foreign countries. The experience that occurs is one of "positive growth that naturally occurs when fun-loving youngsters with varied backgrounds are challenged in a noncompetitive atmosphere." The Navajo Trails motto is "Building youth better for a brighter future." The Sampsons raised five children with this motto in mind. They aim "to serve the youngster as well as the world community."

Parent Comment: "Our two sons attended Navajo Trails. Both boys learned a healthy independence based on self-confidence. They also learned many outdoor skills and the ability to live together in a group."

TETON VALLEY RANCH CAMP
Kelly, Wyoming

Single sex, male (first half of summer); single sex, female (second half of summer)

Ages: 10–16

Campers: 125

Religious affiliation: None

Fees: $1,995, 34 days

Extra fees: Transportation to Jackson Hole, canteen

Founded: 1939

Program: A structured, noncompetitive program with some electives in a Western ranch setting

Facilities/Activities: *Athletics* baseball field, soccer field, riflery range, archery range, volleyball court, playing field; *Waterfront* spring-fed swimming pool, fishing streams, pond; *Camping* campfire and sleep-out sites, nature areas; *Creative Arts* radio room, photography (darkroom), arts and crafts cabin, fly-tying room, lapidary area; *Miscellaneous* wilderness packhorse trips, hiking, backpacking, horseback riding, barn, arena, tack storage, outdoor chapel, meeting rooms

Boarding: 14 cabins (electricity), showerhouses; dining room (family style); laundry done twice weekly by camp staff

Counselors: 1 to every 7 campers, 22 counselors total; average age, 23; 3% are foreign

Camp Rules: Campers not permitted to use phones except in emergencies; letter required for Sunday dinner; no food in cabins

Medical: Registered nurse in camp, EMT on staff, all counselors certified in first aid, 3-bed infirmary, letter to parents if child is sick, notified immediately in medical emergencies; 14 miles from St. John's Hospital

Directors: Stuart and Susan Palmer, Matt Montagne
Summer: P.O. Box 8, Kelly, WY 83011
         307-733-2958
Winter: Same

Stuart Palmer is a graduate of the University of Arizona and has been on the camp staff since 1967. He is a past president of the Wasatch district of the ACA.

Matt Montagne has a degree in geology from Dartmouth College and has been on the camp staff since 1968. A former Teton Valley camper, he has also been a past regional ski coach of the U.S. Olympic biathlon team.

Susan Palmer has a degree in wildlife biology from Kansas State University and has been on the camp staff since 1976. A mother of three daughters, she spent three summers as a naturalist in Glacier National Park.

Philosophy: The goal of Teton Valley Ranch Camp is to provide each camper with broadening experiences. Backpacking and hiking trips venture into the Grand Teton mountains of Jackson Hole. Horseback riding is an important component and each session includes a four- to five-day horse pack trip into the wilderness. Safety and well-being are primary concerns. The staff hopes to "open new worlds of excitement, character growth, and confidence so that Teton Valley Ranch Camp is a milestone for each boy in becoming a finer man and for each girl in becoming a finer woman."

Parent Comment: "Both our daughters had a wonderful summer at Teton Valley Ranch and are enthusiastically looking forward to returning next year. Teton Valley Ranch has been a great life experience for both of them, and they have developed a love for the outdoors and for nature which will last for their lifetimes. Both girls have matured greatly and gracefully through their camp experiences."

WILDERNESS VENTURES

Jackson, Wyoming

Coed

Ages: 13–18

Campers: Varies (in 1990 approximately 450)

Religious affiliation: None

Fees: $1,890–$3,590 (24- to 44-day trips)

Extra fees: Transportation to and from point of departure, weekly spending money

Founded: 1973

Program: Challenging, noncompetitive wilderness expeditions for teens

Facilities/Activities: Wilderness expeditions—canoeing, sea kayaking, white-water rafting, backpacking, rock climbing, bicycle touring, snow climbing, mountaineering, camping in Wyoming, Alaska, Montana, Oregon, Idaho, Washington

Boarding: 2-person tents; students plan and prepare all meals with supervision of staff (cannot accommodate special diets); laundry done weekly at Laundromats by campers

Counselors: 1 to every 5 campers, total number of counselors varies with season; average age, 26; no foreign counselors

Camp Rules: Campers may call home when not in the backcountry; letter writing encouraged, designated "mail stops" where campers can pick up mail

Medical: Every staff member certified in first aid and CPR, parents notified immediately in medical emergencies, secondary contacts required in case parent not available; use medical facilities in the areas being traveled through

Directors: Mike and Helen Cottingham
Summer: P.O. Box 2768-F, Jackson, WY 83001
            307-733-2122
Winter: Same

Mike has an undergraduate degree from Notre Dame and a graduate degree from Xavier University. He has taught high school in Cincinnati. Helen is a graduate of St. Mary's College and has also taught in the Cincinnati schools. Both are members of the ACA.

Philosophy: Wilderness Ventures aims to provide a sharing, cooperative atmosphere where each individual can grow as a person and learn to live within a group. "We also hope to enhance camper self-confidence through challenging wilderness experiences and to broaden the individual's understanding of the natural world and man's effect upon it." The entire summer is spent out of doors.

Parent Comment: "Our daughter has had nothing but positive things to say about her summer with you. Without the very able leaders you attract for Wilderness Ventures, the close feeling wouldn't occur among the group. Obviously, you are quite good at getting fine, mature people who are able to cajole youth into being responsible and caring about each other and their environment. They ask and get the youth to reach inside themselves for inner strength and resources. Again, I want to commend you for a wonderful program."

CANADA

CAMP AROWHON
Ontario, Canada

Coed

Ages: 7–16

Campers: 211

Religious affiliation: None

Fees: $1,900, first 4 weeks / $1,700, second 4 weeks / $3,000, 8 weeks (Canadian currency)

Extra fees: Transportation to and from camp, medical insurance, laundry, and tuck shop (canteen)

Founded: 1932

Program: Completely elective, noncompetitive program with the exception of compulsory swimming

Facilities/Activities: *Athletics* baseball field, soccer field, 4 hard-surface tennis courts, basketball court, volleyball court, archery range; *Waterfront* lake, swimming, 25 sailboats, 20 sailboards, 60 canoes; *Camping* campfire and sleep-out sites, nature areas; *Creative Arts* 300-seat theater, arts and crafts; *Miscellaneous* horseback riding (14 horses), stables, 3 rings, trails, Ping-Pong

Boarding: 33 cabins (electricity), 1 showerhouse for every 4 cabins; dining room (family style), vegetarian menus available; laundry done weekly by commercial service

Counselors: 1 for every 3 campers, 48 counselors total; average age, 19; 30% are foreign

Camp Rules: Campers may use pay telephone anytime except during activity periods and may receive calls at mealtimes; campers must write home twice a week; no food in cabins

Medical: Physician, registered nurse, and nursing student in camp, 5-bed infirmary, parent notified at discretion of camp doctor and director; 35 miles from Huntsville General Hospital

Director: Joanne Kates
Summer: Algonquin Park, Ontario, Canada CN P0A 1K0
705-633-5651
Winter: 297 Balliol Street, Toronto, Ontario, Canada M451C7
416-483-4393

Joanne Kates, the director, was literally raised at Camp Arowhon, which her grandmother founded in 1932 and her father took over in 1949. She grew up being trained on the job to run Camp Arowhon, and was head of the girls camp by age nineteen. She attended Wellesley College and has since had a double career—as a journalist in the winter and a camp director in the summer. In the wintertime she also teaches peer counseling and attends numerous counseling workshops that provide her with ongoing support and education as a camp director.

Philosophy: Arowhon simultaneously nurtures and challenges children so they discover new parts of themselves: A seven-year-old sailboards across the lake—and back! A twelve-year-old goes on a horseback cookout and feels he's conquered the wilderness. A fifteen-year-old who has never stuck with anything in the city is given the constant support she needs to practice every day for a month—and gets her sailing award.

"Our one-to-three staff/camper ratio allows us to give each camper loving attention. Instructional staff are trained to ask children to do their best—in supportive and entertaining ways. Campers rise to the occasion partly because our program allows almost unlimited free choice of activities. With the exception of compulsory instructional swimming, nobody feels forced to do anything." Campers fall in love with Arowhon, which is in the heart of a 3,000-square-mile national park/wilderness preserve. They make the friends of a lifetime, while mastering the art of group living. They learn to sail, sailboard, ride horses, canoe, canoe trip, and play tennis. They do arts and crafts, act in camp plays, and fall under the spell of the wilderness to the tune of the loon's call.

Parent Comment: "I originally sent my daughter to Camp Arowhon because I went there and so did my father. Children learn independence and get to know themselves at camp. Camp Arowhon emphasizes skill development in swimming, canoeing, sailing, tripping, sailboarding, horseback riding, drama, and land sports. The children feel good about themselves that they achieve these skills. The friendships made at Arowhon are very strong. The children return from Camp Arowhon very fit, happy, and confident. Camp Arowhon is an excellent camp as is attested by the children who return year after year."

CANADIAN ADVENTURE CAMP
Ontario, Canada

Coed

Ages: 6–16

Campers: 130

Religious affiliation: None

Fees: $1,410, 4 weeks (U.S. currency)

Extra fees: Transportation to and from camp, tuck shop (canteen) deposit

Founded: 1974

Program: A structured and elective program. Campers in elective program choose 5 activities each day; campers in specialized program commit half the day to either waterskiing, gymnastics, or trampoline, with 2 periods for other activities

Facilities/Activities: *Athletics* archery range, volleyball courts, extensive gymnastics (indoor gym with fully equipped men's and women's apparatus and trampoline), aerobics; *Waterfront* Lake Temagami, swimming, sailboarding, waterskiing, canoeing, inner tubing, kayaking, sailing; *Camping* campfire and sleep-out sites, nature areas and building; *Creative Arts* theater, plays, dance, music, arts and crafts; *Miscellaneous* recreation rooms, pioneering, woodlore

Boarding: 18 cabins (no electricity), 2 showerhouses; dining room (family style); laundry done weekly by camp

Counselors: 1 to every 2 campers, 60 counselors total; average age, 23; 8% are foreign (non–North American)

Camp Rules: No telephone calls are allowed by campers; letter writing is strongly encouraged; no food in cabins

Medical: Physician and registered nurse in camp, 2-bed infirmary, parents notified if major medical problem occurs; 56 miles from North Bay Civic Hospital, 34 miles from Temiskaming Hospital

Director: F. B. (Skip) Connett
Summer: Adventure Island, Temagami, Ontario, Canada P0H 2H0
    705-237-8906
Winter: 31 Helen Avenue, Thornhill, Ontario, Canada L4J 1J6
    416-226-2672

F. B. (Skip) Connett is a full-time camping professional who has been leading youth in camping and outdoor activities for over thirty-five years. He is currently a member of the executive board of the Canadian Camping Association and is the founder and president of Canadian Adventure Camp.

Philosophy: Canadian Adventure Camp (CAC) seeks to help young people grow into responsible, well-rounded citizens through a fun camp atmosphere. It features programs in general camping, gymnastics, and waterskiing. Children attend CAC from Canada, the United States, and other parts of the world. Campers are under the direction of a "mature and safety-conscious staff. The health and safety of your child are our first priorities at Canadian Adventure Camp. We are continually updating our equipment to meet the highest safety standards as well as training our staff in the latest instructional techniques."

Parent Comment: "Just a note to let you know how very much my daughter enjoyed her four weeks at CAC. There was such enthusiasm and so many positive experiences—she loved it. Her counselor wrote a lovely letter with specific information rather than glowing generalities. Thank you for taking such good care of my precious girl and for helping to give her the kind of wonderful, warm memories everyone should have when they think back on childhood summers."

THE HORSE PEOPLE
Ontario, Canada ————————————————————————

Coed

Ages: 9–18

Campers: 80

Religious affiliation: None

Fees: $865, 2 weeks / $1,700, 4 weeks / $2,550, 6 weeks / $3,400, 8 weeks (Canadian currency)

Extra fees: None

Founded: 1976

Program: A structured, noncompetitive English riding camp

Facilities/Activities: *Athletics* baseball field, soccer field, volleyball courts; *Waterfront* swimming pool; *Camping* campfire and sleep-out sites, nature areas; *Miscellaneous* horseback riding, indoor arena, 2 dressage rings, Hunter Jumper courses, steeplechase course, championship "event" course, trails, lounges, recreation room

Boarding: 14 cabins (electricity), dorm, indoor showers; dining room (family style), special diets accommodated, salad bar; laundry done weekly by camp

Counselors: 1 to every 5 campers, 16 counselors total; average age, 19; 1% are foreign

Camp Rules: Campers may receive telephone calls from parents on special occasions; letter writing encouraged; no food in sleeping accommodations

Medical: Doctor on call, staff trained in first aid and CPR, parents notified immediately in medical emergencies; 30 miles from Children's Hospital of Eastern Ontario

Directors: Wolf and Bev Schinke
Summer: RR 1, Wendover, Ontario, Canada K0A 3K0
        613-673-5905, fax: 613-673-4787
Winter: Same

Wolf's love affair with horses began as a child in Germany, where he was a successful show rider and member of the national junior equestrian team of the state of Lower Saxony. He has been in camping since 1967 and has been an equestrian coach for over twenty years. Bev has an M.A. in child counseling. She started out in camping as a camper and has been an owner of The Horse People for fifteen years.

Philosophy: The Horse People's equestrian camping experience is based on the knowledge that each camper must be allowed to progress at his or her own level and be praised for his or her efforts. Riding lessons (primarily English) range from novice to advanced and include games and gymnastics on horseback. The advanced rider has the opportunity to compete in equestrian competitions. Staffing is central to The Horse People and all counselors are former campers who have gone through a training program to enable them to be "professional in helping to develop confidence in the novice rider, while challenging the youngster who wishes to reach the advanced level."

Parent Comment: "There is something magic about The Horse People. Everyone is happy. Every child belongs to the family and endeavors to do his or her share of the work. Each child has a horse to care for throughout his or her stay, which develops a fine four-legged friendship. There are no winners at The Horse People. Every child is a star. Our success was finding this riding camp where good training allows a child to channel his or her enthusiasm and determination to best advantage. Beyond every level of achievement there is a future challenge. Our son and daughter long to be Horse People again so they can meet a new challenge."

CAMP OTTERDALE
Ontario, Canada ——————————————————

Coed

Ages: 7–16

Campers: 200

Religious affiliation: None

Fees: $600, 10 days / $1,200, 3 weeks / $1,650, 4 weeks (U.S. currency)

Extra fees: Transportation to and from camp, tuck deposit (canteen), provincial sales tax

Founded: 1955

Program: A combination of structured mornings and elective afternoons

Facilities/Activities: *Athletics* baseball field, 2 soccer fields, hard-surface tennis court, basketball court, archery range, volleyball courts; *Waterfront* lake, swimming, sailing, sailboarding, canoeing, kayaking; *Camping* campfire and sleep-out sites; *Creative Arts* arts and crafts; *Miscellaneous* horseback riding, recreation room, video, rappel tower

Boarding: 20 cabins (electricity), indoor showers; dining room (family style), salad bar; laundry done weekly by commercial service

Counselors: 1 to every 5 campers, 50 counselors total; average age, 20; 2%–5% are foreign

Camp Rules: Campers not permitted to use telephone; letters home encouraged; reasonable snacks allowed in cabins

Medical: Physician and registered nurse in camp, 8-bed infirmary, parents notified in case of medical emergency; 12 miles from Smiths Falls Community Hospital

Director: Michael W. Southam
Summer: Lombardy, Ontario, Canada K0G 1L0
    613-283-1539
Winter: 1632B Bayview Avenue, Toronto, Ontario, Canada M4G 3B7
    416-322-6500

Michael W. Southam became owner and director of Camp Otterdale in 1981. He is a professional camp director who has been involved with various summer camps for over fifteen years.

Philosophy: Camp Otterdale's goal is to ensure that campers learn new skills in a healthy and safe environment as they are having fun, developing new friendships, and enjoying new experiences and adventures. "The competence of the staff at any summer camp is the most important single factor that contributes to a camper's enjoyment and ensures that campers achieve their greatest potential." All counselors are eighteen and older and take part in an extensive training program each year before camp.

Parent Comment: "When we first sent our kids off to camp almost six years ago, we were the typical anxious parents. To our delight (and surprise) we found the staff to be very loving and sensitive to our children's very different needs. As parents we are delighted with the safe and happy environment at Camp Otterdale. I know my kids look forward to the day when they can apply their years of experience and learned leadership skills to being camp counselors at Otterdale."

CAMP WHITE PINE
Ontario, Canada ————————————————————

Coed

Ages: 8–17

Campers: 380

Religious affiliation: None

Fees: $2,400, 4 weeks / $3,800, 8 weeks (Canadian currency)

Extra fees: Transportation to and from camp, laundry

Founded: 1956

Program: A structured, noncompetitive program with camper choice of activities

Facilities/Activities: *Athletics*   3 baseball fields, soccer field, 8 hard-surface tennis courts (5 lit), basketball court (lit), street hockey court (lit), gymnastics area, archery range, volleyball courts, fitness area, sports field, indoor gym; *Waterfront*   5 swimming pools, lake, swimming, waterskiing, sailing, sailboarding, canoeing, kayaking, fishing; *Camping*   campfire and sleep-out sites, nature areas; *Creative Arts*   outdoor theater, plays, voice, music, other instruction, arts and crafts, silk screening, printmaking, silk painting, model rocketry, dance; *Miscellaneous*   horseback riding, ropes course, recreation rooms

Boarding: 42 cabins (electricity), indoor showers; dining room (family style), special diets accommodated, kosher style, salad bar; laundry done weekly by commercial service

Counselors: 1 to every 2 campers, 200 counselors total; average age, 23; 20% are foreign

Camp Rules: Telephone calls not permitted by campers; letter writing encouraged; no food in cabins

Medical: Physician and 2 registered nurses in camp, 11-bed infirmary, parents notified by phone if child spends night in infirmary; 5 miles from St. John's Hospital

Directors: Joseph Kronick, Adam Kronick
Summer: Haliburton, Ontario, Canada K0M 1S0
　　　　705-457-2131
Winter: 40 Lawrence Avenue West,
　　　　Toronto, Ontario, Canada M5M 1A4
　　　　416-322-6250

Joseph Kronick, who has an M.S.W., has been director of Camp White Pine ever since he founded it in 1956. He is an executive member of the Ontario Camping Association and has been a youth director for various community organizations. His son Adam is carrying on the family tradition by directing the camp with his father. Before becoming co-director in 1985, Adam earned an M.B.A. and served as a White Pine staff member for ten years.

Philosophy: Camp White Pine believes that it is through its policy of small-group living and small camper-to-counselor ratio that young people are given the best opportunity for positive emotional and intellectual growth. In order to create the most effective environment possible for this type of growth, Camp White Pine also believes that it is important for campers to learn from other young people who come from various countries and who offer different perspectives about the world.

Parent Comment: "Our older daughter, at the age of ten, decided that it was time to switch from day camp to sleep-away camp and she requested White Pine because some of her friends had been going there. My husband and I checked the credentials of the camp and its director and we felt confident in registering her for the first half of the season. On Visitors' Day, she begged to remain for the rest of the summer. Our younger daughter, at eight years of age, also began attending. Both girls returned each summer, completed the counselor-in-training years, and subsequently applied to be on staff. White Pine has been a positive influence on their personal growth. It has given them an opportunity to learn new skills, acquire friendships, and relate to others."

CAMP EDPHY
Québec, Canada ────────────────────────

Coed

Ages: 4–16

Campers: 300

Religious affiliation: Catholic

Fees: $345 per week (2- to 9-week sessions offered; Canadian currency)

Extra fees: Transportation to and from camp, laundry

Founded: 1965

Program: A structured, competitive program with camper choice of activities

Facilities/Activities: *Athletics* baseball field, soccer field, 3 tennis courts (2 hard surface, 1 lit, 1 indoor), basketball court (lit), indoor gymnastics area, handball, touch football, track and field, judo, racquetball, volleyball court, archery range, golf; *Waterfront* 2 swimming pools, indoor swimming pool, lake, scuba diving, war canoeing, canoeing, sailboarding, diving; *Camping* campfire and sleep-out sites, nature area; *Creative Arts* dance, theater, arts and crafts, model rocketry; *Miscellaneous* computers (IBM), recreation room, video, circus workshop (juggling, trampoline, trapeze), mountain climbing, horseback riding, cycling, canoe trips

Boarding: Dorms, indoor showers; dining room (cafeteria style), salad bar; laundry done every 12 days by camp

Counselors: 1 to every 3 campers, 150 counselors total; average age, 19; 10% are foreign (non–North American)

Camp Rules: Telephone calls permitted by campers; letter writing encouraged; no food in dorms

Medical: 1 registered nurse in camp, 10-bed infirmary, parents notified by phone if child spends night in infirmary; 10 miles from Centre Hospitalier Laurentien, Sainte-Agathe, Québec

Director: Yvan Dubois
Summer: 100 des Prairies Boulevard, Suite 102-B,
           Laval, Québec, Canada H7N 2T5
           514-669-9068, 514-669-2797, fax 514-668-2827
Winter: Same

Yvan Dubois, the founder of Camp Edphy International, has had a wide variety of experiences in the area of sports and camping. He served as the director of sporting events during Expo '67 in Montréal and was the general manager and mayor of the Olympic Village for the 1976 Montréal Olympic Games. He earned his B.A. in physical education and recreation from the Université de Montréal.

Philosophy: Camp Edphy International is committed to developing the personalities, the initiatives, and the sense of responsibility of its campers. The camp director and counselors are "especially committed to ensuring that the first-time camper's summer experience is a positive and enriching one." Camp Edphy believes that this can most effectively be accomplished by encouraging its campers to participate in its wide variety of activities, with emphasis on team and individual sports.

Parent Comment: "Very pleased! My child is very positive about the camp and hasn't stopped talking about the exciting activities and great group spirit. The first thing he said when he got off the bus was 'I'm going back next year!' "

CAMPS FOR CHILDREN WITH SPECIAL NEEDS

BEHAVIOR DISORDERS

CA   Speech and Language
     Development Center
     Camp
     City of Riverside Parks
     Department
     Riverside, CA 92502
     714-659-2466

     Max Strauss
     1041 Shirlyjean Street
     Glendale, CA 91208
     213-852-1234

IN   Bradford Woods Out-
     door Education and
     Camping Center
     Camp Riley
     5040 State Road 67
     North
     Martinsville, IN 46151
     317-342-2915

MN   Buckskin, Inc.
     P.O. Box 389
     Ely, MN 55731
     218-365-2121

NY   Ramapo Anchorage
     Camp
     P.O. Box 266
     Rhinebeck, NY 12572
     914-876-4273

NC   Talisman Summer
     Camp
     601 Camp Elliot Road
     Black Mountain, NC
     28711
     704-669-8639

OK   Camp Takatoka
     Route 1, Box 287
     Chouteau, OK 74337
     918-476-5191

OR   Mt. Hood Kiwanis
     Camp, Inc.
     P.O. Box 1642
     Beaverton, OR 97075
     503-272-3288

PA   Ken-Crest Camp
     Route 29
     Mont Clare, PA 19453
     215-935-1581

UT   Achievement Founda-
     tion, Inc., Camps
     P.O. Box 1916
     Orem, UT 84057
     801-224-8333

CANCER/ONCOLOGY

AZ   Arizona Camp Sunrise
     American Cancer
     Society
     2929 East Thomas Road
     Phoenix, AZ 85016
     602-478-4500

CA   Dream Street
     405 South Beverly
     Drive, Suite 400
     Beverly Hills, CA 90212
     213-277-6776

     Rainbow
     P.O. Box 24-D-19
     Los Angeles, CA 90024
     213-277-6776

Reach for the Sky
YMCA Camp Marston
Julian, CA 92036
619-765-0861

Ronald McDonald for
  Good Times
520 South Sepulveda
  Boulevard, #208
Los Angeles, CA 90049
213-476-8488

A Special Place
Robert J. Sturhahn
  Foundation
2171 Francisco Boule-
  vard, Suite L
San Rafael, CA 94901
415-485-0872

MD   Sunrise
      Camp Glyndon
      407 Central Avenue
      Reisterstown, MD 21136
      301-529-7272

MN   Trowbridge
      Vegas, MN 56587
      218-342-2811

MO   YMCA of the Ozarks–
        Camp Lakewood
      Route 2
      Potosi, MO 63664
      314-438-2154

NE   Eastern Nebraska 4-H
        Center
      21520 West Highway 31
      Gretna, NE 68028
      402-332-4896

NJ   Happiness Is Camping/
        Camp Gramercy
      62 Sunset Lake Road
      Blairstown, NJ 07825
      201-362-6733

NY   Mid-Hudson Valley
        Camp
      P.O. Box 186
      Esopus, NY 12429
      914-384-6620

PA   Kweebec
      Park Avenue
      Schwenksville, PA
        19473
      215-287-8117

DIABETES

AL   Seale Harris
      Route 7, Box 758
      Wetumka, AL 36092
      205-567-4933

AZ   AZDA–American
        Diabetes Association
      YMCA Chauncey
        Ranch
      Mayer, AZ 86333
      602-632-7704

CA   Bearskin Meadow
      P.O. Box 887
      Kings Canyon National
        Park, CA 93633
      209-335-2403

      Chinnock
      Jenks Lake Road East
      Angelus Oaks, CA
        92305
      916-925-0199

De los Niños Camp
YMCA Camp Campbell
1261 Lincoln Avenue,
#208
San Jose, CA 95125
408-287-3785

Ideal
Santa Cruz Mountains
Soquel, CA 95073
916-925-0199

Wilshire Boulevard
Temple Campus
11495 East Pacific Coast
Highway
Malibu, CA 90265
213-457-7861

CO Diabetes Youth Camp–
Shady Brook
2450 South Downing
Street
Denver, CO 80210
303-778-7556

YMCA Camp Shady
Brook
P.O. Box 1694
Colorado Springs, CO
80901
719-471-9790

FL Florida Camp for Children and Youth with
Diabetes
P.O. Box 14136, Univer-
sity Station
Gainesville, FL 32604
904-392-4123

GA Liwidia
3783 Presidential Park-
way, #102
Atlanta, GA 30340
404-545-8401

Barney Medintz
Route 3, Box 3828
Cleveland, GA 30528
404-865-2715

HI Camp Erdman Adah
Youth Camp
Farrington Highway
Wailua, HI 96791
808-941-3344

ID Hodia
1528 Vista Avenue
Boise, ID 83705
208-342-2774

IN Happy Hollow Chil-
dren's Camp, Inc.
Route 2, Box 382
Nashville, IN 47448
812-988-4900

John Warvel
American Diabetes
Association
222 South Downey
Avenue, Suite 320
Indianapolis, IN 46219
317-352-9226

IA ADA–Camp Hertko
Hollow
YMCA Camp
Route 4, Box 182
Boone, IA 50036
515-432-7558

Des Moines YMCA
Camp
Route 4, Box 182
Boone, IA 50036
515-288-0131

Camp Good Health
1614 Mt. Vernon Road
Mt. Vernon, IA 52314
319-363-0681

KS   Discovery
3210 East Douglas
Street
Wichita, KS 67208
316-684-6091

KY   Camp Hendon at
KYSOC
1902 Easterday Road
Carrollton, KY 41008
502-732-5333

LA   Louisiana Lions Camp
for Diabetic Youth
P.O. Box 171
Leesville, LA 71446
504-588-5375

Wawbansee–American
Diabetes Association
Route 2
Simsboro, LA 71275
328-263-8895

Whispering Pines Dia-
betes Session
P.O. Box 379
Independence, LA
70443
504-878-2173

MA   Clara Barton Camp for
Girls with Diabetes
68 Clara Barton Road
North Oxford, MA
01537
508-987-2056

Elliott P. Joslin for Boys
with Diabetes
Richardsons Corner
Road
P.O. Box 100
Charlton, MA 01507
617-248-5220

MI   Midicha
4205 Hollenbeck Road
Columbiaville, MI 48421
313-793-6600

Midicha–Up Bay Cliff
Health Camp
Big Bay, MI 49808
906-345-9314

MO   Edi Camp
YMCA of the Ozarks
Route 2
Potosi, MO 63664
314-968-3196

Hickory Hill
P.O. Box 1942
Columbia, MO 65205
314-443-2447

YMCA of the Ozarks–
Camp Lakewood
Route 2
Potosi, MO 63664
314-438-2154

MT   Diamont
Hyalite Canyon
Bozeman, MT 59715
406-761-0908

NE Floyd Rogers
    P.O. Box 31536
    Omaha, NE 68131
    402-341-0866

NJ Nejeda
    P.O. Box 156, Saddle-
      back Road
    Stillwater, NJ 07875-
      0156
    201-383-2611

NY NYDA
    Burlingham, NY 12722
    914-733-4528

NC YMCA Camp Hanes
    Route 5, Box 99
    King, NC 27021
    919-983-3131

ND Sioux
    Turtle River State Park
    Arvilla, ND 58214
    701-746-4427

OH Highbrook Lodge
    12944 Aquilla Road
    Chardon, OH 44024
    216-286-3121

    Ko-Man-She
    2256 Clifton Road
    Yellow Springs, OH
      45387
    513-767-7552

OK YMCA Camp Classen
    Route 1
    Davis, OK 73030
    405-369-2272

PA ADA–Camp Setebaid
    P.O. Box 475
    Bloomsburg, PA 17815
    717-784-9133

    Crestfield
    RD 2, Box 71
    Slippery Rock, PA
      16057
    412-794-4022

    Firefly
    Haim Road
    Spring Mount, PA
      19478
    215-287-7675

TN Tennessee Camp for
      Diabetic Children
    Double G Ranch
    2622 Lee Drive
    Soddy, TN 37379
    615-870-0600

TX Sweeney
    P.O. Box 918
    Gainesville, TX 76240
    817-665-9502

    Texas Lions Camp
    P.O. Box 247
    Kerrville, TX 78029
    512-896-8500

UT Utada Camp
    643 East 400 South
    Salt Lake City, UT
      84102
    801-363-3024

VA Camp Jordan
    3008 Lafayette Avenue
    Richmond, VA 23228
    804-262-1111

WI   American Diabetes
     Association–
     Wisconsin
     N2155 Lakeshore Drive
     Chilton, WI 53014
     414-849-4597

     Needlepoint
     YMCA Camp St. Croix
     532 County Road F
     Hudson, WI 54016
     612-593-5333

     Triangle D Camp for
     Children with Dia-
     betes at Covenant
     Harbor
     1724 Main Street
     Lake Geneva, WI 53147
     414-248-3600

EMOTIONAL DISORDERS

CA   Erutan
     2700 Los Osos Valley
     Warden Lake
     Los Osos, CA 93402
     213-666-1900

     Alex A. Krem
     102 Brook Lane
     Boulder Creek, CA
       95006
     408-338-3210

     Speech and Language
       Development Center
       Camp
     City of Riverside Parks
       Department
     Riverside, CA 92502
     714-659-2466

     Max Strauss
     1041 Shirlyjean Street
     Glendale, CA 91208
     213-852-1234

GA   Camp Lookout, Inc.
     Route 2, Highway 157
     Rising Fawn, GA 30738
     404-820-1163

IN   Bradford Woods Out-
       door Education and
       Camping Center
     Camp Riley
     5040 State Road 67
       North
     Martinsville, IN 46151
     317-342-2915

MN   Buckskin, Inc.
     Box 389
     Ely, MN 55731
     218-365-2121

     Knutson
     Manhattan Beach, MN
       56463
     218-543-4232

MO   Rotary–Mattie Rhodes
     1740 Jefferson Street
     Kansas City, MO 64108
     816-471-2536

NM   Santa Fe Mountain
       Center
     Route 4, Box 34C
     Santa Fe, NM 87501
     505-983-6158

NY   Presbyterian Center at
Holmes
RR 1, Box 183
Holmes, NY 12531
914-878-6383

Ramapo Anchorage
Camp
P.O. Box 266
Rhinebeck, NY 12572
914-876-4273

OH   Allyn
1414 Lake Allyn Road
Batavia, OH 45103
513-732-0240

Breezewood Acres
633 Ross Road
Sunbury, OH 43074
614-221-9115

OR   Mt. Hood Kiwanis
Camp, Inc.
P.O. Box 1642
Beaverton, OR 97075
503-272-3288

PA   Helping Hands, Inc.
RD 1, Box 360
Bechtelsville, PA 19505
215-754-6491

Rock Creek Farm
RD 1, Box 53
Thompson, PA 18465
717-756-2706

UT   Achievement Founda-
tion, Inc., Camps
P.O. Box 1916
Orem, UT 84057
801-224-8333

EPILEPSY

AR   Camp Aldersgate, Inc.
2000 Aldersgate Road
Little Rock, AR 72205
501-225-1444

KY   KYSOC
1902 Easterday Road
Carrollton, KY 41008
502-732-5333

MN   Friendship
RR 3, Box 162
Annandale, MN 55302
612-274-8376

YMCA Camp Ihduhapi
Box 37
Loretto, MN 55357
612-479-1146

NH   Camp Allen, Inc., for
Individuals with
Disabilities
RFD 9
Bedford, NH 03102
603-622-8471

Friendship
Star Route 62, Box 469
Center Harbor, NH
03226
603-253-9506

OR   Easter Seal
Boat Route Worth Lake
Lakeside, OR 97449
503-759-3226

PA Ken-Crest Camp
Route 29
Mont Clare, PA 19453
215-935-1581

Lee Mar
Route 590
Lackawaxen, PA 18435
717-685-7189

Samuel Thompson
Scout Camp
Elwyn Institutes
Elwyn, PA 19063
215-891-2299

SC Burnt Gin Camp
Wedgefield, SC 29168
803-494-3145

TX YMCA Camp Carter
6200 Sand Springs Road
Fort Worth, TX 76114
817-738-9241

GENERAL PHYSICAL DISABILITIES

AL Camp ASCCA
P.O. Box 21
Jackson Gap, AL 36861
205-825-9226

AZ Easter Seal
General Delivery
Williams, AZ 86046
602-635-2944

CA Cabrillo Beach Youth
Waterfront
Sports Center
3000 Shoshonean Road
San Pedro, CA 90731
213-831-1984

Costanoan
13851 Stevens Canyon
Road
Cupertino, CA 95014
408-867-1115

Easter Seal Camp
Harmon
P.O. Box 626
Santa Cruz, CA 95061
408-338-3383

Hawley Lake Camp
1911-C Oak Park
Boulevard
Pleasant Hill, CA 94523
415-939-7353

CT Hemlocks Recreation
Center
P.O. Box 198
Hebron, CT 06248
203-228-9496

DE Children's Beach House
1800 Bay Avenue
Lewes, DE 19958
302-645-9184

ID Easter Seal East
Worley, ID 83873
208-689-3220

IL   Easter Seal Camp
       Heffernan
       206 South Linden
       Street, Suite 4A
       Normal, IL 61761
       309-452-8074

       Easter Seal Summer
       Camp
       Hoover Outdoor Education Center
       Yorkville, IL 60560
       312-896-1961

       Camp Little Giant
       Southern Illinois
       University
       Touch of Nature
       Carbondale, IL 62901
       618-453-1121

       Peacock Camp for Crippled Children
       38685 North Deep Lake
       Road
       Lake Villa, IL 60046
       312-356-5201

IN   Bradford Woods Outdoor Education and
       Camping Center
       Camp Riley
       5040 State Road 67
       North
       Martinsville, IN 46151
       317-342-2915

       Isanogel Center
       7601 West Isanogel
       Road
       Muncie, IN 47304
       317-288-1073

Kiwanis Twin Lakes
   Camp
15543 Twelfth Road
Plymouth, IN 46563
219-936-8320

Koch Outdoor Center
P.O. Box 39
Troy, IN 47588
812-547-5581

Millhouse, Inc.
25600 Kelly Road
South Bend, IN 46614
219-287-9833

MD   Greentop
       15001 Park Central
       Road
       Sabillasville, MD 21780
       301-293-0801

       Melwood Recreation
       and Travel Center
       Nanjiemoy, MD 20662
       301-870-3226

MI   Fowler, Inc.
       2315 Harmon Lake
       Road
       Mayville, MI 48744
       517-673-3666

       Indian Trails Camp,
       Inc.
       0-1859 Lake Michigan
       Drive
       Grand Rapids, MI 49504
       616-677-5251

       O the Hills
       2100 Pink Street
       Brooklyn, MI 49230
       517-592-6373

MN Courage
3915 Golden Valley
     Road
Minneapolis, MN 55422
612-963-3121
Attn. Mark Moilanen

Courage North
Box 1626
Lake George, MN 56458
218-266-3658

Friendship
RR 3, Box 162
Annandale, MN 55302
612-274-8376

NE Camp Easter Seal
Route 1, Box 51B1
Milford, NE 68405
402-761-2875

NH Camp Allen, Inc., for
     Individuals with
     Disabilities
RFD 9
Bedford, NH 03102
603-622-8471

Friendship
Star Route 62, Box 469
Center Harbor, NH
     03226
603-253-9506

NM Kamp Kiwanis
Easter Seal Camp
     Program
General Delivery
Vanderwagen, NM
     87326
505-778-5796

NY Clover Patch Camp
Helping Hand Lane
Scotia, NY 12302
518-399-4759

Goodwill–NY Easter
     Seal Camp
Rotary Park, Route 13
Chittenango, NY 13037
315-655-9735

Presbyterian Center at
     Holmes
RR 1, Box 183
Holmes, NY 12531
914-878-6383

OH Allyn
1414 Lake Allyn Road
Batavia, OH 45103
513-732-0240

Cheerful
15000 Cheerful Lane
Strongsville, OH 44136
216-238-6200

Echoing Hills
36272 County Road 79
Warsaw, OH 43844-
     9990
614-327-2311

OR Easter Seal
Boat Route North Lake
Lakeside, OR 97449
503-759-3226

Mt. Hood Kiwanis
     Camp, Inc.
P.O. Box 1642
Beaverton, OR 97075
503-272-3288

PA   Daddy Allen Camp
      RD 1, Hickory Run
        State Park
      White Haven, PA 18661
      717-939-7801

      Easter Seal Camp
      RD 4, Laurel Hill State
        Park
      Somerset, PA 15501
      717-939-7801

      Harmony Hall Camp
      1500 Fulling Mill Road
      Middletown, PA 17057
      717-939-7801

      Lend a Hand Camp
      RD 2, Box 1019
      Conneaut Lake, PA
        16316
      717-939-7801

      YMCA Camp Fitch on
        Lake Erie
      North Springfield, PA
        16430
      814-922-3219

SC   Burnt Gin Camp
      Wedgefield, SC 29168
      803-494-3145

TN   Easter Seal Camp
      Route 1, Box 84
      Mt. Juliet, TN 37122
      615-444-2829

TX   Soroptimist
      Route 1, Box 191A
      Argyle, TX 76226
      817-455-2213

UT   Camp Kostopoulos
      2500 Emigration
        Canyon
      Salt Lake City, UT
        84108
      801-582-0700

VA   Easter Seal East
      Route 1, Box 111
      Milford, VA 22514
      804-633-9855

      Easter Seal West
      Route 2
      Newcastle, VA 24127
      703-864-5750

WA   Easter Seal West
      17719 South Vaughn
        Road
      Vaughn, WA 98394
      206-884-2722

WI   Easter Seal Center for
        Camping and
        Recreation
      N9888, Highway 13
        North
      Wisconsin Dells, WI
        53965
      608-254-8319

MENTAL RETARDATION

CA   All Nations Camp
      P.O. Box 1710
      Wrightwood, CA 92397
      619-249-3822

      Easter Seal Camp
        Harmon
      P.O. Box 626
      Santa Cruz, CA 95061
      408-338-3383

Alex A. Krem
102 Brook Lane
Boulder Creek, CA
  95006
408-338-3210

Speech and Language
  Development Center
  Camp
City of Riverside Parks
  Department
Riverside, CA 92502
714-659-2466

Westminster Woods
6510 Bohemian
  Highway
Occidental, CA 95465
707-874-2426

CO   Rocky Mountain Village
Box 115
Empire, CO 80438
303-892-6063

Sky Ranch Lutheran
  Camp
307 East Stuart Street
Fort Collins, CO 80525
303-493-5258

CT   Hemlocks Recreation
  Center
P.O. Box 198
Hebron, CT 06248
203-228-9496

FL   Thunderbird
909 East Welch Road
Apopka, FL 32712
407-889-8088

GA   Camp Lookout, Inc.
Route 2, Highway 157
Rising Fawn, GA 30738
404-820-1163

ID   Easter Seal East
Worley, ID 83873
208-689-3220

IL   Easter Seal Summer
  Camp
Hoover Outdoor Educa-
  tion Center
Yorkville, IL 60560
312-896-1961

Henry Horner
P.O. Box 232
Round Lake, IL 60073
708-546-4435

Camp Little Giant
Southern Illinois
  University
Touch of Nature
Carbondale, IL 62901
618-453-1121

IN   Koch Outdoor Center
P.O. Box 39
Troy, IN 47588
812-547-5581

Lake Luther Bible
  Camp
RR 3, Box 575
Angola, IN 46703
219-833-2383

Millhouse, Inc.
25600 Kelly Road
South Bend, IN 46614
219-287-9833

KY KYSOC
1902 Easterday Road
Carrollton, KY 41008
502-732-5333

ME Bancroft Camp
Lighthouse Road
Owls Head, ME 04854
207-594-5022

MD Melwood Recreation
and Travel Center
Nanjiemoy, MD 20662
301-870-3226

MI Fowler, Inc.
2315 Harmon Lake
Road
Mayville, MI 48744
517-673-3666

O the Hills
2100 Pink Street
Brooklyn, MI 49230
517-592-6373

Roger
8356 Belding Road NE
Rockford, MI 49341
616-874-7286

MN Friendship
RR 3, Box 162
Annandale, MN 55302
612-274-8376

Knutson
Manhattan Beach, MN
56463
218-543-4232

Minnie-Wa-Kan
Route 2, Box 143
Cass Lake, MN 56633
218-335-6159

Winnebago
RR 1, Box 44
Caledonia, MN 55921
507-724-2351

MS Lake Stephens United
Methodist Camp
P.O. Box 1083
Oxford, MS 38655
601-234-3350

MO Lions Den Outdoor
Learning Center
3602 Lions Den Road
Imperial, MO 63052
314-296-4480

Sunnyhill
P.O. Box 246
Dittmer, MO 63023
314-942-2264

NE Camp Easter Seal
Route 1, Box 51B1
Milford, NE 68405
402-761-2875

NH Camp Allen, Inc., for
Individuals with
Disabilities
RFD 9
Bedford, NH 03102
603-622-8471

Friendship
Star Route 62, Box 469
Center Harbor, NH
03226
603-253-9506

NJ   Aldersgate Center
Sprout Hill Road, Box
  122
Swartswood, NJ 07877
201-383-5978

Beisler Camping and
  Retreat
RD 1, Box 106
Port Murray, NJ 07865
201-832-7264

NM   Kamp Kiwanis
Easter Seal Camp
  Program
General Delivery
Vanderwagen, NM
  87326
505-778-5796

NY   Clover Patch Camp
Helping Hand Lane
Scotia, NY 12302
518-399-4759

Huntington
Bruceville Road
High Falls, NY 12440
914-687-7840

Mid-Hudson Valley
  Camp
P.O. Box 186
Esopus, NY 12429
914-384-6620

Presbyterian Center at
  Holmes
RR 1, Box 183
Holmes, NY 12531
914-878-6383

OH   Allyn
1414 Lake Allyn Road
Batavia, OH 45103
513-732-0240

Breezewood Acres
633 Ross Road
Sunbury, OH 43074
614-221-9115

Echoing Hills
36272 County Road 79
Warsaw, OH 43844-
  9990
614-327-2311

PA   Daddy Allen Camp
RD 1, Hickory Run
  State Park
White Haven, PA 18661
717-939-7801

Easter Seal Camp
RD 4, Laurel Hill State
  Park
Somerset, PA 15501
717-939-7801

Elliott
RD 3, Box 266
Volant, PA 16123
412-533-3162

Helping Hands, Inc.
RD 1, Box 360
Bechtelsville, PA 19505
215-754-6491

Ken-Crest Camp
Route 29
Mont Clare, PA 19453
215-935-1581

Keystone Poconos Resi-
  dence and Camp
RD 1
Gouldsboro, PA 18424
717-842-4521

Lee Mar
Route 590
Lackawaxen, PA 18435
717-685-7189

Lend a Hand Camp
RD 2, Box 1019
Conneaut Lake, PA
16316
717-939-7801

Samuel Thompson
Scout Camp
Elwyn Institutes
Elwyn, PA 19063
215-891-2299

YMCA Camp Fitch on
Lake Erie
North Springfield, PA
16430
814-922-3219

SC   Clemson University
Outdoor Laboratory
263 Lehotsky Hall
Clemson University
Clemson, SC 29634
803-646-7502

TN   Easter Seal Camp
Route 1, Box 84
Mt. Juliet, TN 37122
615-444-2829

TX   Greene Family Camp
Smith Lane
Bruceville, TX 76630
817-859-5411

Soroptimist
Route 1, Box 191A
Argyle, TX 76226
817-455-2213

Texas 4-H Center
Route 1, Box 527
Brownwood, TX 76801
915-784-5482

UT   Camp Kostopoulos
2500 Emigration
Canyon
Salt Lake City, UT
84108
801-582-0700

VA   Baker
7600 Beach Road
Chesterfield, VA 23832
804-748-4789

Easter Seal East
Route 1, Box 111
Milford, VA 22514
804-633-9855

Easter Seal West
Route 2
New Castle, VA 24127
703-864-5750

Overlook
Route 1, Box 203
Keezletown, VA 22832
703-269-4765

Presbyterian Point
Route 1, Box 182
Clarksville, VA 23927
804-252-1603

Virginia Jaycee
Route 1, Box 860
Blue Ridge, VA 24064
703-947-2972

WA   Burton
Route 4, Box 66
Vashon Island, WA
98070
206-622-3935

Easter Seal West
17719 South Vaughn
  Road
Vaughn, WA 98394
206-884-2722

WI Wisconsin Badger
      Camp
    Route 2, Box 351
    Prairie du Chien, WI
      53821
    608-988-4558

    Wisconsin Lions Camp
    46 County Road A
    Rosholt, WI 54473
    715-677-4761

OBESITY

CA Camelot at Whittier
      College
    Whittier, CA 90608
    800-421-4321

    Del Mar
    Point Loma College
    San Diego, CA 92110
    619-450-3376

    La Jolla–San Diego
    P.O. Box 4000, Blake
      Hall
    La Jolla, CA 92093
    619-452-2212

    La Jolla–Santa Barbara
    Tropicana Gardens
    6585 El Colegio Road
    Goleta, CA 93117
    415-924-8725

Murrieta–San Diego
University of San Diego
Alcala Park
San Diego, CA 92111
619-260-7923

Weight Watchers–Camp
  California
The Dunn School
P.O. Box 98
Los Olivos, CA 93441
805-688-6181

Weight Watchers–Camp
  Golden Gate
Woodside Priory School
302 Portola Road
Portola Valley, CA
  94025
800-223-5600

Weight Watchers–Camp
  Ojai
Villanova School
12096 Ventura Avenue
Ojai, CA 93023
800-223-5600

CO Weight Watchers–Camp
      Rocky Mountain
    Colorado Rocky Moun-
      tain School
    Carbondale, CO 81623
    212-889-9500 (NY
      number)

FL Weight Watchers–
      Vanguard
    Vanguard School
    2249 Highway 27 North
    Lake Wales, FL 33853
    800-223-5600

HI   La Jolla–Hawaii
Brigham Young Univer-
    sity Hawaii Campus
Laie, Oahu, HI 96762
818-914-5711

IN   Weight Watchers–Camp
    Hoosiers
Lamure Preparatory
    School
P.O. Box 5005
Laporte, IN 46350
212-889-9500

MA   Camelot at Springfield
    College
Springfield, MA 01109-
    3797
800-421-4321

Kingsmont
RFD 2
West Stockbridge, MA
    01266
413-232-8518

Weight Watchers–New
    England
North Adams State
    College
North Adams, MA
    01247
800-223-5600

MO   YMCA of the Ozarks–
    Camp Lakewood
Route 2
Potosi, MO 63664
314-438-2154

NY   Shane Trim Down
    Camp
Ferndale, NY 12734
914-292-4644

NC   Weight Watchers–Camp
    Asheville
Warren Wilson College
701 Warren Wilson
    Road
Swannanoa, NC 28778-
    2099
212-889-9500 (NY
    number)

PA   Camelot at Millersville
    University
Millersville, PA 17551
800-421-4321

Weight Watchers–Camp
    Colang
Lackawaxen, PA 18435
717-685-7151

Weight Watchers–
    Perkiomen
Camp Perkiomen at the
    Perkiomen School
Pennsburg, PA 18073
215-679-8238

TX   Weight Watchers–Lone
    Star
Selwyn School
P.O. Box 2146, Univer-
    sity Drive West
Denton, TX 76201
800-223-5600

VT   Camp Vermont
University of Vermont
460 South Prospect
    Street
Burlington, VT 05401
800-365-8746

CAN   Weight Watchers–
    Camp Canada
St. Andrew's College in
    Aurora
Aurora, Ontario, Can-
    ada L4G 3H7 CN
212-889-9500 (NY
    number)

SPEECH IMPAIRMENTS

AZ   Easter Seal
General Delivery
Williams, AZ 86046
602-635-2944

CA   Speech and Language
    Development Center
    Camp
City of Riverside Parks
    Department
Riverside, CA 92502
714-659-2466

CT   Shadybrook Learning
    Center
P.O. Box 365
Moodus, CT 06469
203-873-8800

DE   Children's Beach House
1800 Bay Avenue
Lewes, DE 19958
302-645-9184

IL   Easter Seal Summer
    Camp
Hoover Outdoor Educa-
    tion Center
Yorkville, IL 60560
312-896-1961

Peacock Camp for Crip-
    pled Children
38685 North Deep Lake
    Road
Lake Villa, IL 60046
312-356-5201

MD   Melwood Recreation
    and Travel Center
Nanjiemoy, MD 20662
301-870-3226

MI   O the Hills
2100 Pink Street
Brooklyn, MI 49230
517-592-6373

MN   Courage
3915 Golden Valley
    Road
Minneapolis, MN 55422
612-963-3121
Attn. Mark Moilanen

Courage North
Box 1626
Lake George, MN 56458
218-266-3658

NH   Friendship
Star Route 62, Box 469
Center Harbor, NH
    03226
603-253-9506

OH   Echoing Hills
36272 County Road 79
Warsaw, OH 43844-
   9990
614-327-2311

PA   Helping Hands
RD 1, Box 360
Bechtelsville, PA 19505
215-754-6491

Lee Mar
Route 590
Lackawaxen, PA 18435
717-685-7189

Samuel Thompson
   Scout Camp
Elwyn Institutes
Elwyn, PA 19063
215-891-2299

Variety Club and De-
   velopmental Center
Valley Forge and Pot-
   shop Roads
Worcester, PA 19490
215-584-4366

VA   Easter Seal West
Route 2
New Castle, VA 24127
703-864-5750

VISUAL IMPAIRMENTS

AL   Camp ASCCA
P.O. Box 21
Jackson Gap, AL 36861
205-825-9226

AZ   Easter Seal
General Delivery
Williams, AZ 86046
602-635-2944

CA   Bloomfield Foundation
   for the Junior Blind
35375 Mulholland
   Highway
Malibu, CA 90265
213-457-5330

CT   Wapanacki
RR 1, Box 1086
Hardwick, CT 05843
802-472-6612

ID   Easter Seal East
Worley, ID 83873
208-689-3220

IL   Easter Seal Camp
   Heffernan
206 South Linden
   Street, Suite 4A
Normal, IL 61761
309-452-8074

Camp Little Giant
Southern Illinois
   University
Touch of Nature
Carbondale, IL 62901
618-453-1121

IN   Isanogel Center
7601 West Isanogel
   Road
Muncie, IN 47304
317-288-1073

KY   KYSOC
1902 Easterday Road
Carrollton, KY 41008
502-732-5333

MI   Echo Grove Salvation
       Army Camp
1101 Camp Road
RR 2
Leonard, MI 48038
313-628-3108

Fowler, Inc.
2315 Harmon Lake
   Road
Mayville, MI 48744
517-673-3666

MN   Courage
3915 Golden Valley
   Road
Minneapolis, MN 55422
612-963-3121
Attn. Mark Moilanen

Courage North
Box 1626
Lake George, MN 56458
218-266-3658

MO   YMCA of the Ozarks–
       Camp Lakewood
Route 2
Potosi, MO 63664
314-438-2154

NH   Camp Allen, Inc., for
       Individuals with
       Disabilities
RFD 9
Bedford, NH 03102
603-622-8471

NJ   Lighthouse Vacation
       Center
Waretown, NJ 08758
609-698-5061

NM   Kamp Kiwanis
Easter Seal Camp
   Program
General Delivery
Vanderwagen, NM
   87326
505-778-5796

OH   Echoing Hills
36272 County Road 79
Warsaw, OH 43844-
   9990
614-327-2311

Highbrook Lodge
12944 Aquilla Road
Chardon, OH 44024
216-286-3121

SC   Clemson University
       Outdoor Laboratory
263 Lehotsky Hall
Clemson University
Clemson, SC 29634
803-646-7502

TX   Soroptimist
Route 1, Box 191A
Argyle, TX 76226
817-455-2213

Texas Lions Camp
P.O. Box 247
Kerrville, TX 78029
512-896-8500

VA Camp Blue Ridge
P.O. Box 120
Montebello, VA 24464
703-377-2413

Easter Seal East
Route 1, Box 111
Milford, VA 22514
804-633-9855

WA Easter Seal West
17719 South Vaughn
  Road
Vaughn, WA 98394
206-884-2722

Sealth
Vashon Island
Burton, WA 98013
206-463-3174

WI Wisconsin Lions Camp
46 County Road A
Rosholt, WI 54473
715-677-4761

GLOSSARY

ACA American Camping Association.

ALPINE TOWER (RAPPELLING TOWER) Man-made structure thirty to fifty feet high from which to practice rappelling.

BATIK Technique of dyeing fabrics by using wax to cover parts of design not to be dyed.

BMX BIKE Nonmotorized bicycle used on an off-the-road course.

CAMPCRAFT Art or practice of camping outdoors.

CANTEEN Store where campers can buy snacks or personal items (toiletries or batteries), or an account for spending money.

CLAY TENNIS COURT Surface composed of clay, making for a slower game.

CLIMBING WALL Rectangular wooden wall of varying heights in which epoxy handholds are in place for individuals to practice rock climbing or physical fitness.

DRESSAGE Precision-control movement of horses.

EMT Emergency medical technician.

FLYTYING ROOM Place where campers make or tie flies for flyfishing.

FUN BUG or FUNYAK Boat similar to kayak used in small-craft activities.

GYMKHANA Place where a sports meet occurs or a combination of different activities (e.g., horseback riding and gymnastics).

HARD-SURFACE TENNIS COURT One of the following surfaces: asphalt, cement, macadam, concrete, composition, all-weather, Plexi-Pave, Laykold, or other material or combination resulting in a faster game, in contrast to clay and Har-Tru.

HAR-TRU TENNIS COURT Surface composed of clay, granular materials, and limestone. It is similar to clay and plays a slower game.

HUNTER JUMPER English-style riding obstacle used on a fox-hunt trail.

LAPIDARY The cutting, polishing, and engraving of precious stones.

ORIENTEERING Means of traveling through an outdoor area using maps, charts, compasses, and natural reference points.

PHANTOM Sailboat.

PONTOON Boat with a hollow float.

RAPPELLING Descent by a mountain climber, as down the sheer face of a cliff.

ROPES COURSE Problem-solving course comprising high and low elements that include tires, cables, ropes, nets, and platforms. Individuals work in groups to accomplish certain goals. This activity encourages cooperation and team effort.

SCULLING Propelling a boat with an oar at the stern.

SHOWERHOUSE Building containing bathroom and shower facilities.

SKEET RANGE   Range where a shooter fires a gun from eight different angles at clay targets thrown from traps (also known as trapshooting).

SPANISH WEBB   Four-inch rope covered by cloth tape and used to perform aerial ballet.

SUNFISH   Sailboat.

TACK ROOM   Room where horseback riding equipment is stored.

TRAPSHOOTING   Sport of shooting clay pigeons thrown into the air.

WATER BIKE   Boat propelled by pedals.

ZIP LINE   Wire or rope between two points which is crossed by pulley.

INDEX